Harold Pinter Collected Screenplays Two

Harold Pinter was born in London in 1930. He is married to
Antonia Fraser. In 1995 he won the David Cohen British
Literature Prize, awarded for a lifetime's achievement in
literature. In 1995 he was given the Laurence Olivier Award
for a lifetime's achievement in theatre.

by the same author

plays
ASHES TO ASHES
BETRAYAL
THE BIRTHDAY PARTY
THE CARETAKER
CELEBRATION and THE ROOM
THE COLLECTION and THE LOVER
THE HOMECOMING
LANDSCAPE and SILENCE
NO MAN'S LAND
OLD TIMES
ONE FOR THE ROAD
OTHER PLACES
(A Kind of Alaska, Victoria Station, Family Voices)
THE ROOM and THE DUMB WAITER
A SLIGHT ACHE and other plays
TEA PARTY and other plays
MOUNTAIN LANGUAGE
PARTY TIME
MOONLIGHT

PLAYS ONE (The Birthday Party, The Room, The Dumb Waiter,
A Slight Ache, The Hothouse, A Night Out, The Black and White,
The Examination)

PLAYS TWO (The Caretaker, The Dwarfs, The Collection, The Lover,
Night School, Trouble in the Works, Request Stop, Last to Go,
Special Offer)

PLAYS THREE (The Homecoming, Tea Party, The Basement, Landscape,
Silence, Night, That's Your Trouble, That's All, Applicant, Interview,
Dialogue for Three, Tea Party (short story), Old Times, No Man's Land)

PLAYS FOUR (Betrayal, Monologue, One for the Road, Mountain Language,
Family Voices, A Kind of Alaska, Victoria Station, Precisely,
The New World Order, Party Time, Moonlight, Ashes to Ashes)

screenplays
HAROLD PINTER COLLECTED SCREENPLAYS ONE
(The Servant, The Pumpkin Eater, The Quiller Memorandum, Accident,
The Last Tycoon, Langrishe, Go Down)

HAROLD PINTER COLLECTED SCREENPLAYS THREE
(The French Lieutenant's Woman, The Heat of the Day,
The Comfort of Strangers, The Trial, The Dreaming Child)

poetry and prose
COLLECTED POEMS AND PROSE
THE DWARFS (a novel)
100 POEMS BY 100 POETS
99 POEMS IN TRANSLATION
VARIOUS VOICES
(Prose, Poetry, Politics: 1948–1998)

HAROLD PINTER

Collected Screenplays Two

The Go-Between

The Proust Screenplay

Victory

Turtle Diary

Reunion

Introduced by the author

faber and faber

First published in this collection in 2000
by Faber and Faber Limited
3 Queen Square London WCIN 3AU

Photoset by Parker Typesetting Service, Leicester
Printed in England by Mackays of Chatham plc

2 4 6 8 10 9 7 5 3 1

CONTENTS

INTRODUCTION

When I first read *The Go-Between* I burst into tears on the
last page so that when Joe Losey asked me if I'd like to write
a screenplay of it I said, 'Impossible. I can't write a
screenplay with tears streaming down my face.' However, I
managed to pull myself together and get down to work. Joe
and I decided quite early on that we would bring the present
into the past throughout the film. This entailed the arrival of
Michael Redgrave (the elderly Leo) to the village he last saw
as a boy in 1912, where he witnessed or rather participated in
the disintegration of a society. This structure was not
popular with the distributors. Coming away from an early
screening I heard a moneyman say, 'If they just get rid of all
that Michael Redgrave crap it could do well.' Pressure was
brought to bear on us but Joe and I would not budge. I'm
very glad we stuck to our guns.

Someone enquired once why I kept so much of L. P.
Hartley's dialogue. I replied 'Because it could not be
bettered.'

Early in 1972 Nicole Stephane, who owned the film rights
to *A la Recherche du Temps Perdu,* asked Joseph Losey if he
would like to work on a film version of the book. He asked
me if I was interested.

For three months I read *A la Recherche du Temps Perdu*
every day. I took hundreds of notes while reading but was
left at the end quite baffled as to how to approach a task of
such magnitude. The one thing of which I was certain was
that it would be wrong to attempt to make a film centred
around one or two volumes, *La Prisonnière* or *Sodome et
Gomorrhe,* for example. If the thing was to be done at all, one
would have to try to distil the whole work, to incorporate the
major themes of the book into an integrated whole. We

decided that the architecture of the film should be based on
two main and contrasting principles: one, a movement,
chiefly narrative, towards disillusion, and the other, more
intermittent, towards revelation, rising to where time that
was lost is found, and fixed forever in art.

In *Le Temps Retrouvé*, Marcel, in his forties, hears the bell
of his childhood. His childhood, long forgotten, is suddenly
present within him, but his consciousness of himself as a
child, his memory of the experience, is more real, more
acute than the experience itself.

Working on *A la Recherche du Temps Perdu* was the best
working year of my life.

The money to make the film was never found.

I worked on the script of *Victory* with Richard Lester. I
had found Joseph Conrad's book immensely powerful, with
a very rich collection of characters. I was also excited to write
a film based in East Asia in 1900. But the American
production company did not share my enthusiasm. They
decided that 'period' films cost too much money,
particularly when they dealt with Conradian moral
complexities, so they withdrew. This screenplay has never
been shot, although another film of the book was made a few
years ago.

Turtle Diary, a wry, secretive book by Russell Hoban, I
found a very attractive proposition. The film, I think,
succeeds on a number of counts but finally disappoints. This
is because it fails to give proper expression to the inner life of
the two protagonists. The failure does, I think, lie in the
screenplay itself, although it's difficult to put one's finger on
it. The film is funny but not, perhaps, sufficiently *earthed*.

I believe *Reunion* is a very underrated film. Fred
Uhlmann's book focuses on the life of two boys (one a
German aristocrat, the other the son of a Jewish doctor) in
Germany in the early thirties. The framework of the novella
is the Jewish boy fifty years later, now a lawyer in America. I
took the lawyer on a trip to Germany and juxtaposed past

and present, gradually revealing both. The contrast, in Jerry Schatzberg's film, of Germany then and now and Jason Robard's almost silent journey through the city of his childhood I found extremely telling.

I have never written an original film. But I've enjoyed adapting other people's books very much. Altogether, I have written twenty-four screenplays. Two were never shot. Three were rewritten by others. Two have not yet been filmed. Seventeen (including four adaptations of my own plays) were filmed as written. I think that's unusual. I certainly understand adapting novels for the screen to be a serious and fascinating craft.

Harold Pinter
13 September, 2000

The Go-Between

The Go-Between is a World Film Services Production
presented by EMI/MGM in July 1971 with the following cast:

MARIAN Julie Christie
TED Alan Bates
MRS MAUDSLEY Margaret Leighton
MR MAUDSLEY Michael Gough
TRIMINGHAM Edward Fox
LEO Dominic Guard
MARCUS Richard Gibson
DENYS Simon Hume-Kendall
KATE Amaryllis Garnet
CHARLES Roger Lloyd-Pack
BLUNT John Rees
STUBBS Keith Buckley
RECTOR Gordon Richardson
COLSTON Michael Redgrave

Directed by Joseph Losey

The action of this film takes place during a span of 3 weeks in August in the summer of 1900 except for certain scenes, which take place in the present. The 'present' is any time in the last 20 years.

EXT. ENGLISH COUNTRYSIDE. A RIVER. SUMMER. DAY.

The river comes out of the shadow of a belt of trees. It flows gently through the weeds and rushes. Heat haze.

Steam rising from rushes.

Sound of approaching horses' hooves. A pony carriage drives by on the road, glimpsed only fragmentarily through the leaves. It passes.

Silence.

The camera is still, looking through the leaves towards the silent road. In the distance, a 1900 farm machine, horse drawn, can be seen, moving slowly.

Sound of the flowing river.

The voice of an elderly man, Colston, heard over:

> COLSTON
> (*VO*)
> The past is a foreign country. They do things differently there.

EXT. GRAVEL ROAD. LONG SHOT.

The pony and carriage trotting. On it are Marcus, Leo, a Footman and an Undercoachman.

Marcus is pointing across the fields.

From viewpoint of the carriage see Brandham Hall in the distance.

The carriage goes downhill. Brandham Hall lost.

INT. HOUSE. BACK STAIRS.

The back stairs are rambling and narrow. Marcus and Leo, followed by footman, climb up. Doors, other passages glimpsed.

The reach Marcus's room.

INT. MARCUS'S ROOM.

There is one small window high in the wall. An old terrier jumps from the four-poster bed as the door opens and Marcus and Leo enter.

The dog jumps up at them.

MARCUS

This is Dry Toast.

EXT. FRONT OF HOUSE. LAWN.

In foreground the shape of a girl lying in a hammock. The wide lawn falls away before the house on a gentle slope. Cedars, elms. The hammock, faded crimson canvas, swings gently. In background figures in white playing croquet.

INT. HOUSE. MAIN HALL.

A butler carrying a bowl of flowers walks up the double staircase, which is shaped like a horse-shoe, and goes out of shot.

Marcus and Leo appear at the top of the staircase.

They run down it at different sides. At the foot of it Leo turns to look up.

EXT. LAWN.

Men in white flannels, white boots and straw boaters, women in white dresses and hats playing croquet.

INT. HOUSE. MAIN HALL.

Leo turns from staircase, glances through open double doors to a long room with large windows.

The camera pans to see into the room. A long shining mahogany table.

INT. HOUSE. OPEN FRONT DOOR.

Marcus turns from the door.

> MARCUS
>
> Come on, slug.

Leo moves quickly and threateningly after him to the front of the house.

Framed in the door a girl in a hammock can be seen, on the lawn, in the distance.

EXT. LAWN.

Hammock in foreground, the girl in it is still not clearly seen. Indistinguishable shapes of several people lounging in the shade.

In background Leo and Marcus run out of the house.

> A GUEST
> *(VO)*
>
> Who's that?

EXT. DERELICT OUTHOUSES.

Leo and Marcus wander about derelict outhouses, rubbish heap and disused vegetable gardens, swishing twigs about them. The paths are overgrown. Flies. They walk into denser undergrowth.

MARCUS

My sister is very beautiful.

LEO

Yes.

They approach a roofless outhouse. In it is a large glossy shrub with bell-shaped flowers. They stop. The camera goes before them and stops, regarding the shrub. Their voices over:

LEO

What's that?

MARCUS

It's a deadly nightshade, you oaf!

LEO

Atropa belladonna.

MARCUS

Atropa what?

LEO

Atropa belladonna. It's poisonous. Every part of it is poison.

TWO SHOT. MARCUS AND LEO.

Marcus thrusts Leo towards the shrub.

MARCUS

Die.

Leo resists. Marcus runs through the outhouses, Leo following. The camera watches them with the bell-shaped flowers of the shrub in foreground.

EXT. MARIAN IN HAMMOCK. LAWN.

Her eyes are closed in the sun. They open.

6

Leo walking alone along grass verge of the garden. He slowly comes to halt, looks down.

Marian in hammock from Leo's point of view.

Close-up of Marian.

Her eyes are half closed.

INT. HOUSE. BACK STAIRS.

Leo standing in dark passage. Sudden laughter from servants' quarters.

Leo's point of view. Kitchen door half open.

Glimpsed in the kitchen, two women: The cook and the under-cook, both fat. They are giggling. Steam from saucepans.

EXT. CLOSE-UP OF MARIAN. LAWN.

Her head turns quickly on her shoulder, her eyes are open.

INT. MARCUS'S ROOM. EVENING.

Leo is washing his hands in a bowl. He wipes them and looks at himself in a small mirror.

INT. HALL. EVENING.

Leo descending the stairs. He draws near the half-open door of the drawing-room and stops. Voices:

> MRS MAUDSLEY
> Didn't you say his mother is a widow, Marcus?

> MARCUS
> I think so. I don't really know very much about him.

> MR MAUDSLEY
> Seems to be a nice lad.

MARCUS

I do have an impression that he lives in rather a small house with his mother.

MRS MAUDSLEY

Yes. He seems to be a very nice boy. Now – is everyone here?

Leo opens the door and goes in.

INT. DRAWING-ROOM.

Leo at the door.

MRS MAUDSLEY

Ah, Leo. Good evening.

LEO

Good evening Mrs Maudsley.

MRS MAUDSLEY

Now, let us go into dinner.

They all move to the door.

A GUEST

You were in cracking form to-day at croquet, Marian.

MARIAN

Was I?

DENYS

Marian is quite formidable at croquet.

MARIAN

Am I?

INT. HALL.

The party moving through the hall. Mrs Maudsley with Leo.

MRS MAUDSLEY

I believe we must be wary of you, Leo, I understand
you're a magician. Is that true?

LEO

Well . . . not really . . . only, you know . . . at school.

Leo glances over his shoulder at Marcus.

Anyway it was supposed to be a secret actually.

INT. DINING-ROOM. NIGHT.

*Candlelight. Glow of silver. The family and guests move to the
table.*

MARCUS

His curses are fearful. He cast a fiendish spell on two
boys at school. They fell off the roof and were severely
mutilated.

DENYS

Did they die?

LEO

Oh no. They were just a little . . . you know . . . severly
mutilated.

MR MAUDSLEY

Was it difficult to arrange? I mean to get them to fall off
the roof without killing them.

LEO

Well, it wasn't a killing curse, you see. There are curses
and curses. It depends on the curse.

MRS MAUDSLEY

How frightening.

Mrs Maudsley sits. They all sit. Marian leans forward.

MARIAN

You're not going to bewitch us here, are you?

LEO

Oh no, I shouldn't think so.

Laughter.

INT. BEDROOM. NIGHT.

Marcus and Leo in bed. Marcus asleep. Leo awake.

Laughter from the lawn below. A piano playing. A girl's voice singing. Leo looks up at the high window above his bed. Clear night sky. Voices float in.

EXT. HOUSE. DISUSED GAME LARDER UNDER A YEW TREE. DAY.

This structure is empty but for a thermometer which hangs on the wall.

Leo is staring at it. The temperature is eighty-three.

He turns. Mr Maudsley is behind him.

MR MAUDSLEY

Hello. Enjoying yourself?

LEO

Yes sir.

MR MAUDSLEY

Good. Pretty warm. What does it say?

LEO

Eighty-three.

MR MAUDSLEY

Warm.

Mr Maudsley studies Leo's clothes.

Suit a little warm, is it?

> LEO

No, sir.

Mr Maudsley taps the thermometer.

> MR MAUDSLEY

Enjoying yourself?

> LEO

Yes thank you, sir.

> MR MAUDSLEY

Good.

INT. BEDROOM. DAY.

Leo wiping his sweating face with a handkerchief.

> LEO

Do you think I should sport my cricket togs?

> MARCUS

I wouldn't. Only cads wear their school clothes in the holidays. And another thing. When you undress you mustn't fold your clothes and put them on the chair. You must leave them lying wherever they happen to fall. The servants will pick them up. That's what they're for.

Close-up of Denys.

> DENYS

You are looking hot. Haven't you something cooler to wear?

The camera withdraws to find Leo and Denys with a group of young people in the hall.

> LEO

I'm not hot, really.

DENYS

Isn't that a Norfolk jacket?

LEO

Yes.

DENYS

Well it's quite appropriate then, isn't it? After all we are in Norfolk.

They move through the open front door on to the lawn.

EXT. LAWN.

Close-ups of large silver tea-pot pouring tea into tea-cups.

The camera shifts to look along the tea table which is laden with watercress, tomato, cucumber and lettuce sandwiches, scones, muffins, cream cakes, pastries etc. Voices over:

DENYS

Have we a pair of bellows, Mother?

MRS MAUDSLEY

Why?

DENYS

To cool Leo.

MRS MAUDSLEY

Does Leo need cooling?

LEO

I may look hot, but I'm really quite cool underneath.

The camera shifts and settles to look at the gathering.

MRS MAUDSLEY

Did you leave your summer clothes at home?

LEO

I expect Mother forgot to put them in.

Silence. Stirring of cups.

MRS MAUDSLEY

Why don't you write and ask her to send them?

MARIAN

Oh that would take too long, Mama. Let me take him
into Norwich tomorrow and get him a new outfit.
Would you like that, Leo?

LEO

I haven't any money. At least only –

MARIAN

They can be your birthday present from us. When is
your birthday?

LEO

Well . . . it's on the twenty-seventh of this month,
actually. I was born under the sign of Leo.

MARIAN

Good. I can give you a lionskin.

DENYS

Or a mane.

Close-up of Marian.

She is sipping her tea.

MARIAN

Well, we'll go tomorrow.

Close-up of Mrs Maudsley.

Mrs Maudsley raises her eyes and looks at Marian.

MRS MAUDSLEY

Wouldn't you rather wait until Monday, when Hugh
will be here, and make a party to go to Norwich?

DENYS
(*VO*)
Trimingham? I thought he'd gone to Goodwood.

MR MAUDSLEY
(*VO*)
Hugh coming?

MRS MAUDSLEY
Yes, I had a letter from him. He comes on Saturday and stays until the end of the month.

Close-up of Marian. Her eyes are hooded.

She sips her tea. Mrs Maudsley's voice over:

Are you sure you couldn't wait until Monday?

Marian looks up and smiles.

MARIAN
Norwich will hardly be a treat for Hugh, Mama, trailing round the shops. Besides, by Monday Leo will have melted into butter. And all he'll need will be a muslin bag.

Close-up of Mrs Maudsley.

She holds her tea-cup faintly smiling.

Close-up of Marian.

May we go, Mama?

Close-up of Mrs Maudsley.

MRS MAUDSLEY
Yes, of course you may.

EXT. COUNTRY ROAD. DAY.

Pony and carriage trotting. Marian and Leo on it. It trots into the distance.

14

COLSTON
(*VO*)
(*murmuring*)
You flew to near the sun and you were scorched.

EXT. CATHEDRAL SQUARE. NORWICH.

A footman sits waiting on the carriage. Parcels and boxes are piled up.

INT. HOTEL RESTAURANT. NORWICH.

Marian and Leo at a table. Leo wears a new green suit.

MARIAN
What did your father do?

LEO
He worked in a bank actually. And he was a pacifist.

MARIAN
Ah.

LEO
Mmm. And he was a book collector. He liked books very much. And so he collected them. That was his hobby. Mother said they're quite valuable. We might have to sell them.

MARIAN
Here's your pudding.

The waiter places a large plum pudding in front of Leo. He begins to eat.

What's it like?

LEO
Very good.

Marian is served with coffee. She sips it.

MARIAN

Used any Black Magic on anyone lately?

LEO
(*through food*)

Not lately, no.

MARIAN

I envy you your power. What's it like to have such power at your finger tips?

LEO

Oh it makes you feel fairly good. But I only ever use it at school, you know.

MARIAN

Can you teach me? I could use it here.

LEO

Would you really want to?

MARIAN

Oh not really. The results might be too alarming.

EXT. LOBBY HOTEL.

Marian and Leo.

MARIAN

Would you like to amuse yourself in the Cathedral for an hour? I have some shopping to do.

LEO

Yes. Certainly.

MARIAN

Can you amuse yourself in a Cathedral?

She giggles.

EXT. CATHEDRAL.

Leo wanders through the crowded market and stands to look up at the Cathedral.

EXT. VILLAGE STREET. LONG SHOT. VERY STILL. MORNING. PRESENT.

The sky is overcast. (The sky is constantly overcast in all present-day shots.)

The street is more or less deserted. A couple of parked cars.

Colston stands in the distance, looking down the street.

LEO
(*VO*)

Well, it wasn't a killing curse, you see. There are curses and curses. It depends on the curse.

The man begins to walk down the street.

INT. CATHEDRAL. PAST.

Leo looking up at the vaulted roof.

EXT. SQUARE. THE PONY CARRIAGE.

The coachman raises his whip in salute. The camera pans to Leo, who raises his hand and walks towards a statue in the centre of the square where he stands waiting.

Leo's point of view. The square.

Drowsy traffic of carriages. Men and women walking through the market, which is now much quieter.

Suddenly the camera concentrates on a distant corner of the square. Marian is talking to a man, not identifiable. The man raises his hat. Marian turns and threads her way slowly through the traffic. She suddenly sees Leo, waves her parasol and quickens her step.

EXT. THE RIVER. AFTERNOON.

Silence.

INT. THE HOUSE. DRAWING-ROOM.

Leo is standing on a chair in his new suit revolving. Group of people admiring him.

AD LIB

Superb! Dazzling! Most impressive! What a splendid green! Remarkably elegant! Most fetching! Charming!

DENYS

Did you get the tie at Challow and Challow?

MARIAN

Of course.

DENYS

And where did you get the shoes?

MARIAN

At Sterling and Potter.

DENYS

What green is this?

MARIAN

Lincoln green.

DENYS

I thought so. I shall dub you Sir Robin Hood.

A GIRL

Do you feel different?

LEO

Yes. I feel quite another person.

Laughter. Leo gets off the chair. Mrs Maudsley leads him to the window.

MRS MAUDSLEY

Let me have a proper look at you.

She feels the material and examines the smoked pearl buttons.

Yes, I think it does very well, and I hope your mother will think so too. Have you written to her, Leo?

LEO

Oh yes I have.

MRS MAUDSLEY

Good. You've chosen very well, Marian. Did you do any shopping for yourself?

MARIAN

Oh no, Mama. That can wait.

MRS MAUDSLEY

It mustn't wait too long. You didn't see anyone in Norwich, I suppose?

MARIAN

Not a soul. We were hard at it all the time, weren't we Leo?

Pause.

LEO

Yes, we were.

INT. PLATFORM NORWICH STATION. LONG SHOT. PRESENT.

Colston walks along the platform carrying a small case. He declines a porter's help. The camera watches him move into the ticket hall where a chauffeur in a peak cap approaches him.

Colston and Chauffeur walk to a car. The man gets in, the Chauffeur puts the case in the boot. Over this last shot the following dialogue heard, fragmentarily:

THE GO-BETWEEN

MRS MAUDSLEY

I'm afraid he can't without his mother's permission.
Your mother has written to me that you're liable to
colds. But you can watch the others bathe, of course.

Pause.

MARCUS

Why are you bringing your bathing suit if you're not
allowed to swim?

LEO

Well, it is a bathing party.

MARCUS

But you're not going to swim.

LEO

I know I'm not.

MARCUS

In that case why –?

The car moves away from the station.

EXT. THE RIVER. DAY. PAST.

Silence.

*Voices heard approaching. Indecipherable chatter. Giggling.
Immediately voices are heard the camera moves along the river
bank, in front of and at a distance from the characters.*

*A black peeling construction (a diving pier) is suddenly found. A
man emerges from the rushes. The camera stops abruptly. The
man is wearing tight woollen trunks. The voices cease. The man
climbs onto the platform, stands a moment, and then dives into
the river. He swims away.*

DENYS
(*VO*)

What cheek! The man's trespassing. What shall we do?

GUEST
(*VO*)

Order him off.

DENYS

What cheek!

EXT. RIVER BANK. THE GROUP.

Marian and Kate are in foreground.

KATE

Who can he be?

MARIAN

I don't know.

KATE

He's a good swimmer. And really rather well built.
Don't you think?

Marian turns away.

MARIAN

Come on, Kate, we'll go and change.

Marian and Kate go towards a small hut among the rushes. The others walk down to the river.

DENYS

Shall we order him off?

Point of view of group. Man swimming in river.

The man sees them and swims towards them.

DENYS

It's Ted Burgess.

MAN

Who's he?

DENYS

The tenant of Black Farm. We can't be rude to him. He farms the land on the other side.

MAN

Perhaps you'd better be nice to him.

DENYS

I'll just say how do you do to him. We don't know him socially of course, but I think I should be nice to him, don't you?

MAN

I would say so.

DENYS

In that case I shall. I shall be particularly nice to him.

Ted hauls himself up from the water by means of a fixed spiked post. For a moment he appears to be about to impale himself on it. But he jumps onto the bank. Denys moves forward to shake his hand.

What a way to land! There are some steps over there.

TED

Oh I've always done it this way.

He looks at the group.

I didn't know anyone was going to be here. Just started on the harvest . . . got so hot . . .

DENYS

Don't worry at all, please. We were hot too . . . up at the Hall . . . very hot . . .

Pause.

Trimingham's coming to-night.

TED

Uh. Is he?

Pause.

I won't be long. Just one more header.

DENYS

Absolutely. Absolutely.

Ted raises his hand, turns, runs up to the platform, the camera panning up to watch him, and dives into the water.

Denys turns to the others.

I think I put him at his ease, don't you?

EXT. THE RUSHES.

Denys and his friend undressing in the rushes. The camera moves to find Marcus undressing, Leo watching. Leo begins to untie his tie.

MARCUS

You don't intend to put on your bathing suit, do you? I shouldn't put on a bathing suit if you're not going to bathe. It would look absurd.

Leo reties his tie, and strolls away, his bathing suit over his shoulder.

Ted climbing on to river bank.

Denys, Guest and Marcus, splashing in river.

Leo watching.

Marian and Kate pushing each other, giggling.

They wear long bathing dresses.

Leo suddenly crouching in rushes.

Through the rushes glimpse a glistening body, moving. The body sinks to the ground. Leo raises himself to peer through the rushes.

Ted lies down in the sun, stretches his arms, and scratches his chest.

Leo watching.

> MARIAN
> (*VO*)
> My hair's come down! It's all wet!

Leo turns his head quickly.

Ted jumps up, pulls on his clothes swiftly, swears as he fastens his leather belt and moves swiftly away.

EXT. RIVER BANK.

Marian standing holding the long coils of her hair in front of her.

Leo runs down to her.

> MARIAN
> It's all wet. I shall never get it dry.

She looks at Leo.

> Oh you do look so dry and smug. I should like to throw you in the river.

She laughs.

> Has that man gone?

> LEO
> Yes. He went off in a hurry. His name is Ted Burgess, he's a farmer. Do you know him?

> MARIAN
> I may have met him.

EXT. VILLAGE STREET. MORNING. PRESENT.

A car appears round the corner and draws slowly to a halt. The engine is cut off. No one emerges. The village street is silent. Over this shot, Marian's voice:

MARIAN

It's dripping on my dress.

EXT. RIVER BANK. TWILIGHT. PAST.

Close-up of Leo.

LEO

Here's my bathing suit. It's *quite* dry. If you fasten it round your neck, so that it hangs down your back, then you can spread your hair on it, and your hair will get dry and your dress won't get wet.

Two shot. Marian and Leo.

Marian is pinning the bathing suit at her throat. Leo drapes it over her shoulders.

MARIAN

Spread my hair on it. Take care not to pull it.

Leo does so. She cries out. Leo looks at her in alarm. She smiles. Leo drapes her hair delicately.

Is it well spread?

EXT. LONG SHOT. PATH THROUGH THE TREES.

Marian and Leo walking through the lengthening shadows. The others straggling behind.

MARIAN

Is it dry?

Leo touches her hair. She cries out. Leo takes his hand away sharply. She giggles.

What a comfort . . . your bathing suit on my shoulders.
Is my hair well spread?

LEO

Oh yes. It is.

EXT. FRONT OF HOUSE. EVENING.

*The house is lit. Marian and Leo walk up the slope. She stops,
takes the bathing suit from her shoulders and hands it to him.*

MARIAN

Is it dry?

He touches her hair. She does not cry out.

LEO

Yes.

She touches her hair.

MARIAN
(*smiling*)

Yes, it is.

INT. HOUSE. MAIN HALL. MORNING.

*The gong sounds. One or two figures walk across the hall. Leo
appears at the top of the stairs and bounds down.*

*Camera follows him as he walks swiftly into the breakfast room.
Mr Maudsley is seated at the top of the table. All other chairs
drawn back and ranged round the walls. On the sideboard stand
the breakfast dishes.*

*Leo makes for a particular chair, sits down on it, and moves
about to test its creak. It does not creak. He moves to another
chair, sits and does the same. It creaks sharply. He relaxes in the
chair. One or two guests take their seats. The servants file in and
take theirs. From the servants: 'Good morning Mr Maudsley.'
'Good morning, Mrs Maudsley'.*

*The servants comprise: An elegant housekeeper, three round cooks,
a short elderly gardener, a neat slender butler, a tall footman, two
burly coachmen, two very young maids and a skinny pantry
maid, even younger. Close shot. Leo kneeling.*

Mr Maudsley begins to say morning prayers in the background.

*A figure kneels beside Leo. He looks up. The man is a stranger.
His face is scarred. Trimingham.*

Two shot. Leo and Trimingham.

*Mr Maudsley saying prayers in background. Leo observes
Trimingham sideways.*

INT. BREAKFAST ROOM. MEN WALKING ABOUT EATING
PORRIDGE.

The ladies are seated. Leo holds his plate very carefully.

MRS MAUDSLEY
Now, everybody. Let us decide what we shall do today.
Hugh . . .?

She looks at Trimingham. Leo looks at Trimingham.

Come, sit down and advise us.

Trimingham sits down next to her.

Now what do you suggest?

INT. HOUSE. MARCUS AND LEO'S BEDROOM DOOR.

An envelope is fixed on the door, with NO ADMITTANCE *written
on it. Leo opens the door and goes in.*

INT. BEDROOM.

Marcus is in bed. The dog growls.

LEO

What's up?

MARCUS

Decent of you to trickle along, but don't come in. I have a headache and some spots. Mama thinks it may be measles.

LEO

Hard cheese.

MARCUS

See Trimingham?

LEO

Is he the man with the face?

MARCUS

Yes. Got it in the war. He was gored by the Boers.

LEO

Hard cheese.

EXT. VILLAGE. MORNING.

Church bells.

The house party is passing down the village street on its way to the church.

They pass a cottage. The camera rests momentarily on the cottage.

EXT. CHURCH. LONG SHOT.

The party, going through the church door.

EXT. CHURCH DOOR.

Leo looking into the church.

THE GO-BETWEEN

INT. CHURCH. LEO'S POINT OF VIEW.

Bell ringers at the back of the church, pulling the bell ropes.

EXT. COTTAGE. DAY. PRESENT.

The camera, motionless, looking at the same cottage door.

Church bells heard over.

Colston's back comes into shot.

EXT. VILLAGE STREET. DAY. PAST.

The procession passing the cottage on the way back from church. Trimingham joins Leo.

> TRIMINGHAM
> I don't think we've been introduced. My name is Trimingham.

> LEO
> How do you do, Trimingham.

> TRIMINGHAM
> You can call me Hugh, if you like.

Leo looks at him.

> Or Trimingham, if you prefer.

> LEO
> Why not Mister Trimingham?

> TRIMINGHAM
> I think Trimingham is slightly more in order, if you prefer it to Hugh.

> LEO
> But why not Mister?

> TRIMINGHAM
> Well as a matter of fact I'm a Viscount.

LEO

Viscount Trimingham?

TRIMINGHAM

That's right.

LEO

Oughtn't I to call you My Lord?

TRIMINGHAM

No, no. Hugh will do . . . or Trimingham if you like.
What's your name?

LEO

Colston.

TRIMINGHAM

Mister Colston?

LEO

Well, Leo, if you like.

TRIMINGHAM

I'll call you, Leo, if I may.

LEO

Oh yes that's quite all right.

High shot. Group walking along lane.

Two shot. Leo and Trimingham.

TRIMINGHAM

Does Marian call you Leo?

LEO

Oh yes. I think she's ripping. I'd do anything for her.

TRIMINGHAM

What would you do?

LEO

Oh anything. Anything.

Would you like to take her a message for me?

Oh yes. What shall I say?

Tell her I've got her prayer book. She left it behind in
church.

Leo runs off.

EXT. VILLAGE STREET. PRESENT.

Car drawing to a halt. Engine cuts off. Silence.

(*VO*)
How careless. I forget everything. Please thank him for me.

INT. HOUSE. BACK STAIRS. PAST.

Leo passes Marcus's room. He glances at the NO ADMITTANCE
sign, pauses, and then goes on to a green baize door.

INT. LEO'S ROOM.

Leo enters and looks at it.

*The room is very small. Narrow bed. On the sideboard his
hairbrush, red collar box. Another largish locked box. He opens
this and takes out two dry sea urchins, stumps of sealing wax, a
combination lock, twists of whip cord. Under this gradually
disclosed a locked book. He unlocks it, opens first page. We see
'Diary for the year 1900' in copper plate script. Round this cluster
the signs of the zodiac; The Fishes, The Crab, The Scorpion, The
Ram, The Bull, The Lion, The Archer, The Virgin and The
Water Carrier. Leo studies this page. He then turns the pages of
the diary and stops at a page which contains incomprehensible
lettering and in the centre:*

CURSE THREE
AFTER CURSE THREE THE VICTIM DIES!
*Given under my hand
and written in my* BLOOD!
by order of

THE AVENGER

Leo shuts the book.

EXT. BACK OF THE HOUSE. THE THERMOMETER.

Leo staring at thermometer. The temperature is eighty-four.

EXT. FRONT OF HOUSE. LAWN.

Marian in hammock. She lies still, gazing up into the trees.

EXT. RIVER. THE DIVING PIER.

Leo walks on to pier. Looks down into water.

EXT. CORNFIELD.

Leo wanders through the corn. The stubble pricks his ankles. He comes to a gate, opens it, the camera with him. He turns into a farm road caked with hard mud and then into a farmyard.

Leo looking at a strawstack, a ladder running up it, in the farmyard. He opens the gate and walks into the yard. He stands looking at the height of the stack, and glances towards the silent farmhouse.

He climbs the ladder to the strawstack, he looks down. He slides. A swift rush through the air. His knee, at the bottom, hits a chopping block. He falls off clutching his knee.

Medium shot Ted.

Ted stands at the corner of the farmhouse holding two pails of water. He puts the pails down and strides towards Leo.

TED

What the hell do you think you're doing? I've a good mind to give you the biggest thrashing you've ever had in your life.

Ted from Leo's point of view.

Ted looking down at him.

LEO

My knee!

TED

Get up! What the hell are you doing here? Who are you?

LEO

I know you! We've met!

TED

Met?

LEO

At the bathing place. You were bathing. I came with the others.

TED

Oh. You're from the hall.

Pause.

Can you walk?

Wide shot. Farmyard.

Ted helps Leo up. They walk.

LEO

I saw you dive. You did it jolly well.

INT. FARMHOUSE.

Leo is sitting down. Ted swabbing his knee with carbolic.

33

TED

You were lucky. You might have spoiled your suit.

LEO

Miss Marian gave it to me. Miss Marian Maudsley.

TED

Oh did she? Is it stinging?

LEO

Yes.

TED

You're a spartan.

Ted takes out a handkerchief and ties it around the knee.

LEO

Won't you want that?

TED

I've got plenty more. Try walking.

Leo hobbles about the kitchen.

LEO

Thank you very much, Mr Burgess. Is there . . .
anything I can do for you?

Pause.

TED

Well, perhaps there is.
                    (*Pause.*)
Could you take a message for me?

LEO

Of course. Who to?

Shot across kitchen sink.

*Ted approaches sink with bowl of discoloured water, empties it
and swills it. Leo remains in background.*

34

TED

How old are you?

LEO

I shall be thirteen on the twenty-seventh of this month.

Leo's point of view. Ted turning to him from sink. Ted looks at him in silence.

TED

Can I trust you?

Close-up of Leo.

Leo looks at him expressionless.

Close-up of Ted.

Can I?

Close-up of Leo.

LEO

Of course you can.

Wide shot. Kitchen.

Ted begins to walk around the room.

TED

There's a boy, isn't there? A lad of your age.

LEO

He's in bed, with measles.

TED

Oh, is he?
(*Pause.*)
Are you . . . ever alone with anybody . . . in the house?

LEO

Nobody talks to me much. They're all grown up, you
see. Except Marcus and he's in bed. Marian talks to me.
Miss Marian.

TED

Oh does she?

LEO

She often talks to me. She talks to me most. When her
hair was wet I . . .

Medium shot. Ted sitting at table.

TED

Are you ever alone with her? I mean, just the two of you
in a room, with no one else.

LEO

Well, sometimes. Sometimes we sit together on a sofa.

TED

On a sofa?

Wide shot of room.

Ted stands, walks about the room.

Could you give her a letter without anybody else seeing?

LEO

Of course I could.

Close-up of Ted.

Ted regards him thoughtfully.

TED

But can I trust you . . . to keep your mouth shut?

Close-up of Leo.

Leo looks at him with some disdain.

Close-up of Ted.

Because . . . you see . . . it's a secret.
                    (*Pause.*)
All right. I'll trust you.

36

Wide shot. Room.

Ted takes pen, ink and paper from the sideboard and sits down at the table.

We do some business together.

LEO

Secret business?

TED

That's right. No one else must see this letter. You understand?

LEO

Yes.

TED

If you can't get her alone don't give it to her. Put it in the place where you pull the chain.

INT. HOUSE. TEA-TIME. SITTING-ROOM.

Leo sitting with handkerchief round his knee.

MR MAUDSLEY

Yes, Ted Burgess, good-looking chap, rides well, I'm told. Good to know he was kind to you.

DENYS

Yes, how nice of him to be so nice. But I was very nice, of course, at the bathing place, wasn't I?
(*To his mother.*)
I put him very much at his ease, you know.

MRS MAUDSLEY

Did you?

MARIAN

I think I'd better dress that knee for you, Leo. It's looking a bit messy.

INT. BATHROOM.

Leo's knee under the running tap. Marian bathing it.
Handkerchief on the edge of the bath.

> MARIAN
>
> Mmmm. There.

She wipes it with towel.

Camera rises as she stands. She collects bandage.

Shot over bath edge.

Marian glances at the handkerchief and bends to fix bandage.

> Is that his?

> LEO
>
> Yes. He said he wouldn't want it back. Shall I throw it
> on the rubbish dump?

> MARIAN
>
> Oh I don't know. Perhaps I'll wash it out. It seems quite
> a good handkerchief.

> LEO
>
> Oh he asked me to give you this.

He takes a letter from his back pocket.

> It's a bit crumpled.

She snatches the letter, standing.

> MARIAN
>
> Oh these dresses.

She tucks the letter up her sleeve.

> Now the bandage.

> LEO
>
> You've put it on.

MARIAN

Oh yes.

She bends to him.

Now I'll put on your stocking.

LEO

Oh I can do that.

MARIAN

No, no, I'll do it.

Close two shot.

Marian drawing the stocking up.

You won't . . . tell anyone about this letter will you?
You won't . . . will you?

LEO

Of course I won't.

Marian's hand smooths the stocking and touches the bandage.

Close-up of Marian doing this.

MARIAN
(*softly*)

There.

EXT. OUTHOUSES. THE DEADLY NIGHTSHADE.

The camera is still, looking at it. It glistens.

Voices heard over:

COLSTON
(*VO*)

Of course I won't.

MARIAN'S VOICE YOUNG
(*softly*)

There.

EXT. MEADOW BY STREAM. DAY.

A picnic party. Numerous open hampers. Ladies and gentlemen sitting on multi-coloured rugs. Footmen serving food. Ham, cheese, eggs etc.

Over this shot and the next two shots the following spasmodic dialogue is heard:

A GIRL

But Gussy doesn't dance.

A MAN

Doesn't he really?

GIRL

Not a step.

ANOTHER MAN

Shall you be going to Goodwood?

FIRST MAN

How odd. I thought I saw him dancing at Lady Mary's.

THIRD MAN

I think I shall go to Goodwood. Shall you?

GIRL

But he doesn't dance a step, I promise you.

SECOND MAN

Yes, I think I shall.

Amber wine being poured from tall bottles into goblets.

Leo holding glass. A footman bends to him, pours fizzy lemonade into it from a bottle with a glass marble for a stopper.

Leo drinks lemonade and stands. In the background Marian and Trimingham are sitting together. He is talking intently to her. Leo strolls close to them. Trimingham looks up.

TRIMINGHAM
Hello, there's Mercury!

MARIAN
Why do you call him Mercury?

TRIMINGHAM
Because he takes messages.

Over the back of Marian's head, rigid, to Trimingham and Leo.

Marian turns away.

You took a message for me, didn't you old chap? To this young lady, on the way from church. But it didn't fetch a very warm response.

Marian laughs.

Three shot. Relaxed.

Marian laughing.

(*To Leo.*)
Do you know who Mercury was?

LEO
Mercury is the smallest of the planets.

TRIMINGHAM
Ah, but before that he was the messenger of the gods. He went to and fro between them.

EXT. PICNIC MEADOW. LATE AFTERNOON.

Leo asleep in the grass. Marian and Mrs Maudsley seen in background. His eyes flicker.

MARIAN

I think he must be bored to tears, trailing round with us.
He'd be much happier pottering about on his own.

MRS MAUDSLEY

Do you think so? He's so devoted to you, he's your little
man. Still, I can ask him. It is unfortunate about
Marcus.

MARIAN

If Marcus has got the measles, I suppose we shall have
to put off the ball.

MRS MAUDSLEY

Oh I don't think so. We should disappoint so many
people. You wouldn't want to do that, would you?

Marian and Mrs Maudsley rise and stroll away.

Leo sits up.

From his viewpoint on the grass:

*The carriages drawn up in the shade. Horses whisking their tails.
The coachmen high up on their boxes, hats almost touching the
branches.*

EXT. ROAD. MOVING CARRIAGE.

*Leo and Coachman Buff on the box seats of the carriage. Below
them in the well of the carriage a roof of parasols.*

EXT. A SMALL VILLAGE.

*Carriages passing through the village. Children run along the
road as they pass. The Coachmen throw pennies to them. The
children scrabble for them.*

Medium shot. Leo and Coachman.

Leo is watching the children. He turns abruptly to the Coachman.

LEO

Do you know Ted Burgess?

BUFF

Ted Burgess? We all know him. He's a bit of a lad, Ted Burgess.

LEO

What do you mean by a lad? I should have said he was a full grown man.

The carriage has reached the top of a steep hill.

BUFF

Hold on, hold on. Here we go!

The descent begins, the coachman grinding the brakes, the horses' hindquarters sweating. Leo clutches the rail and turns sharply to look behind him up the hill. His face into the camera.

Quick cut. Close shot. A car door bangs shut. PRESENT.

Long shot.

Colston's back standing by car in village street. He begins to walk down the street away from the camera.

Marian's skirt glimpsed flashing quickly by through weeds.

The thermometer.

The marker points to ninety-four.

Leo staring at it. His hand to his mouth.

A voice behind him.

MR MAUDSLEY

Enjoying yourself?

LEO

Oh yes thank you, sir.

MR MAUDSLEY

Miss your mother?

LEO

Yes, sir – I mean . . . no, sir. A little, sir.

Mr Maudsley peers at the thermometer.

MR MAUDSLEY

Pretty hot today.

LEO

Is it a record?

MR MAUDSLEY

I shouldn't be surprised. I shall have to look it up. Hot weather suit you?

LEO

Yes. sir.

EXT. BACK OF HOUSE.

Leo looking back at game larder. Mr Maudsley's back is bent towards the thermometer.

EXT. THE DERELICT OUTHOUSES.

Camera, still, looks through tangled bush towards the half-hidden outhouses.

Flies. Silence.

EXT. FRONT OF HOUSE. LAWN.

Leo walking past in foreground. In background figures strolling.

Trimingham turns in background and calls:

TRIMINGHAM

Hi! Mercury! Come here! I want you.

Shot over Trimingham to Leo, strolling in the distance.

Trimingham walks towards Leo. They meet in the centre of the lawn.

Trying to sneak past in dead ground.
>   (*Pause.*)
Where were you off to?

LEO

Nowhere.

TRIMINGHAM

Ah. Nowhere. Well, would you like to go somewhere?

LEO

Well, yes . . . where?

TRIMINGHAM

That's up to you.

LEO

Oh.

Trimingham laughs.

TRIMINGHAM

I want you to find Marian. We need her to make a four at croquet. No idea where she is. Can you find her?

LEO

I don't know.

TRIMINGHAM

No one else could. But you can. Will you do that?

LEO

Yes.

Leo turns and begins to trot away.

Trimingham calls after him.

TRIMINGHAM

You must bring her back dead or alive!

EXT. BACK OF THE HOUSE.

Leo wandering along, looking vaguely about, picks up a stone, throws it. Suddenly stops.

Marian is walking along the cinder track from the outhouses.

Close-up of Marian.

She stops.

MARIAN

What are you doing here?

LEO
(VO)

Hugh asked me to find you.

MARIAN

Why?

LEO
(VO)

He wants you to play croquet.

Marian does not reply. She moves away.

Silence.

Leo stands a moment, and then follows.

Two shot.

He said I was to bring you back dead or alive.

MARIAN

Well, which am I?

They laugh and begin to walk slowly towards the house.

We're going to luncheon with some neighbours

tomorrow. They're very old and mossy. I don't suppose
you want to come, do you?

LEO

Oh no. I can stay here.

MARIAN

What will you do?

LEO

Oh . . . anything.

MARIAN

But what?

LEO

I might go for a walk.

MARIAN

Where to?

They stop. Marian sits on a bench.

LEO

I might slide down a strawstack.

MARIAN

Oh. Whose?

LEO

Farmer Burgess.

MARIAN

Oh, his. Oh well, Leo, if you go that way perhaps you'd
give him a letter for me.

LEO

I was hoping you'd say that.

MARIAN

Why? Because you like him?

THE GO-BETWEEN

LEO

Yes. But there's another reason.

MARIAN

What is it?

LEO

Because I like you.

Close-up of Marian.

She smiles.

MARIAN

That's very sweet of you.

EXT. CORNFIELD. DAY.

Ted riding on a reaper, horse drawn, cutting corn. Three labourers binding the sheaves. Leo appears, walks beside the reaper. The reaper and Leo go through the corn.

Medium shot of Reaper.

Ted stops the horse and gets down. Leo gives him a letter. Ted opens it, reads it, stuffs it into his pocket.

TED

Tell her it's all right.

INT. HOUSE. LONG CORRIDOR. EVENING.

Marian walking alone. She pauses, looks at a painting on a wall. Leo walks towards her, speaks quietly to her. She walks on.

EXT. CORNFIELD. DAY.

Ted standing with gun, pointed at a small area of uncut corn. Leo watches from a distance. A labourer moves through the corn calling 'sshoo'.

Close-up of Ted with gun.

He shoots.

Close-up of rabbit.

The rabbit is flung into the air.

Close-up of Leo.

Two shot.

Ted holds out his hand for the letter. His hand is smeared with blood. He takes the letter from the envelope. The letter is smeared with blood.

> LEO
> Look what you've done.

Ted stuffs the letter into his pocket.

> TED
> Tell her it's no go.

INT. PASSAGE. DOOR OF MARCUS'S ROOM.

Sign on door SAFE ENTRY. Leo opens door, peeps round it.

> MARCUS
> You may enter boldly. My disease has fled.

> LEO
> You don't look better.

> MARCUS
> Of course I'm better. I shall be down this afternoon.
> You can bore me with your life story.

Leo standing alone at the top of a flight of stairs in the back of the house. He runs down it.

INT. FRONT OF HOUSE.

Leo walking quickly down a passage.

INT. WRITING ROOM.

Marian sitting at desk writing. She puts the letter in an envelope. Leo enters quickly, closes the door.

LEO

Marian, Marcus is –

The latch clicks. She slips envelope into his hand, he slips it into his pocket. Trimingham enters.

TRIMINGHAM

Ah! A conspiracy. A love scene. May I seize you from this fortunate fellow?

MARIAN

Is seize an appropriate word?

TRIMINGHAM

Gather then.
> (*He holds out his hand to her.*)
May I gather you from this fortunate fellow.

MARIAN
> (*to Leo*)
Do you mind if I'm gathered, Leo?

LEO

Oh, not at all.

Trimingham bows to Leo and leads Marian out.

Leo alone in writing room.

He takes the letter from his pocket and looks at it.

It is unsealed.

EXT. SIDE OF THE HOUSE. A PART OF THE LAWN.

Sounds of croquet. Smack of the mallet on the ball. Taps of the balls hitting each other. Voices in the distance.

                              A GIRL
Charles! Do come over here. Look at this beautiful bird.

                              CHARLES
What is it?

                              GIRL
Isn't it pretty? Look at the pretty colours.

                              CHARLES
Never seen one like it, I must admit.

Leo passes quickly through the shot.

EXT. WOODS.

Leo walking towards farm.

He stops, takes the unsealed envelope from his pocket, looks at it, puts it back.

He continues walking, stops, sits on a hillock, thinks.

He stands, walks, stops to look down into a valley.

Close-up of Leo.

He takes out the envelope and looks at it. He turns it to the open flap. Handwriting can be discerned on the paper. He looks at it upside down and swiftly turns it right side up. The camera concentrates on the writing on the paper.

The words exposed are:

> Darling, Darling, Darling,
> Same place, same time, this evening.
> But take care not to –

Close-up of Leo, his mouth open.

Leo sits down by a tree.

His expression is one of utter disappointment and disbelief. He leans on his elbow. He grimaces.

He emits a number of short noises, grunts, and 'hahs', hollow laughs. He sits baffled. Looks at the words again.

He sighs, stands, seals the letter. He walks on, uttering further short noises. The loudest of these alarm some birds. They fly up.

EXT. FARMYARD GATE.

In foreground Leo is crouching looking into the farmyard. In background Ted can be seen emerging from the stable door. Leo watches him move across the yard.

EXT. FARMYARD. REVERSE SHOT.

In background Leo stands up. Ted stops.

> TED
>
> Hullo, how's the postman?

> LEO
>
> Very well thank you.

> TED
>
> Brought anything for me?

Leo hands him the letter. Ted reads it.

> LEO
>
> I'm afraid I shan't be able to bring you any more letters.

Ted stares at him.

> TED
>
> Why not?

> LEO
>
> Marcus has got over his measles. I'll be with him all day. You said he wasn't to know. If he came here with me he would know.

> TED
>
> Have you told Miss Marian this?

LEO

No.

TED

She won't know what to do. Nor shall I.

LEO

What did you do before I came?

TED

Well . . . it wasn't so easy then.

INT. FARMHOUSE. KITCHEN.

The door opens. Ted comes in. Leo appears on the threshold, and stands in the doorway. Ted walks about the room.

TED

She likes you doesn't she? You want her to like you, don't you? You wouldn't want her to stop liking you. No . . . you wouldn't.
    (Pause.)
She won't be the same to you, if you don't take the letters. That's the truth. They're not just ordinary letters. She'll miss them. So shall I. She'll cry perhaps. Do you want her to cry?
    (Pause.)
It isn't hard to make her cry. She used to cry, before you came along.

LEO

Did you make her cry?

TED

She cried when she couldn't see me.

LEO

How do you know?

TED

Because she cried when she did see me.

Leo walks into the room and sits down.

Silence.

(*To himself.*)
I've been busy. Smiler's going to have a foal. She's ill.

LEO

Why does she have it then if it makes her ill?

TED

She hasn't much choice.

LEO

What made her have one?

Ted looks at him.

TED

What?

LEO

What made her have one?

Ted is silent for a moment, then laughs.

TED

Between you and me she did a bit of spooning.

LEO

Spooning? I didn't know horses could spoon.

TED

Oh it's a silly word really.

LEO

What does it *mean*?

TED

You seem to know something about it.

LEO

I don't know anything about it. That's the point. It's all
this kissing, isn't it? That's what it is. All that silly
kissing. I've seen it on postcards at the seaside. You
can't tell me horses do that.

TED

No, horses don't do that.

LEO

Well, what do they do? What does anyone do? There's
more to it than just kissing, I know that. But what?

TED

You'll find out.

Pause.

LEO

Could you marry someone without ever spooning with
them?

TED

Spooning's a silly word.

LEO

Well whatever the word is. Could you marry someone
and never do . . . whatever it is?

TED

You could. But it wouldn't be a very lover-like thing to
do.

Pause.

Leo stares at him.

LEO

Lover-like?

TED

That's enough questions anyway.

LEO

But you haven't told me anything.

TED

All right. Let's make a bargain. I'll tell you all about it on the condition you go on being our postman.

Close-up of Leo.

LEO

All right.

INT. HOUSE. DRAWING-ROOM.

Marian is arranging flowers by the window.

Leo runs in in cricket flannels.

MARIAN

Hello. Don't you look marvellous? Are you in the team?

LEO

Well, not exactly. I'm twelfth man. Marcus, you see, is convalescent.

MARIAN

What's twelfth man?

LEO

First reserve.

MARIAN

Ah. Well maybe someone will drop dead and then you can play.
(*She pricks her finger on a thorn.*)
Blast!

LEO

I've got a message for you from Hugh. He wants to know if you'll sing at the concert.

MARIAN

Oh does he? Well, tell him . . . that I'll sing . . . if he sings too.

EXT. VILLAGE STREET. DAY. PRESENT.

The back of Colston crossing the street towards a young man who glances at him.

TRIMINGHAM
(*VO*)

But I don't sing.

EXT. LANE. PAST.

The house team walking to the ground, dressed in white. The camera finds Leo and Marcus.

LEO

Why did you say I couldn't wear my cap?

MARCUS

Because it's a school cap. If it was an England cap, or a county cap, or a club cap, then, of course, you could wear it. But to wear a school cap in a private match simply isn't done.

LEO

Stomach pump!

EXT. CRICKET PAVILION.

The village team stands in a line. Trimingham leads Leo along it.

TRIMINGHAM

Burdock, this is our twelfth man, Colston.

Burdock and Leo shake hands and mutter 'how do you do'. This formula is repeated in all cases, with the following men: Stubbs, Mersham, Toms, Blunt, Hollyoak, Bates, Handson, Thorburn, Bolt and lastly Ted Burgess.

Close-up of Leo.

Three shot.

Ted smiles.

> **TED**
> Oh we know each other, m'lord, Master Colston and I,
> he comes to slide down my strawstack.

> **TRIMINGHAM**
> Of course. He's told us all about it.

> **LEO**
> Are you a good batsman?

> **TED**
> No, not me. I'm not much of a cricketer, really.

> **TRIMINGHAM**
> He can be very dangerous, Leo. We've got to get him
> out quickly.

> **TED**
> I'm not a cricketer. I just hit.

> **TRIMINGHAM**
> Well, we're going to get you out before you get the
> chance.

EXT. CRICKET GROUND.

*Four old men sitting on a bench smoking pipes. The camera pans
from them to see the ground filling up with spectators.*

*Trimingham and Burdock on the field. Burdock spins a coin.
Trimingham calls 'heads'. The coin lands. He looks at the coin,
turns to the pavilion, and makes a gesture of batting.*

EXT. PAVILION.

Leo jumping across a bench to Marcus.

                         LEO
He's won the toss! We're batting!

EXT. GROUND SCOREBOARD.

*A boy approaches the scoreboard with two mugs of tea and hands
them to the scorers.*

*A shout from the spectators. The scorer looks up and takes down
the last batsman's score from the board.*

EXT. PAVILION.

*The ladies of the house, including Mrs Maudsley and Marian,
walk to the pavilion to their seats. The gentlemen standing. They
settle in their seats. The rector sits beside Mrs Maudsley.*

*Marian sits in front of them with Kate. Trimingham comes out of
the pavilion, inclining his head to the ladies as he passes them.
Applause.*

*The camera pans from the ladies to find Denys with Leo and the
rest of the team.*

                        DENYS
He's a pretty bat. A very pretty bat. I have great
confidence in him.

EXT. THE PITCH.

Trimingham driving gracefully.

Marian applauding.

Denys and Leo.

                        DENYS
Isn't he fine? Such command and elegance. Don't you
think he's fine?

LEO

Yes, I do.

A shout. They lean forward, shocked.

Trimingham leaving the wicket. His stumps are down.

Marian applauding vigorously as Trimingham returns to the pavilion. Mr Maudsley comes out of the pavilion. Applause.

Denys turns to Leo.

DENYS

We're in trouble. There's only me to come. I mean that's any good, quite frankly.

EXT. THE PITCH.

Mr Maudsley tapping his bat on the ground, waiting for the ball. It is bowled. He places it calmly between two fielders and runs.

Mr Maudsley steering the ball calmly off his legs. He runs.

EXT. PAVILION.

DENYS

He's in some command. But he mustn't tire himself.

A shout. Denys jumps up.

That's me. It's absolutely up to me. But I mustn't tire him. He's not young.

EXT. PITCH.

Mr Maudsley leaning on bat waiting. Denys comes to arrive at the wicket.

Shot over Denys to Mr Maudsley batting.

Mr Maudsley plays the ball and starts to run. Denys's hand shoots up.

DENYS
(*loudly*)

No!

Mr Maudsley looks at him with irritation.

Long shot. Ground.

Mr Maudsley plays the ball and starts to run. Denys flings up his hand.

DENYS
(*loudly*)

No!

EXT. GROUND. LEO AND MARCUS.

LEO
Why does he keep saying no?

MARCUS
He wants to save my father's strength. Which is a little unnecessary I think.

EXT. PITCH.

Mr Maudsley plays the ball and begins to run. Denys flings up his hand.

DENYS

No!

MR MAUDSLEY
(*shouting*)

Come on!

Mr Maudsley runs up the pitch. Denys, late, begins to run. The ball is thrown in. Denys stumbles, falls headlong, flat on his face. The ball has hit the wicket. He is out. He stands, dusts himself, and walks away.

Close shot. Mr Maudsley.

He stands calmly, his hands on his hips.

INT. PAVILION.

The teams are having tea. The camera tracks down the table.

> TRIMINGHAM
> Beautifully played, sir.

> MR MAUDSLEY
> Thank you very much. Now we have to get Burgess out.

The camera tracks. Sandwiches, buns etc.

> LEO
> What about Burgess? Isn't he dangerous?

> DENYS
> He's a strong hitter, I grant you. But he's no sense of
> culture or discipline. Trimingham will be far too
> cunning for him.

EXT. CRICKET PITCH.

Ted hitting six.

A tree.

The ball soars into a tree.

Close-up of Leo.

*In foreground Marian intent. In background Mrs Maudsley
intent.*

They are both watching the game.

Ted hitting six.

*Leo applauding suddenly. He stops. Looks about him. The
camera looks with him towards Marian. She is biting her lip.*

The back of Mrs Maudsley's head in foreground.

The back of Marian's head in background.

They are both still.

Close shot. Ted.

He hits the ball hard.

A fielder half stops the ball with his hand, falls. The ball careers on.

EXT. PAVILION.

The ball hurtling into the pavilion. It lands near the ladies' seats. Mrs Maudsley jumps up with a cry. Marian puts her hand to her mouth. The other ladies jump up.

>   RECTOR
> Mrs Maudsley! Are you all right?

>   MRS MAUDSLEY
> Yes, yes. Perfectly all right.

>   RECTOR
> That was a close shave.

>   KATE
> What a shock. He's terribly savage.

Close shot. Leo picking up the ball.

He looks up.

>   TRIMINGHAM
>   (VO)
> Where's our twelfth man?

Two shot. Mrs Maudsley and Marian.

Mrs Maudsley leans over.

MRS MAUDSLEY

Are you all right, Marian?

MARIAN

Yes, Mama. Thank you.

MRS MAUDSLEY

The ball didn't hurt you?

MARIAN

It didn't touch me, Mama.

EXT. PITCH.

Trimingham walking with Leo.

TRIMINGHAM

(*muttering*)

We've got to get him out or he'll beat us on his own.

Trimingham, tossing the ball, walks to the bowler's end. The camera with Trimingham looks down the wicket at Ted. Trimingham runs up to bowl. Bowls. Ted swings, the ball beats him but misses the wicket. Trimingham flings up his arms. Ted grins. The ball is returned to Trimingham.

Close-up of Leo watching.

Close-up of Trimingham turning.

Close-up of Ted waiting for the ball.

Trimingham bowls.

Ted drives.

The ball landing in the crowd.

Leo standing. Biting his thumb.

Trimingham bowls fast.

Shot over Leo's shoulder.

In background Ted swings. Hits the ball. It hurtles through the air towards Leo. Leo jumps up and catches it.

Leo on his back on the grass. The ball in his hand.

Applause. Trimingham comes into the shot, helps him up, pats him on the back.

TRIMINGHAM
Magnificent catch.

Shot from behind Mrs Maudsley and Marian.

Their backs are still. In background the players are returning to the pavilion.

The players.

Leo runs to Ted who is walking alone.

LEO
I didn't really mean to catch you out.

TED
It was a damn good catch.
          (*He laughs. Then murmurs.*)
I never thought I'd be caught out by our postman.

Applause grows. Ted goes forward. Shouts of his name. He goes into the pavilion alone. Trimingham stops the team at the pavilion gates and ushers Leo in alone. Applause for Leo. As the team follows Leo up the steps the camera rests on Marian. She is still. Her head is bent.

EXT. CRICKET FIELD. EVENING. PAST.

The field is silent. As we have just seen it, but empty. Long shadows across it.

COLSTON
(*VO*)
Isn't it dull for you to live here alone?

                    MARIAN'S VOICE OLD (OVER)
Alone? But people come in shoals. I'm quite a place of
pilgrimage.

INT. VILLAGE HALL.

The concert.

*Union Jacks, paper streamers etc. Food, wine. Mr Maudsley on
the platform.*

                         MR MAUDSLEY
And last but not least, except in stature, our young
David, Leo Colston, who slew the Goliath of Black
Farm, if I may so describe him, not with a sling but with
a catch.

Close shot of Ted. In high starched collar.

He winks at Leo.

Leo surrounded by applause.

Mr Maudsley on platform.

And now, I believe, it is time for the music. Who I
wonder will be prepared to give us the first song?

The assembly.

*A proportion of the assembly is slightly drunk, particularly Blunt
and Stubbs. A number of people turn to look at Ted and call for
him.*

                            BLUNT
Ted's the one! He's the big hitter!

                            STUBBS
And he's the best shot with a gun!

                            BLUNT
But is he the best singer?

Calls of 'Yes, come on, Ted' 'Ted's the one' and 'Give us a song'.

Ted stands boldly. A shout of acclaim from the audience. Ted walks with confidence up to the platform. Shouts of 'Good old Ted'.

The platform.

Ted puts his music down on the piano and grins. He suddenly looks at the piano stool, goes to it and lifts it up, looking at it carefully. He turns to the audience.

TED

I can't see the pianist.

The audience.

Some of the audience laugh and then a murmur begins. Voices: 'Where's the pianist?' 'What's happened to him?' etc.

VOICE

He's in bed. Ill.

Cries of 'In bed?' 'He should be here'.

He's caught a fatal finger disease.

A laugh and then sudden silence falls on the assembly.

TRIMINGHAM

We can't manage without a pianist.

The platform.

Ted holding piano stool uncertain.

The audience from Ted's point of view.

BLUNT

Come on, Ted. Don't be shy. You don't need music.

STUBBS

Yes, give us a song.

                          BLUNT
    But take your collar off first! It's going to strangle you!

Medium shot. Ted.

*He puts the piano stool down and stands dogged and unhappy.
He shakes his head.*

Close-up of Mrs Maudsley.

She sits with a very faint smile in her eyes.

                          BLUNT
                          (*VO*)
    Come on, be a gentleman. You're dressed up like one.

                          STUBBS
    A sheep in wolf's clothing.

A sudden rustle. Silence. A murmur from the audience.

The audience from Ted's point of view.

*Marian moving swiftly down the aisle towards the platform.
Applause from the audience.*

The platform. Long shot.

*Marian climbing the steps to the platform. Ted still. He moves
abruptly to help her up. Ironic applause from some members of the
audience. She goes to the piano stool and sits down. She picks up
the top sheet of music and holds it up to Ted questioningly. Ted
nods miserably. She places it on the music rest. Ted turns to the
audience.*

                          TED
                          (*very low*)
    Take a pair of sparkling eyes.

                          BLUNT
    What did you say? Speak up.

TED

Take a pair of sparkling eyes.

STUBBS

Well, cheer up it isn't a funeral.

Close-up. Ted begins to sing.

Close-up of Marian playing the piano.

INT. COTTAGE. THE SITTING-ROOM. LONG SHOT. PRESENT.

Colston standing with his back to the camera. A maid comes into the room. She says something unheard. Colston shakes his head. The maid leaves the room. Colston stands.

Over this Ted's voice singing 'Take a pair of sparkling eyes'.

INT. VILLAGE HALL. PAST.

Audience clapping.

Close-up of Leo clapping.

Shouts of encore.

Ted and Marian on platform.

Ted begins to leave the platform. Shouts of encore. Trimingham smoking, looking up at the platform. Mr Maudsley looking across at Trimingham. He glances down.

Applause. Marian rises from her stool. She bows to Ted. He jerks his head towards her and away. The audience laughs. He slowly turns towards her and bows. Then they bow to the audience.

EXT. CRICKET FIELD. EARLY EVENING. PRESENT.

The field is silent. A modern mower stands in the centre of the field. The shot is held in silence. Suddenly Marian's voice:

MARIAN
(*VO*)

Well, Leo, what's it to be?

Close-up of Leo. Quick cut. PAST.

Leo is now on the platform.

Platform. Long shot. Leo approaches the edge of the platform. The audience is still. He sings:

> Angels! Ever bright and fair,
> Take, oh take me to your care.
> Speed to your own courts my flight
> Clad in robes of virgin white
> Clad in robes of virgin white.

During this song the camera gently cuts between Stubbs and Blunt, totally sober and attentive, Trimingham, Mr Maudsley, Mrs Maudsley and Ted. Close-ups of Marian and Leo. Gleam of Marian's white arms and neck from Ted's and Leo's point of view.

The final shot of this sequence of shots is from the back of the hall as Leo finishes the song, the audience quite still, before the applause.

EXT. LANE. MOONLIGHT. NIGHT.

The party walking back to the house. Marcus and Leo straggling behind.

MARCUS

Well, thank goodness we've said good-bye to the village for a year. Did you notice the stink in that hall?

LEO

No.

MARCUS

What a whiff! I suppose you were too busy mooing and

rolling your eyes and sucking up the applause. Still,
toadstool, I must admit you didn't do too badly.

LEO

Oh thank you.

MARCUS

Except that it was rather horrific to see your slimy
serpent's tongue stuck to the roof of your mouth and
your face like a sick cow.

Leo seizes him.

LEO

You po-faced pot-bellied bed wetter!

MARCUS

Pax! I'll tell you a secret.

LEO

What?

MARCUS

Marian's engaged to marry Trimingham. It'll be
announced after the ball. Are you glad?

Leo lets him go.

LEO

Yes, I am. I'm sure I am.

EXT. HOUSE. THE LONG SHOT. LAWN. DAY.

*Marian and Trimingham playing croquet. They play slowly and
with concentration. He moves towards her and whispers
something to her. They laugh. The camera suddenly observes that
Leo is watching them.*

INT. HOUSE. THE HALL LOOKING THROUGH TO DINING-
ROOM.

*The end of luncheon. The house party sitting at the long table
eating peaches.*

Marcus and Leo come out of the dining-room.

MARCUS

Are you going out?

LEO

Yes. Shall we?

MARCUS

I'm afraid I can't.

LEO

Why not, sewer rat?

MARCUS

Nanny Robson isn't well. She lives in the village.
Marian says I have to spend the afternoon with her.
Isn't it boring? Marian said she was going herself after
tea. What will you do? Where will you drag your evil
smelling carcase?

LEO

Oh I might hang round the rubbish heap for a bit. And
then –

MARCUS

Well, don't get carted away by mistake.

The boys tussle in the hall.

EXT. BACK OF HOUSE.

*Leo strolling away from the thermometer. He turns in the direction
of the rubbish dump. Marian's voice stops him:*

MARIAN

Hello, Leo. Just the man I was looking for.

She comes into shot.

Will you do something for me?

LEO

Oh yes. What?

MARIAN

Take this letter.

She holds out the letter.

Leo looks at it and then at her.

LEO

But . . . who to?

MARIAN

Who to? Why to the farm. You silly.

Close-up of Leo.

He stares at her.

Two shot.

What's the matter?

LEO

But I can't.

MARIAN

Can't? Why not?

Pause.

LEO

Because of Hugh.

MARIAN

Hugh? What has Hugh to do with it?

LEO

He . . . might be upset.

MARIAN

What has Hugh got to do with it? I told you, this is a
business matter between Mr Burgess and myself. It has
nothing to do with anyone else, no one else in the
world. Do you understand? Or are you too stupid?

Close-up of Leo.

LEO

But you and Hugh . . . you and Trimingham . . .
you . . .

Close-up of Marian.

MARIAN

What are you talking about? You come into this house,
our guest, a poor nothing out of nowhere, we take you
in, we know nothing about you, we feed you, we clothe
you, we make a great fuss of you – and then you have
the damned cheek to say you won't do a simple thing
that any tuppeny-ha'-penny rag-a-muffin in the street
would do for nothing!

Long shot.

Marian and Leo alone on the path.

Nothing!

*She raises her hand. Leo starts back. They are still. Close-up of
Marian.*

You want paying, I suppose. I see. How much do you
want?

Two shot.

Leo snatches the letter and runs.

EXT. COUNTRY LANE. VERY HIGH SHOT.

Leo, a tiny figure in the landscape, walking, kicking a stone.

> MARIAN'S VOICE OLD (OVER)
> So you met my grandson?

> COLSTON
> (*VO*)
> Yes I did.

> MARIAN'S VOICE OLD (OVER)
> Does he remind you of anyone?

> COLSTON
> (*VO*)
> Of course. His grandfather.

> MARIAN'S VOICE OLD (OVER)
> That's it, that's it. He does. Yes, he does.

The stone is kicked against a gate.

Shot over farmyard gate to Leo.

His face is stained with tears.

INT. FARM. KITCHEN.

Ted is sitting alone holding a gun between his knees. His chest is naked. The barrel is pressed against it. The muzzle just below his mouth. He is peering down the barrel.

The shot holds.

Sound of a knock and a door opening.

Ted looks up.

> TED
> Hullo! It's the postman!

Shot of kitchen.

Ted stands.

How are you?

He comes closer to Leo and peers at him.

You've been crying. What's the matter?

Ted takes out a handkerchief and gives it to him.

Would you like to have a shot with my gun? I was just going to clean it but I can do that afterwards.

Leo shakes his head.

Come and watch me then. There's some old rooks round here that could do with a peppering.

EXT. FARMYARD.

Ted standing in the yard. Gun at his shoulder. Leo by the door.

Ted shoots. Leo starts.

Leo's point of view.

The bird twirls slowly to earth. Ted picks it up and throws it into a bed of nettles.

The sky.

Rooks wheeling away.

TED
(*VO*)
They won't come back in a hurry.

INT. SCULLERY.

Ted putting the kettle on to boil on the grate.

TED
Have you got a letter for me?

INT. KITCHEN.

*Ted walks in with tablecloth and drapes it over the table. Leo
hands him the letter.*

TED

Looks as though you've been sleeping on it.

Ted reads it quickly, puts it away.

You'd like some tea, wouldn't you? I'm on my own today. My daily woman doesn't come on Sundays.

LEO

Oh, do you have a woman every day?

Ted looks at him.

TED

No. I told you she doesn't come on Sundays.

LEO

Have you any message for her?

TED

Who?

LEO

Marian.

TED

I might have, but do you want to take it?

LEO

Not very much. But she'll be angry if I don't.

Ted lights a cigarette.

TED

So it was her.
(*Pause.*)
It isn't fair to ask you to do it for nothing. What can I do
to make it worth your while?

77

Close-up of Leo.

                    LEO
Last time I was here you said you'd tell me something.

Close-up of Ted.

                    TED
Did I?

                    LEO
Yes, you said you'd tell me about . . . spooning.

Close-up of Leo.

I don't know any other word. Is there another word?

The kitchen.

Ted goes to the dresser, brings some tea-cups and saucers and puts them on the table.

You said you'd tell me.

                    TED
                (*collecting plates*)
Yes. But now I'm not sure that I shall.

                    LEO
Why not?

                    TED
It's a job for your dad, really.

                    LEO
My father's dead. And I'm quite sure he never did it!

                    TED
Are you?

Pause.

                    LEO
You can't break your promise.

78

Pause.

> TED
>
> Well . . . it means putting your arm round a girl, and kissing her. That's what it means.

Leo jumping out of chair.

> LEO
>
> I know that! But it's something else too. It makes you *feel* something.

> TED
>
> What do you like doing best?

> LEO
>
> Oh . . .

Hissing of the kettle from the scullery.

> TED
>
> The kettle's boiling.

Ted goes into the scullery. Leo stands. Ted comes out with a tea-pot and a jug of milk and puts them on the table.

> It's like whatever you like doing best, and then some more.

Close-up of Leo.

> LEO
>
> Yes, but *what more*? What is lover-like? What does it mean? What is a lover? What does a lover do? Are you a lover? What do you do? You know. I know you know. And I won't take any more messages for you unless you tell me!

Ted from Leo's point of view.

Ted towers above him, and moves towards him.

TED

Clear out of here quick.

Leo's back darts out of shot.

INT. COTTAGE. HALL AND FRONT DOOR. PRESENT.

The back of Colston walking through the hall, down a step into the sitting-room. The maid closes the door and follows. She leaves the room by another door. Colston stands.

Over this Leo's voice:

LEO'S VOICE
(*as if writing*)

Dear Mother, I am sorry to tell you I am not enjoying myself here. I would like to come home.

EXT. ROAD OUTSIDE FARM. PAST.

Leo running away from farm. Ted waving and shouting at farmyard gate, receding into the distance.

INT. HOUSE. TEA. THE SILVER TEA-POT.

The camera withdraws to find Marian presiding over tea. Trimingham sits beside Marian, on a low stool, half in shadow. She regards her guests with a smile, pouring milk in one cup, a slice of lemon in another and lumps of sugar into some. The cups and plates of cakes are passed round. When it is Leo's turn for tea Marian drops four lumps of sugar into his cup, giggling.

This shot is silent. Over the shot hear Marian's voice as an old lady.

MARIAN'S VOICE (OLD)

I rarely went to parties. People came to see me, of course, interesting people, artists and writers, not stuffy country neighbours. There *are* stuffy people, aren't there? No, no, interesting people came to see me.

Artists and writers. Modern people with modern views.

INT. HOUSE. HALL. BRASS POSTBOX.

Leo popping letter into the postbox.

EXT. BACK OF THE HOUSE. EARLY EVENING.

Leo and Marcus pushing each other.

> MARCUS
>
> What shall we do? Where shall we go?

> LEO
>
> What about the rubbish dump?

> MARCUS
>
> Oh no, it's so boring. What about those mysterious
> outhouses?

> LEO
>
> Good idea.

> MARCUS
>
> Not that there's anything worth seeing, apart from a lot
> of dreary old outhouses.

> LEO
>
> There's the deadly nightshade.

> MARCUS
>
> Oui, le belladonne.

> LEO
>
> You mean atropa belladonna.

*They begin to walk towards the outhouses. Marcus's voice
receding.*

> MARCUS
>
> I don't mean that at all. I mean deadly nightshade.

Marcus and Leo walking through the tangled undergrowth.

Mama is ill in bed.

LEO

Why?

MARCUS

I don't know.

They walk on.

What do you think of my mother?

Leo glances at him.

LEO

I think she has a lot to look after . . . with the house and everything, and organizing the ball and everything.

MARCUS

She has, yes. She undoubtedly has.

They walk on.

My sister is very beautiful, isn't she?

LEO

Yes. She is very beautiful.

They walk on.

MARCUS

She's going to London tomorrow.

LEO

What for?

MARCUS

Firstly to buy a dress for the ball, you oaf. The engagement ball, you oaf, and then to get something for you.

LEO

What do you mean?

MARCUS

A birthday present, frog-spawn. Now shall I tell you
what it is or shall I not?

LEO

Do you *know* what it is?

MARCUS

Yes, but I don't tell little boys.

Leo grapples with him and holds him in a firm grip.

Well swear that you won't tell anyone I told you.

LEO

I swear.

MARCUS

It's a bicycle.

Leo lets Marcus out of his grip.

LEO
(*with great pleasure*)

What?

MARCUS

Do you know what colour it is? It's green, green, you
imbecile. Bright green. And do you know why? Because
you are green yourself. It's your true colour, Marian
said so.

Leo standing with Marcus dancing round him.

Green. Green. Green!

LEO

Did she say that?

MARCUS

But of course.

Marcus continues to dance around Leo.

Green. Green. Green!

Close-up of Leo.

LEO
(*violently*)
Do you know where Marian is at this moment?

Two shot.

Marcus stops still.

MARCUS

No. Do you?

LEO

Yes.

MARCUS

Where?

LEO

I don't tell little boys.

Leo dances round Marcus.

Little boy, little boy, wouldn't you like to know?

MARCUS

Pax!

Leo walks away.

Leo and Marcus walking.

Do you really know where she is?

LEO

Ah-hah!

84

They walk on in silence, kicking stones as they go. Suddenly Leo stops.

The deadly nightshade.

It has grown out of its door, and spread. It emerges over the roofless wall. It is heavy, purple, oppressive.

MARCUS
(VO)

Shall we push past it into the shed?

Close-up of Leo.

LEO

No, you mustn't.

Suddenly the low murmur of a man's voice heard. Marcus and Leo freeze. The voice is insistent, cajoling, tender. The words are indecipherable. Marcus whispers to Leo.

MARCUS

A loony talking to himself. Shall we go and see?

A second voice heard, low, toneless, light.

There are two of them. They're spooning. Let's go and rout them out.

Quick close-up of Leo.

LEO
(hushed whisper)

No! It would be too boring!

EXT. OUTHOUSES.

Leo walks away. Marcus stands a moment, looking back, and then follows. He joins Leo in foreground.

MARCUS

What confounded cheek. Why should they come here?

This is private property. I wonder what Mama would say.

LEO

Oh, I shouldn't tell her. What's the point?

MARCUS

What confounded cheek!

They disappear from shot.

The camera holds on the view of the outhouses, including the deadly nightshade.

INT. HOUSE. HALL. THE POSTBOX.

Leo looks through the pane into the postbox. He sees his letter. He fingers the door. It opens. He takes the letter out, looks at it, puts it back quickly. Closes the door.

The camera pans to watch him run up the centre stairs.

INT. HOUSE. CORRIDOR. FIRST LANDING.

Leo appears and sees Trimingham going into the smoking-room. The door closes.

Leo hesitates, then walks to the smoking-room door, hesitates, knocks at the door, opens it.

INT. SMOKING-ROOM.

Trimingham picking up a newspaper. Leo pokes his head round the door.

TRIMINGHAM

Hello.

Leo hesitates at the door.

Come in.

Leo closes the door.

Never been in here before?

LEO

No.

TRIMINGHAM

Sit down. Cigar?

LEO

No thank you.

Trimingham sits down and lights a cigar.

Can I ask you something?

TRIMINGHAM

You can.

LEO

I was reading a book. And in this book . . . two men fought a duel . . . over a quarrel . . . about one of the men's wife. And then . . . in this duel . . . the wife's husband . . . the husband . . . was shot.

TRIMINGHAM

Mmn-hmnm

(*Pause.*)

What's your question?

LEO

Well, I thought . . . when I read it . . . that it was probably the lady's fault, but she didn't have to fight the duel and I just thought that it was a little unfair.

Close-up of Trimingham.

TRIMINGHAM

Nothing is ever a lady's fault.

Close-up of Leo.

LEO

Oh.

Close-up of Trimingham.

TRIMINGHAM

Does that answer your question?

Shot across Trimingham to Leo.

LEO

Yes.

TRIMINGHAM

Any other questions?

LEO

Er . . . what do you think of Ted Burgess?

TRIMINGHAM
(*ruminatively*)
What do I think of Ted Burgess?
(*Pause.*)
He's a powerful hitter.

Leo chuckles.

But you had the measure of him.

Leo smiles.

You defeated him, didn't you?
(*Pause.*)
Yes, Ted Burgess is quite a decent fellow. A bit wild.

LEO

Wild? Do you mean he's dangerous?

TRIMINGHAM

He's not dangerous to you or to me. He's a bit of a lady-killer, that's all.

LEO
(baffled)

A lady-killer?

The door opens. Mr Maudsley comes in.

Trimingham and Leo rise.

MR MAUDSLEY

Sit down, please sit down. Ah! A new recruit to the
smoking-room. Have you been telling him some
smoking-room stories?

Trimingham laughs.

Or showing him the pictures?
(He turns to Leo.)
Have you looked at the pictures?

*Mr Maudsley indicates a row of small dark canvases, set deep in
heavy frames.*

Leo turns to look at the pictures.

*Men sitting on tubs, drinking. Women serving them. One woman
leaning on the back of a man's chair watching the card game.
The chair back pressing against her breasts, which bulge over its
rim.*

Leo turns away from the pictures.

Close-up of Mr Maudsley.

He doesn't like them.

Three shot.

TRIMINGHAM

Teniers is an acquired taste, in my opinion. We were
talking about Ted Burgess when you came in. I told Leo
he was a lady-killer.

89

MR MAUDSLEY

He has that reputation, I believe.

TRIMINGHAM

I've been talking to him about joining the army. A likely man. Single. No ties. And a pretty good shot too with a rifle, by all accounts.

MR MAUDSLEY

He has that reputation, I believe.
                    (*Pause.*)
Do you think he'll go?

TRIMINGHAM

I think he may. He was quite interested.

MR MAUDSLEY

He won't altogether be a loss to the district.

TRIMINGHAM

Why?

MR MAUDSLEY
                    (*vaguely*)
Oh, what you were saying just now.

Mr Maudsley goes to the cabinet to pour sherry from a decanter.

They say he's got a woman up this way.

LEO

I know.

Close-up of Mr Maudsley.

Mr Maudsley, in the act of pouring sherry, stops and looks over his shoulder at Leo.

Trimingham and Mr Maudsley looking at Leo.

Close-up of Leo.

But she doesn't come on Sundays.

Trimingham and Mr Maudsley.

> TRIMINGHAM
> (*to Mr Maudsley*)

Cigar?

EXT. CORNFIELD. LONG SHOT. DAY.

*Leo stands in foreground looking across the field. Ted is driving
the reaper. Leo waves. Ted does not see him. A labourer sees Leo
and signals to Ted. Ted stops the horse and dismounts. The
labourer gets up on the reaper and continues the work.*

*Ted walks slowly across the fields towards Leo. The camera moves
with Leo as he walks towards Ted. They stop at a short distance
from each other.*

Silence.

> TED
> I didn't think you'd come again.
> (*Pause.*)
> I'm sorry I shouted at you. I didn't mean to. I just
> didn't feel like telling you – what you wanted to know –
> that's all. But I'll tell you now if you like.
> (*Pause.*)
> Do you want me to tell you? Because I'll tell you now. If
> you want me to.

Close-up of Leo.

> LEO
> No, no. I wouldn't dream of troubling you. I know
> someone who'll tell me. As I matter of fact I know
> several people who can tell me.

Two shot.

> TED
> As long as they don't tell you wrong.

LEO

How could they? It's common knowledge, isn't it?

Pause.

TED

What are you doing with your bathing suit?

They begin to stroll along the edge of the cornfield.

LEO

I told Marcus you were going to give me a swimming lesson. I've come to say good-bye, you see.

Long shot. Across cornfield.

Leo and Ted walking along its rim. Their voices:

TED

Oh, you're off are you?

LEO

Yes. I'm expecting to hear from my mother by Friday at the latest. I think I really should go home. She does miss me, you know.

TED

I'm sure she does.

Pause.

LEO

Is it true you're going to the war?

TED

Who told you that?

LEO

Lord Trimingham.
                    (*Pause.*)
Did you know Marian was engaged to him?

TED

Yes. I did.

Close two shot. Ted and Leo stopping.

LEO

Is that why you're going?

TED

I don't know that I *am* going. That's for her to say. It isn't what I want, but what she wants.

Close-up of Leo staring at him.

Two shot.

LEO

Well, good-bye.

TED

So long, postman.

They shake hands. Leo turns, turns back.

LEO

Shall I take one more message for you?

Close-up of Ted.

TED

Yes. Say tomorrow's no good, but Friday at half-past five, same as usual.

Close-up of Marian.

MARIAN

Did you miss me?

LEO
(*VO*)

Well . . . I've been quite busy.

MARIAN

That's the first unkind thing I've ever heard you say.

Two shot Marian and Leo.

They are sitting in a small writing room.

MARIAN

I've been to London on a special mission.

LEO

Did you enjoy yourself?

MARIAN

No.

LEO

I'm sorry.

MARIAN

No you're not. You couldn't care less if I dropped dead in front of you. You're a hard-hearted boy, but then all boys are.

LEO

What about men?

MARIAN

You're all alike, blocks of granite. Or the beds here. They're *really* hard.

LEO

Mine isn't.

MARIAN

You're lucky. Mine is, harder than the ground.

LEO

I know a boy who slept on the ground once. He said it made his hips sore. Did you find that?

Marian looks at him.

MARIAN

What makes you think I've slept on the ground?

LEO

Because you said your bed was harder.

MARIAN

Well, so it is.

(*Pause.*)

I'm sorry I was so nasty to you the other day. I'm not really nasty. I'm a good natured girl, really.

Close-up of Leo.

LEO

Do . . . soldiers have to sleep on the ground?

MARIAN

Yes, I suppose so.

LEO

Will Ted have to?

Close-up of Marian.

MARIAN

Ted?

LEO

Yes, when he goes to the war.

MARIAN

Ted going to the war, what do you mean?

Two shot.

LEO

Hugh told me. Hugh asked him to join up and he said he might.

MARIAN

Hugh? Hugh! Do you mean that Hugh has persuaded Ted to enlist?

She stands and goes to the window.

Marian foreground. Window. Leo background.

> (*Quietly.*)
> No. No he won't, he won't go to the war. I'll see to that.
> I'll tell Hugh . . . that it's out of the question. One word
> would do it.

Leo comes to her at the window.

LEO

No, you mustn't say any word. You see, Hugh doesn't
know.

MARIAN

Doesn't know? Then why does he want Ted to go to the
war?

LEO

He's patriotic.
> (*Pause.*)
Perhaps he *wants* to go.

MARIAN

He couldn't.

Pause.

LEO

Why don't you marry Ted?

MARIAN

I can't . . . I can't. Can't you see why?

LEO

But why . . . are you marrying Hugh?

MARIAN

Because I must. I must. I've got to.

Wide shot. Room.

Marian suddenly cries quietly. Leo stares at her and then begins to cry himself.

They stand, crying. They hold each other. Leo forces himself to stop.

LEO

I have a message for you.

She looks up.

Friday at 5.30.

MARIAN

Yes.

LEO

But can you be back in time?

MARIAN

For what?

LEO

For my birthday. For cutting the cake.

Marian takes his hand.

MARIAN

Of course. Of course.

EXT. VILLAGE STREET. PRESENT.

Colston standing by the car. At the far end of the village the figure of a young man appears. He slowly draws nearer on the other side of the street. Colston moves a few steps, stops and watches the young man. As the young man comes closer, Colston begins to cross the street towards him.

Zoom in to young man's face turning sharply, seeing Colston approach.

Leo's Mother's voice over this (as if writing):

LEO'S MOTHER'S VOICE

I think it would be ungrateful to Mrs Maudsley after all her kindness to you if you were to leave so suddenly. I think it would be a mistake.

INT. LEO'S ROOM. NIGHT. PAST.

Leo at the writing table, erecting a structure like a small altar. Four books form the framework. Within stand four candles, a soap dish drainer rests on the books, on the drainer a silver cup, four boxes of matches, a water bottle and a damp sponge, set at precise intervals on the table. Leo looks at his clock. It is 11.15.

Over this shot the woman's voice continues:

LEO'S MOTHER'S VOICE

The ten days will soon pass, my darling, and then you'll be home. We can't expect to be happy *all* the time, can we?

He puts on his slippers and his dressing gown over his nightshirt and opens the door.

INT. HOUSE. STAIRCASE. NIGHT.

Through the closed door of the drawing room sounds of a piano and singing. Marian is singing 'Roaming in the Gloaming'.

The front door is open. Leo creeps down the main staircase, hesitates a moment and then goes out the door.

EXT. BACK OF THE HOUSE. LEO RUNNING THROUGH THE BUSHES.

The sky, cloudy, through moonlight.

The outhouse.

Leo stops dead.

Leo's point of view. The deadly nightshade.

Leo walks towards it slowly. When he is close to it, he stops.

He touches it. He moves quickly past it and into the outhouses.

INT. OUTHOUSE.

Close-up of Leo. The twigs of the deadly nightshade about him.

He shifts his position. A berry touches his face. He whimpers, tries to force his way out, hits a wall, turns, nightshade flowers around his face.

Leo begins to tear at the nightshade. Branches rip and crack. He stumbles, still pulling, out of the outhouse, pulling at the main stem. Leaves fall, the main stem cracks. Roots creak. He pulls with all his might to unearth the plant and suddenly it gives way.

He falls on his back clutching the stump.

High shot. Leo lying with stump.

> LEO
>
> Delenda est Belladonna.

INT. LEO'S ROOM. CLOSE SHOT SILVER CUP ON WRITING TABLE. NIGHT.

Diary open beside it. Incomprehensible writing seen. Leo is crushing a leaf, flower and two berries from the deadly nightshade in the cup, pouring boiling water into it with his left hand.

> LEO
> (*VO, whispering*)
>
> Delenda, delenda, delenda.

INT. LAVATORY.

Leo pouring the mashed contents of the cup into the lavatory.

> COLSTON
> (*VO*)
>
> Delenda est Belladonna.

Leo makes a gesture of exorcism.

EXT. HOUSE. LAWN. RAIN. DAY.

The rain sweeps over the lawn and through the cedars. Close-up of Mrs Maudsley.

MRS MAUDSLEY
And now today . . . is Leo's day.

She smiles.

The camera tracks back to find Mrs Maudsley and the others at the breakfast table. In front of Leo are opened envelopes and packages. Cards, ties etc.

You've opened your presents. At seven o'clock you'll cut your birthday cake, and receive a rather special present, so I believe. Now how would you like to spend the day? Unfortunately the weather . . . has changed, but if it clears perhaps you would like to go for a drive to Beeston Castle, after luncheon? You haven't seen it, have you?

LEO
That would be very nice.

MRS MAUDSLEY
Well, we shall do that, if the weather clears. We shall decide at luncheon.

DENYS
What if the weather doesn't clear, Mama?

MRS MAUDSLEY
Then he shall have to think again. We shall make our decision at luncheon. Don't you think, Hugh?

TRIMINGHAM
Quite a fair plan, I should say.

DENYS

But it may not clear.

EXT. VILLAGE STREET. OVER COLSTON TO THE YOUNG
MAN. PRESENT.

*The young man steps back to point to a cottage at the far end of
the village. Colston nods to the young man. They shake hands
and part.*

Over this the following dialogue:

MR MAUDSLEY

I think it will. The rain seems to have stopped. For the
moment anyway.

DENYS

So it has.

MRS MAUDSLEY

There you are then. It seems that all will be well for
Leo's birthday.

DENYS

There's still a lot of dark cloud about.

MR MAUDSLEY

What's your opinion, Hugh?

INT. HALL. MORNING. PAST.

Guests passing through the hall. Marian stops, alone, and turns.

MARIAN

Leo, come with me and tell me what the weather means
to do.

EXT. FRONT OF HOUSE.

Marian and Leo emerge and look up at the sky. They walk along the path and turn by the side of the house into the rhododendrons, the camera watching them.

Marian and Leo amid the rhododendrons.

LEO

Do you think the summer is over? It's one of the hottest summers on record. You know.

MARIAN

Of course it isn't over. Tell me, would you like to walk?

LEO

Oh yes! Where shall we walk?

MARIAN

I can't, I'm afraid. It's this kind of walk.

Close shot of Marian's hand touching Leo's. A letter in Marian's hand.

Close-up of Leo.

LEO

Oh no!

Close-up of Marian.

MARIAN
(*laughing*)

Oh yes!

Two shot.

Marian, laughing, tries to thrust the letter into Leo's hand. Leo resists. They begin to dodge and feint and lunge, both now laughing.

MRS MAUDSLEY
(*VO*)

Marian! Leo!

They stop still. The camera moves towards them.

What were you fighting about?

MARIAN

Oh I was just teaching him a lesson –

Leo whose hands are at his sides, suddenly drops the letter.

The camera dips slowly to look at it. It lies on the ground, crumpled.

Leo looks sharply into camera. Marian remains composed.

Close-up of Mrs Maudsley.

MRS MAUDSLEY

Was that the bone of contention?

Three shot.

Marian picks up the letter and puts it into Leo's pocket.

MARIAN

Yes it was, Mama. I wanted him to take this note to Nanny Robson to tell her that I will go and see her some time this afternoon. And would you believe it, Leo didn't want to! He pretended he had something on with Marcus.

Leo looks at her.

Yes you did!

MRS MAUDSLEY

I shouldn't let it worry you, Marian. You say she often doesn't remember whether you've been or not. She is certainly growing old, poor Nanny Robson. I think it's about time Leo and I took a walk in the garden.
(*She takes Leo's hand.*)
Come along Leo. I don't believe you've seen the garden properly, have you?
(*She turns to Marian.*)
You can spare Leo now, can't you Marian?

MARIAN

Oh, yes.

Long shot.

Mrs Maudsley with Leo walks away from Marian.

LEO

Would you like Marcus to come with us?

MRS MAUDSLEY

Oh no. Marcus isn't interested in flowers. You are
though, aren't you?

LEO

Yes, I am.

The backs of Mrs Maudsley and Leo walking through the garden.

They arrive at the flower beds.

MRS MAUDSLEY

The rain has certainly stopped.
                    (*Pause.*)
Well, now, here's the garden. What kind of flowers truly
interest you?

LEO

Poisonous ones really.

MRS MAUDSLEY

I don't think you'll find many of those.

LEO

Oh there is one in the out –

Two shot.

Mrs Maudsley stops.

MRS MAUDSLEY

In the what?

LEO

Well . . . I've seen . . .

MRS MAUDSLEY
(*smiling*)

What have you seen, Leo?

LEO

Well, there is a deadly nightshade in one of the
outhouses.

MRS MAUDSLEY

Oh, you mean where the old garden used to be.

LEO

Yes, somewhere there . . .

MRS MAUDSLEY

Do you often go to the outhouses?

LEO

Oh no, not often.

They stop by a magnolia.

MRS MAUDSLEY

This always reminds me of Marian. How sweet of you
to say you'd take her note to Nanny Robson. Does she
often send you with messages?

LEO

Oh no, just once or twice.

MRS MAUDSLEY

It rather worries me that I stopped you going just now.
Perhaps you would like to go? You know the way, of
course?

Pause.

LEO

Well, not quite but I can ask.

MRS MAUDSLEY

You don't know the way? But I thought you had taken messages there before.

LEO

Yes, well, yes I have.

MRS MAUDSLEY

But you don't know the way.
(*Pause.*)
I think perhaps the note should be delivered. You have it in your pocket, haven't you? I'll call one of the gardeners and ask him to take it.

LEO

Oh no, really. It's not a bit important. Please don't bother.

MRS MAUDSLEY

It is important in a way, you see. Stanton, could you come here a minute.

A gardener puts down his tools and comes towards her and into the shot.

We have a note here for Miss Robson, rather urgent. Would you mind taking it?

STANTON

Yes'm.

Leo digs his fingers into his pocket.

LEO

I've . . . lost it. I haven't got it. It must have fallen out of my pocket.

MRS MAUDSLEY

Feel again.

Leo does so.

LEO

I must have dropped it.

MRS MAUDSLEY

Very well, Stanton.

Stanton moves away.

Close-up of Mrs Maudsley.

Take your hands out of your pockets. Has no one ever
told you not to stand with your hands in your pockets?

Close-up of Leo taking his hands out of his pockets.

Two shot over Leo to Mrs Maudsley.

MRS MAUDSLEY

I could ask you to turn your pockets out. But I won't do
that. I'll just ask you one question. You say you have
taken messages for Marian before?

LEO

Well I –

MRS MAUDSLEY

I think you said so. If you don't take them to Nanny
Robson –

EXT. VILLAGE STREET. NO CARS. DAY. TIME NEUTRAL.

EXT. HOUSE. GARDEN. LONG SHOT.

Mrs Maudsley and Leo standing.

INT. HOUSE. LAVATORY.

Leo sitting on lavatory lid.

MRS MAUDSLEY
(*VO*)
– to whom do you take them?

EXT. VILLAGE STREET. PRESENT.

Across Colston to the young man. The young man is listening to Colston.

EXT. HOUSE. GARDEN. RAIN SWEEPING OVER THE GARDEN. PAST.

No one in sight.

INT. COTTAGE. PRESENT.

Colston ushered into the room by the maid.

INT. HOUSE. LAVATORY. PAST.

Leo sitting.

> MARIAN'S VOICE OLD (OVER)
> So you met my grandson.

> COLSTON
> (*VO*)
> Yes, I did.

> MARIAN'S VOICE OLD (OVER)
> Does he remind you of anyone?

> COLSTON
> (*VO*)
> Of course. His grandfather.

> MARIAN'S VOICE (OLD)
> That's it, that's it. He does.

Close-up of Colston. PRESENT.

(NOTE: *In the following shots we see the faces of Colston and Marian old for the first time.*)

> COLSTON
> It must be a comfort for you to have him near you.

Close-up of Marian as an old lady. PRESENT.

> MARIAN
>
> Yes. But he doesn't come to see me very much. I think
> he has a grudge against me.

Close-up of Colston. PRESENT.

> COLSTON
>
> Oh surely not.

Close-up of Marian. PRESENT.

> MARIAN (OLD)
>
> They tell me that he wants to marry a girl – a nice girl –
> but he won't ask her . . . he feels . . . I think he feels . . .
> that he's under some sort of spell or curse, you see.
> That's just plain silly. Now this is where you come in.

> COLSTON
>
> I?

> MARIAN
>
> Yes, you. You know the facts, you know what *really*
> happened. Tell him, tell him everything, just as it was.

Close-up of Colston. PRESENT.

Shot over Colston to Marian. PRESENT.

> Every man should get married. You ought to have got
> married. You're all dried up inside, I can tell that. Don't
> you feel any need of love? Speak to him, tell him there's
> no spell or curse except an unloving heart.

INT. HOUSE. HALL. EVENING. PAST.

Mrs Maudsley descending the stairs.

> MARIAN'S VOICE OLD (OVER)
>
> Tell him that.

THE GO-BETWEEN

Mrs Maudsley walks to the door of the drawing-room and opens it.

From her point of view. See a collection of people standing at windows looking out.

Distant thunder.

INT. DRAWING-ROOM. THE WINDOWS.

Leo turns.

Mrs Maudsley moving into the room.

> MARCUS
> We're watching the lightning, Mama.

> TRIMINGHAM
> Rather good luck we didn't set out for Beeston Castle.

> MRS MAUDSLEY
> Yes, it would have been rather a damp expedition.

The gathering clusters round the tea-table.

> Sit here please, Leo, dear.
> (*She indicates a place.*)
> Do you see what's in front of you?

Across table at Leo. Sitting.

In foreground a birthday cake with twelve candles.

Crackers, flowers. A smaller cake with one candle.

Over Leo to Mrs Maudsley.

> You see I don't like the number thirteen – isn't it silly of me? So we've put twelve candles round the big cake, and then when they're blown out, you shall light this one, and blow this one out.

Mrs Maudsley's hands.

Over Mrs Maudsley to Leo.

LEO

When will that be?

MRS MAUDSLEY

When Marian comes. She has a rather special present
for you. She wants to give it to you herself, naturally.

Long shot. Room.

Let's all sit down.

Everyone does so.

Marian should be back at about six o'clock from Nanny
Robson.

TRIMINGHAM

I haven't seen Nanny Robson for years. How is she?

MRS MAUDSLEY

Remarkably well. Isn't it time that Leo cut the cake?

MARCUS

Yes! If he can do it.

MRS MAUDSLEY

That's unkind. Of course he can do it. He's a man of
great capabilities.

TRIMINGHAM

Considerable. And well loved. Didn't you know he was
Marian's cavalier?

Leo blowing the candles out.

Cries of encouragement. Applause.

MARCUS

He's done it!

The Servants handing round portions of the cake.

DENYS

Leave a piece for Marian.

TRIMINGHAM

She ought to be here now.

MR MAUDSLEY

It's still raining.

(*Pause.*)

We'd better send the carriage down to fetch her. Why didn't we think of it before?

Table in foreground.

Mr Maudsley talking to butler at door in background.

EXT. HOUSE. RAIN. EVENING.

The carriage going into the distance down the drive.

INT. DRAWING-ROOM.

Everyone eating cake.

Silence.

TRIMINGHAM

She should be with us in five minutes now.

A GUEST

She may be walking up in the rain. Poor darling, she'll be soaked.

Pause.

MARCUS

What about your thirteenth candle?

TRIMINGHAM

We must light it first.

It is lit.

Leo blowing the candle out.

DENYS

Now you must cut a piece for yourself.

Leo does so.

He'd rather have his cake than eat it.

Denys laughs. No one else does.

Close-up of Leo.

He nibbles a little at his cake.

Silence.

The room.

Silence.

MR MAUDSLEY

Let's have a round of crackers. Here, Leo, come pull
one with me.

*Leo does so. Everyone, with the exception of Mrs Maudsley, finds
partners.*

Now all together!

*They pull the crackers. They all put on paper hats and blow
whistles.*

Medium shot of Leo turning to look for a cracker.

A cracker is thrust into his hand. He looks up.

Leo's point of view. Mrs Maudsley with cracker.

Over Mrs Maudsley to Leo.

They pull. The cracker cracks.

Back of Butler at door.

The assembly turns to him. Mrs Maudsley in the forefront.

BUTLER

Excuse me, Madam. The carriage has come back but
not Miss Marian. She wasn't at Miss Robson's. And
Miss Robson said she hadn't been all day.

The Butler goes out.

Silence.

DENYS

Where can she be?

Pause.

MR MAUDSLEY

Well, all we can do is wait for her.

DENYS

I've just found a wonderful riddle. Listen to this.

Mrs Maudsley's chair scraping back. Her skirt.

Close-up of Mrs Maudsley.

MRS MAUDSLEY

No. We won't wait. I'm going to look for her. Leo, you
know where she is. You shall show me the way.

Long shot. Room.

Mrs Maudsley seizes Leo's hand. A chair falls.

She takes him to the door.

Close-up of Mr Maudsley.

MR MAUDSLEY

Madeleine!

INT. HALL.

*Mrs Maudsley and Leo going through hall. They pass a green
bicycle standing in the hall, and go out the door.*

INT. ROOM.

Silence. Everyone still.

Close-up of Trimingham sitting quite still.

EXT. HOUSE. NIGHT.

Mrs Maudsley and Leo come out of the front door.

*The Butler follows them swiftly and offers Mrs Maudsley a
lantern and an umbrella. She ignores them both. Mrs Maudsley
and Leo walk along the path, she leading. It is raining heavily.*

EXT. HOUSE. GARDEN. RAIN. NIGHT.

*Mrs Maudsley and Leo moving past the rhododendrons towards
the outhouses.*

INT. COTTAGE. PRESENT.

Colston and Marian sitting. Long shot.

She is speaking, but the words are unheard.

Over this voices:

> MARIAN'S VOICE (YOUNG)
> You won't . . . tell anyone about this letter. You won't
> . . . will you?

> LEO
> (*VO*)
> Of course I won't.

EXT. HOUSE. GARDEN. RAIN. NIGHT. PAST.

*Mrs Maudsley and Leo moving past rhododendrons towards
outhouses.*

THE GO-BETWEEN

EXT. OUTHOUSES. RAIN. NIGHT.

Mrs Maudsley and Leo approach the outhouses.

EXT. COTTAGE. THROUGH WINDOW. PRESENT.

Marian and Colston sitting. She is talking, words unheard. Over this voices:

> MARIAN'S VOICE (YOUNG)
> Tell me. Would you like a walk?

> LEO
> (*VO*)
> Oh yes! Where shall we walk?

> MARIAN'S VOICE (YOUNG)
> I can't, I'm afraid. It's this kind of walk.

EXT. OUTHOUSES. RAIN. NIGHT. PAST.

Mrs Maudsley and Leo approach the outhouses.

Medium shot. Stump of deadly nightshade lying on the path. Camera still. Rain.

INT. DEADLY NIGHTSHADE. OUTHOUSE.

Mrs Maudsley standing. Leo behind her.

> MRS MAUDSLEY
> Not here.

Close-up of Leo whimpering.

Mrs Maudsley's face comes into the shot.

> No, you *shall* come.

She pulls him after her.

Mrs Maudsley dragging Leo towards the row of outhouses. Rain.

Light flickering. Their faces.

They stop.

INT. OUTHOUSE.

A lantern on the ground.

A shadow moving on the wall like an umbrella opening and closing.

Close-up of Leo mystified.

The shadow.

Close-up of Mrs Maudsley.

The shadow.

Close-up of Mrs Maudsley.

Her face contorts. She lets her breath out in a long exhalation and groan.

The shadow ceasing to move.

Close-up of Mrs Maudsley. Her face contorted. No sound.

Close-up of Leo.

The faces of Ted and Marian on the ground.

They are still. Ted's head is buried in Marian's shoulder. Marian looks up through half-open eyes.

EXT. LAWN. FRONT OF HOUSES. DAY.

In foreground a shape of a girl lying in a hammock. The wide lawn falls away before the house on a gentle slope. Cedars, elms. The hammock, faded crimson canvas, swings gently. In background figures in white playing croquet. Over this Marian's voice.

MARIAN'S VOICE (OLD)

You came out of the blue to make us happy. And we made you happy, didn't we? We trusted you with our great treasure. You might never have known what it was, you might have gone through life without knowing. Isn't that so?

Close-up of Colston listening. PRESENT.

MARIAN'S VOICE (OLD)

But you see you can tell him, Leo. You can tell him everything, just as it was.

The camera holds on Colston.

Medium shot of Ted dead.

He is slumped in his chair, his gun against his leg. His shirt is bloody. His head cannot be seen.

Near the end of this shot Marian's voice begins:

MARIAN'S VOICE (OLD)

Hugh was as true as steel, he wouldn't hear a word against me.

Close-up of Marian old. PRESENT.

MARIAN

But everybody wanted to know us, of course. I was Lady Trimingham, you see. I still am. There is no other.

INT. CAR WINDSCREEN. MOVING TOWARDS BRANDHAM HALL. PRESENT.

MARIAN'S VOICE OLD (OVER)

Remember how you loved taking our messages, bringing us together and making us happy. Well this is another errand of love and the last time I shall ever ask you to be our postman.

The car goes down an incline and begins to rise.

INT. CAR. COLSTON'S FACE IMPASSIVE. PRESENT.

> MARIAN'S VOICE OLD (OVER)
> Our love was a beautiful thing, wasn't it? Tell him he
> can feel proud to be descended from our union, the
> child of so much happiness and beauty. Tell him –

The sound stops abruptly.

The car comes to the top of the hill.

EXT. ROAD. DAY. PRESENT.

The south west prospect of Brandham Hall springs into view.

The elms have been cut down.

The car stops.

Brandham Hall.

A cloud of dust from the car slightly obscures the view.

The Proust Screenplay

Yellow screen. Sound of a garden gate bell.

*Open countryside, a line of trees, seen from a railway carriage.
The train is still. No sound. Quick fade out.*

Momentary yellow screen.

*The sea, seen from a high window, a towel hanging on a towel
rack in foreground. No sound. Quick fade out.*

Momentary yellow screen.

*Venice. A window in a palazzo, seen from a gondola. No sound.
Quick fade out.*

Momentary yellow screen.

The dining-room at Balbec. No sound. Empty.

EXT. THE HOUSE OF THE PRINCE DE GUERMANTES. PARIS.
1921. AFTERNOON.

*In long shot a middle-aged man (Marcel) walks towards the
Prince de Guermantes' house.*

His posture is hunched, his demeanour one of defeat.

*Many carriages, a few cars, a crowd of chauffeurs. Realistic
sound.*

INT. LIBRARY. THE PRINCE DE GUERMANTES' HOUSE. 1921.

A waiter inadvertently knocks a spoon against a plate.

Marcel, large in foreground, looks up.

123

INT. DRAWING-ROOM. THE PRINCE DE GUERMANTES'
HOUSE. 1921.

The drawing-room doors open.

The camera enters with Marcel, who hesitates.

*Hundreds of faces, some of which turn towards him, grotesquely
made up, grotesquely old.*

A tumult of voices.

Spoon hitting plate.

*Continue Marcel's progress into the drawing-room. Voices. Faces.
The wigs and make-up, combined with the extreme age of those
who with difficulty stand, sit, gesture, laugh, give the impression
of grotesque fancy dress.*

*In the library, Marcel, a glass by his side, wipes his lips with a
stiff napkin, which crackles.*

Venice. Window in a palazzo. Silent.

In the drawing-room, a group of very old women, talking.

Water pipes in the library.

The shrill noise of water running through the pipes.

Silent countryside from the railway carriage.

EXT. THE HOUSE OF THE PRINCE DE GUERMANTES. 1921.

A car swerves to avoid Marcel.

He steps back, trips on the cobbles.

Chauffeur shouts.

The dining-room at Balbec. Silent.

Yellow screen.

*The camera pulls back to discover that the yellow screen is
actually a patch of yellow wall in a painting.*

The painting is Vermeer's View of Delft.

Marcel 37 in his room at a sanatorium, sitting motionless as an owl.

INT. THE DRAWING-ROOM. THE PRINCE DE GUERMANTES'
HOUSE. 1921.

No sound track.

Old people chattering soundlessly.

Marcel stands detached from them.

The sound of a garden gate bell heard, becoming gently insistent.

(The tempo of the next sequence quickens, and the bell continues over it, irregularly.)

Marcel, in his twenties, in his hotel room at Balbec, bending over his boots, grief-stricken.

Three church steeples, seen from a moving carriage, at sunset. They seem to be dancing together in the last rays of the sun.

Three trees, seen from a moving carriage, at noon. Although the carriage is moving away from them, the trees give the impression of following it.

Marcel bending over his boots.

The trees.

The steeples.

Flash of yellow screen. Music of Vinteuil.

Quick shot of the garden gate at Combray. Very dim.

The steeples.

Calm, still shot of the garden gate.

The bell is slightly shaking but silent.

(NOTE: *In the preceding opening sequence, all scenes in the drawing-room of the Prince de Guermantes' house to be shot on colour stock in black and white.*)

INT. MARCEL'S ROOM. COMBRAY HOUSE. 1888. EVENING.

Marcel, a boy of eight, is sitting on the bed, in his nightshirt. He is writing laboriously. He finishes writing and puts the piece of paper in an envelope.

EXT. THE GARDEN. COMBRAY HOUSE. EARLIER IN THE EVENING.

Marcel, his Father 42, Mother 33, and Grandmother 56 sitting with Dr Percepied 50.

> DR PERCEPIED
> Well, I must be going. I have to look in to see Monsieur Vinteuil. Not in the best of health, poor man.

> FATHER
> Mmmm.

> DR PERCEPIED
> His daughter's friend is staying with them again, apparently.

> FATHER
> (*grimly*)
> Is she?

> DR PERCEPIED
> Yes. She's a music teacher.

> MOTHER
> But Monsieur Vinteuil is a music teacher himself.

> DR PERCEPIED
> His daughter prefers to be taught by her friend. Apparently.

(He bends forward to speak in a lower voice.)
Of course some people say it's not music she teaches his
daughter, that Monsieur Vinteuil must be blind.

Father coughs, glances at Marcel.

But every time you pass the house the piano is tinkling
away, tinkling away. It's a regular music box. Too much
music, in my opinion. Sending Monsieur Vinteuil to his
grave.

Pause.

GRANDMOTHER
Marcel looks tired.

FATHER
Yes, come on, off to bed. We said good night to you
hours ago. Isn't Swann a little late? What time are we
dining?

DR PERCEPIED
Charming man, Monsieur Swann. I was called in to see
his wife yesterday. She had a slight migraine.

Pause.

FATHER
(abruptly, to Marcel)
Come on, come on, how many times do I have to tell
you? Go to bed.

Marcel stands, goes to his Mother, leans forward to kiss her.

No, no, leave your mother alone. You've said good
night to one another. That's enough. All this fuss is
ridiculous. Go upstairs.

THE BACKDOOR OF THE HOUSE. GARDEN IN BACKGROUND.

As Marcel enters the door:

DR PERCEPIED
Monsieur Swann is dining with you alone, I gather?

FATHER
Alone. Yes.

INT. COMBRAY HOUSE.

Marcel walks slowly up the stairs. The kitchen door opens.
Françoise (late 40s) looks up.

FRANÇOISE
That's right. Off to bed. How was your chocolate cake?

Marcel does not reply. Françoise grunts, closes door.

EXT. THE GARDEN GATE.

The bell rings, two peals.

Swann enters. He is forty.

Grandmother walks across the grass towards him.

Father stands up in background.

GRANDMOTHER
Good evening, Monsieur Swann.

INT. MARCEL'S BEDROOM.

Françoise with envelope. Marcel on bed staring at her.

FRANÇOISE
How can you expect me to pester your mother when
she's at dinner? Mmmnn? With Monsieur Swann sitting
at the table. They say he's an intimate acquaintance of
the President of the Republic himself, not to mention
the Prefect of Police and the Prince of Wales of England.
His coachman told me he dines with princesses. At least,
that's what they call them. Still, that's what they say.

Marcel stares at her.

> Anyway, they're still eating their ices. Perhaps I can give
> it to your mother with the coffee. I'll see.

CLOSE-UP. MARCEL, LOOKING AT HER.

EXT. THE GARDEN.

The table. The letter unopened under Mother's coffee cup.

SWANN
When do you go back to Paris?

FATHER
In two weeks' time, I'm afraid.

SWANN
Yes, we shall be leaving shortly.

MOTHER
It's always sad when the summer is over, and we have to
leave Combray.

GRANDMOTHER
It's so much healthier here than Paris for Marcel, so
much better for him.

SWANN
How is he?

FATHER
(tapping chest)
Chest. Have to keep our eye on it.

*Swann observes Marcel peering down, half hidden, at his
window. Their eyes meet. Swann turns to the family.*

SWANN
I have a book I think Marcel might enjoy. I'll send it
round tomorrow.

GRANDMOTHER

How very kind.

FATHER

We were talking about Monsieur Vinteuil before you came. Do you know him?

SWANN

We've never really met, no. But I've often wondered if he's any relation to the composer.

FATHER

Composer?

MOTHER

You must know the Vinteuil sonata!

FATHER

Do I?

SWANN

Don't you know it? It's an enchanting piece of work. I first heard it . . . oh, many years ago.

FATHER

Oh, the Vinteuil *sonata*? Yes, yes, of course, of course. Delightful.

SWANN

I wonder if this fellow's any relation. I must find out.

FATHER

I shouldn't think so.

The envelope remains unopened.

THE GARDEN GATE CLOSES.

The bell shudders.

INT. MARCEL'S ROOM.

Marcel is looking down from the window at Father and Mother alone at the table.

MOTHER

He didn't look too well, I thought.

FATHER

It's his wife. To have thrown his life away for a woman like that. It's beyond me. He could have had any woman he liked. Did, in fact. Are you ready for bed?

MOTHER

You might at least let me ask after his daughter. He's so proud of her.

FATHER

Once you start asking after the daughter you'll end up asking after the wife. And then you'll find she'll be paying you calls. And there can be no question of that.

INT. COMBRAY HOUSE. LANDING. STAIRS.

Marcel stands in the shadows.

A faint glimmer of light from his parents' room.

A flickering candle ascends the stairs. His Mother reaches the landing and sees Marcel.

He rushes to her, clasps her.

MOTHER

What on earth are you doing?

He tries to pull her towards his door.

She stops him.

(whispering)

No. Go back to your room. Do you want your father to catch you behaving like this?

Candlelight appears from end of corridor.

Father emerges from his room.

> FATHER

What's this?

> MOTHER

He wants me to kiss him good night, in his room. He's behaving very stupidly.

Pause.

> FATHER

Go with him then.

> MOTHER

Oh really, we mustn't indulge him.

> FATHER

Rubbish. There's no need to make him ill. Sleep in his room just this once.

> *(Yawns.)*

I'm off to bed anyway. Good night.

INT. MARCEL'S BEDROOM.

Marcel in bed, sobbing, clutching his Mother's hand.

She sits on the bed.

> MOTHER
> *(gently)*

You must stop it. You'll make me cry in a minute, if you don't.

> *(Strokes him.)*

There. There.

MOTHER'S EYES.

INT. MARCEL'S BEDROOM. LATER.

Mother asleep in the other bed.

Marcel turns in his bed, looks across to her.

CLOSE-UP. MARCEL.

INT. THE OPERA. PARIS. LATE 1898.

The audience are taking their seats.

Marcel 19 is seated in the orchestra stalls. Most people in the stalls are looking up at the boxes. The boxes are shadowy. Shafts of light flash as the doors to the boxes open. The entering figures stay in the shadows, then emerge into the light, the ladies with bare shoulders, pearls on their throats, unfurling their fans.

Camera, in long shot, concentrates on one box; that of the Princesse de Guermantes, an extremely beautiful woman of thirty-seven. With her is the Prince de Guermantes, a man of fifty-two.

Marcel stares up. A voice whispers behind him: 'That's the Prince and Princess.'

The Princesse sits on a coral sofa, by a mirror. She wears a net of shells and pearls on her head, with a necklace to match, and a bird of paradise headdress curves round her face. She offers crystallized fruit to a stout man.

The box door opens. Enter the Duc 52 and Duchesse de Guermantes 40.

Marcel's eyes tighten. Voice: 'Who's that?' Other voice: 'The Duchess. Her cousin.' 'And the man?' 'The Duke, you idiot.'

The Duc, a magnificent figure, with monocle and white carnation, drops his hand vertically upon the shoulder of those in the box who are standing for him and his wife. He bows to the

*Princesse. The Princesse and Duchesse greet each other. The
Duchesse is in white muslin, carries a swansdown fan, wears in
her hair a simple aigrette. The Duchesse and Princesse appraise
each other, laughing.*

The Duchesse looks down into the stalls.

*Marcel is watching her, compelling her to see him. She suddenly
does.*

She raises her white-gloved hand and waves.

The Princesse turns to look down herself.

The Duchesse smiles down.

CLOSE-UP. MARCEL, MUCH AFFECTED.

FATHER
(*VO*)

Today we'll walk the Guermantes' way.

EXT. THE RIVER VIVONNE. COMBRAY. DAY. 1893.

Water lilies on the water.

Boys lowering glass jars to catch minnows.

Marcel 13 and family walking along the bank.

FATHER

No, no, of course we can't get as far as the château. It's
much too far.

MOTHER
(*to Marcel, gently*)

But you'll be able to see the Duchess on Sunday. She's
coming to Combray for the wedding.

GRANDMOTHER

I think Marcel's fascinated by the name as much as
anything else. Aren't you?

134

FATHER
The name stands for something. They're one of the oldest and noblest families in France.

GRANDMOTHER
Yes, but I meant the actual sound. It's golden. Guermantes.

INT. MARCEL'S ROOM. NIGHT. 1888.

Marcel 8 alone with a magic lantern.

The image of Geneviève de Brabant (ancestress of the Guermantes family) floats over the walls and ceiling.

MARCEL
(*VO, mumuring*)
Guermantes.

INT. SAINT-HILAIRE CHURCH, COMBRAY. 1893.

Chapel of Gilbert the Bad.

Camera pans down stained-glass window.

The wedding in progress. White hawthorn blossoms over the altar.

INT. CHURCH. CONGREGATION.

The Duchesse de Guermantes 35 seen from Marcel's point of view.

CLOSE-UP. MARCEL.

Looking at her.

CLOSE-UP. THE DUCHESSE.

She turns her head, a slight smile on her lips.

THE CHÂTEAU OF GUERMANTES (IDEALIZED IMAGE).

Long shot across the lake to the château.

In the far distance the figures of the Duchesse and Marcel, walking slowly by the lake. She is holding his hand.

A woman's voice (not the Duchess's) heard over:

> VOICE
> You are a poet. I can tell. Tell me about your poems. Tell me about the poems you intend to write.

EXT. GARDEN. COMBRAY. DAY. 1893. LONG SHOT.

Swann 45 and Marcel 13 are sitting together in the garden. Their heads are close.

Swann is riffling through the pages of a book.

Smiling, he reads a sentence or two to Marcel.

Marcel's reaction is animated. He takes the book from Swann, and studies the page.

Chimes of the church bell.

Bird sounds.

EXT. GARDEN. COMBRAY. SUNSET.

Marcel sitting in a hooded wicker chair, reading.

He is alone in the garden.

Chimes of the church bell.

Françoise with a carving knife suddenly emerges from kitchen chasing a chicken.

Marcel looks up startled.

FRANÇOISE
(*savagely*)

Come here! Come here!

Françoise chases the chicken into the kitchen.

Shouts of 'Come here!' The chicken's squawks cease.

Marcel's hands clench.

INT. COMBRAY HOUSE. LAVATORY.

Marcel at window stares down at the streets of Combray, silent, still, in the heat.

The church steeple.

A young girl, alone, crosses a street, disappears.

Flowering currant cascades through the window.

MARCEL'S EYES.

A sigh, offscreen, is heard from Marcel.

The camera slowly leaves him and rests on the flowering currant, and the view.

EXT. M. VINTEUIL'S HOUSE. MONTJOUVAIN. DAY.

In foreground Marcel and family. M. Vinteuil 60 comes quickly from the front door and walks towards them.

Through the drawing-room window Mlle. Vinteuil 18 and her Friend 21 can be clearly seen playing a duet.

M. VINTEUIL

How very nice to see you. Good afternoon to you all.
(*He glances back to the window.*)
Yes, as you see, the two young ladies are practising away. My daughter's friend is really quite talented. I hope my daughter will benefit from her example, her

enthusiasm. I'm too old now, too old to teach, but my daughter's friend is so able, so charming, so able.

The camera focuses on Mlle. Vinteuil and her Friend, playing. They do not look out of the window.

INT. RAILWAY CARRIAGE. LITTLE TRAIN FROM LA RASPELIÈRE. 1901. NIGHT.

Marcel 21 and Albertine 21. Albertine is in the middle of speaking.

ALBERTINE
I know Vinteuil's daughter almost as well as I know her friend. I always call them my two big sisters.

EXT. SWANN'S HOUSE. TANSONVILLE. 1893.

The path by the side of Swann's park.

A hedge of white and pink hawthorns.

Marcel 13 comes into shot. He stands looking at the hawthorns.

FATHER
(*VO*)
Today we'll walk Swann's way.

FURTHER ALONG THE PATH.

Mother and Father walking ahead. Marcel straggles after. Suddenly he stops.

GAP IN HEDGE.

Through a gap in the hedge he sees a pond. A fishing line rests by the side of the pond, its float bobbing in the water. By the side of the rod a straw bucket.

Along a gravel path a watering pipe is coiled, water emerging from the holes along its length like a fan over the flowers; jasmine, pansies, verbenas, wall flowers.

138

Suddenly his head jolts. A girl with black eyes, holding a trowel, is looking at him. It is Gilberte. She is thirteen.

EXT. PARK AT TANSONVILLE. LONG SHOT.

Marcel at hedge. Mother and Father continuing up the hill.

THE HEDGE.

He stares at her.

She looks at him with a half smile, a curious intensity.

CLOSE-UP. GILBERTE'S FACE.

Her black eyes, smiling.

CLOSE-UP. MARCEL.

His face, bewildered, even alarmed.

GILBERTE'S EYES.

> ODETTE
> (*VO*)
> Gilberte, come along. What are you doing?

THE HEDGE.

Odette (Mme. Swann) dressed in white, comes into view. She is thirty-six.

She is followed by the Baron de Charlus, wearing a white linen suit. He is forty-six.

Gilberte turns to them. They regard Marcel for a moment, and then continue walking.

FURTHER ALONG THE PATH.

Mother and Father have stopped and turned.

Odette, Charlus and Gilberte glimpsed by them moving through trees.

MOTHER
I thought she was in Paris.

FATHER
She's sent Swann to Paris alone, that's what she's done, so that she can be alone with Charlus. That was the Baron de Charlus. I recognized him.

MOTHER
Who is he?

FATHER
Her newest lover. Or her oldest, I don't know. I take no interest in these matters. It's intolerable. And in front of the girl too.

He calls to Marcel, who has not moved. 'Marcel! Come on!'

MOTHER
I don't think Swann cares any more. I honestly think he's quite indifferent.

CLOSE-UP. ODETTE, SEEN THROUGH LEAVES.

CLOSE-UP. ODETTE, FOURTEEN YEARS YOUNGER.

INT. THE VERDURINS' HOUSE, PARIS. 1879.

Over Odette's face, the voice of Mme. Verdurin.

MME. VERDURIN
(*VO*)
She's just a little tiny piece of perfection. Aren't you? Look! She's blushing!

ODETTE
(*demurely*)

Oh, Madame Verdurin.

TWO SHOT: SWANN 31 AND M. VERDURIN 39.

Swann is looking towards Odette. He turns from her as M. Verdurin speaks.

VERDURIN

I'm going to light my pipe. Do light a pipe if you wish. There's no ceremony here.

MME. VERDURIN
(*VO*)

No ceremony, no snobbery, no airs, and no graces.

Swann looks, slightly uneasily, towards Mme. Verdurin.

We're real people here, I hope, not stuffed dummies. That's the kind of house you find yourself in, Monsieur Swann. And we're delighted to welcome you.

SWANN

You're very kind.

VERDURIN

Ah! Dechambre's ready to play. A really original piece we've discovered. A sonata by a man called Vinteuil.

THE ROOM.

Mme. Verdurin 37 is sitting in a high Swedish chair of waxed pinewood. About the room are Dr Cottard 35, Mme. Cottard 31, Brichot 42, and Dechambre 20.

MME. VERDURIN

No, no, no, not my sonata! I shall have to stay in bed for a week. Oh well, I'll have to surrender to it, I suppose. Make myself ill for the sake of art. Monsieur Swann, you're not comfortable – sit by Mademoiselle de Crécy on the sofa. You can make room for him, Odette, can't you, you exquisite little thing?

ODETTE

Oh yes, Madame Verdurin, I think so.

Swann sits next to Odette. She lowers her lashes.

LONG SHOT OF ROOM.

Dechambre plays on the piano the section of the sonata which includes the 'little phrase'.

Mme. Verdurin sits with her eyes tight shut, her hands to her face.

SWANN AND ODETTE.

Swann listens intently, frowning.

INT. ODETTE'S HOUSE IN RUE LAPÉROUSE. PARIS. 1879.

In the lobby leading to the drawing-room a long box filled with chrysanthemums. Palm trees growing out of pots of Chinese porcelain, lamps in porcelain vases, screens upon which are fastened photographs. Fans, bows of ribbon, large cushions of Japanese silk, a dromedary of inlaid silver work and a toad carved in jade on the mantelpiece, a portrait of Odette upon an easel.

Odette's arms and neck are bare. She wears a wrapper of mauve crêpe de Chine. She is playing the 'little phrase' on the piano, badly. Swann looks down at her, listening.

SWANN

Play it again.

ODETTE
(*laughing*)
Again! The little phrase, that's all.

She plays.

I play so badly.

He kisses her neck, throat, mouth, as she falteringly plays. She stops.

Now make up your mind. Do you want me to play the phrase or do you want to play with me?

> SWANN

That music belongs to us. It's our anthem.
> (*Kissing her.*)
Don't you think it's beautiful?

> ODETTE

It's very nice.

> SWANN

There's a painting by Botticelli. Jethro's daughter. It's you. She is you.

> ODETTE
> (*kissing him quickly*)

You are sweet.

INT. ODETTE'S HOUSE. EARLY EVENING. 1880.

Swann is sitting uncomfortably on a sofa as Odette fusses about him, arranging cushions around him. She moves a tray of tea on a side table nearer to him. She places his feet on a footstool and settles further cushions about him, giggling.

Swann takes from his pocket a fat wad of banknotes. He gives it to her.

> SWANN

You said you needed some money.

> ODETTE

Oh darling!

143

She bends to kiss him.

ODETTE FROM SWANN'S POINT OF VIEW.

She bends to kiss him.

Her cheeks, smooth and flushed, come closer to his eye and show a coarser grain.

OVER ODETTE TO SWANN.

She is kissing him.

His eyes are open.

EXT. ODETTE'S HOUSE. NIGHT.

A carriage draws up. Swann gets out, goes to door, knocks.

Silence.

Odette in négligée. She stares at him.

> SWANN
> It's late I know. I'm sorry.

> ODETTE
> But you weren't coming tonight. What happened to
> your banquet?

> SWANN
> I left early. To see you.

> ODETTE
> But I'm asleep. I have a terrible headache. I was asleep.

> SWANN
> Let me come in. I'll . . . soothe you.

> ODETTE
> You say you're not coming, I don't feel well, I go to
> bed, and then you arrive, in the middle of the night.

144

SWANN

It's only eleven o'clock.

ODETTE

It's the middle of the night for me.
(*Softer.*)
Please. Not now. Tomorrow. Tomorrow night. I'll be
better. It will be sweet. Think of that.

EXT. SWANN'S HOUSE. PARIS. NIGHT.

*The carriage draws up. Coachman opens carriage door. Swann
does not move.*

SWANN

Go back. To Rue Lapérouse.

EXT. RUE LAPÉROUSE. NIGHT.

*The lamps in the street are now out. The street is quite dark but
for one light in one house, shining through the slats of the shutters.*

Swann walks quietly to this window and listens outside it.

Murmurs of a man's voice.

He stands, pained, uncertain.

He suddenly knocks on the shutters.

Silence.

He knocks again.

A man's voice: 'Who's that?'

As the window and shutters are being opened Swann speaks.

SWANN

Just happened to be passing. Wanted to know if you
were feeling better.

The shutters open.

*An Old Gentleman holding a lamp stares at him. In the
background of a quite unfamiliar room stands another Old
Gentleman.*

I'm terribly sorry. I'm afraid I have the wrong house.

GENTLEMAN

Good night, sir.

He closes the shutters.

*Swann, in the dark, looks towards Odette's house, which is dark
and silent.*

INT. ODETTE'S BEDROOM.

Odette is combing her hair at her dressing table.

SWANN

Odette, I must ask you a few questions.

ODETTE

What now?

She looks at him.

Nasty ones, I'm sure.

SWANN

Since you have known me have you . . . known any
other men?

ODETTE

I knew it was that kind of question from your face. No. I
have not. Why would I want other men, you silly? I have
you.

Pause.

SWANN

What about women?

146

ODETTE

Women?

SWANN

You remember once Madame Verdurin said to you: 'I
know how to melt you, all right. You're not made of
marble.'

ODETTE

You asked me about that ages ago.

SWANN

I know –

ODETTE

I told you it was a joke. A *joke*, that's all.

SWANN

Have you ever, with her?

ODETTE

I've told you, no! You know quite well. Anyway, she's
not like that.

SWANN

Don't say 'You know quite well'. Say 'I have never done
anything of that sort with Madame Verdurin or with any
other woman'.

ODETTE
(*automatically*)

I have never done anything of that sort with Madame
Verdurin or with any other woman.

Silence.

SWANN

Can you swear to me on the medal round you neck?

ODETTE

Oh, you make me sick! What's the matter with you today?

SWANN

Tell me, on your medal, yes or no, whether you have
ever done those things?

ODETTE

How do I know? I don't even know what you mean.
What things? Perhaps I have, years ago, when I didn't
know what I was doing. Perhaps two or three times, I
don't know.

Pause.

SWANN

How many times exactly?

ODETTE

For God's sake!
           (*Slight pause.*)
Anyway it's all so long ago. I've never given it a thought.
Anyone would think you're trying to put ideas into my
head – just to get me to do it again.

SWANN

It's quite a simple question. And you must remember.
You must remember with whom . . . my love. The last
time, for instance.

Odette relaxes, speaks lightly.

ODETTE

Oh, I don't know. I think in the Bois . . . on the island
. . . one evening . . . you were dining with those
Guermantes. At the next table was a woman I hadn't
seen for ages. She said to me, 'Come round behind the
rock there and look at the moonlight on the water.' At
first I just yawned and said, 'No, I'm too tired.' But she
swore there'd never been any moonlight to touch it.
'I've heard that tale before,' I said to her. I knew quite
well what she was after.

EXT. SWANN'S PARK AND HOUSE AT TANSONVILLE. DAY.

No one in sight.

> SWANN
> (*VO, with fatigue*)
> Perhaps two or three times.

Bird song.

> I knew quite well what she was after.

EXT. M. VINTEUIL'S HOUSE AT MONTJOUVAIN. EARLY
EVENING. 1895.

The camera, still, looking into the drawing-room window.

*Mlle. Vinteuil enters; stands, goes to mantelpiece, takes photograph,
walks to sofa, places photo on table by sofa, lies down on sofa.*

Her Friend enters. Mlle. Vinteuil sits up, makes room on sofa.

Friend looks at her in silence.

Mlle. Vinteuil lies down again, yawns.

> FRIEND
> I wish you'd change that ghastly dress. Are you going to
> mourn your father for ever?

Mlle. Vinteuil rises, walks to window to close shutters.

> Leave them open. I'm hot.

> MLLE. VINTEUIL
> But people can see us.

Friend smiles.

> I mean see us reading, or whatever we're doing.

> FRIEND
> And what if they do see us reading? Who could object to
> that?

Pause.

Where's your book?

MLLE. VINTEUIL

What book?

FRIEND

How can you read without a book, you stupid slut?
Anyway, I'm not reading, I'm thinking.

MLLE. VINTEUIL

What about?

The Friend walks towards Mlle. Vinteuil. She kisses her.

Mlle. Vinteuil breaks away. Friend chases her.

Mlle. Vinteuil falls on sofa. Friend lies on top of her.

My father's looking at us. Stop.

Friend turns, picks up the photograph.

FRIEND

Do you know what I'm going to do to your dear dead
father?

She whispers.

MLLE. VINTEUIL

You wouldn't.

FRIEND

Oh yes I would. Oh yes I will.

Mmle. Vinteuil runs to the window and closes the shutters.

Camera turns slowly away from the window.

Marcel 15, watching.

EXT. COUNTRY ROAD NEAR COMBRAY. SUNSET. 1895.

Long shot. Dr Percepied's carriage driving fast.

He passes Marcel and family walking, stops.

He invites the family into the carriage. They climb in.

Marcel sits with the coachman.

MARCEL'S POINT OF VIEW. FROM MOVING CARRIAGE.

The twin steeples of Martinville church and, in the distance, a third steeple from another village.

At first the distance between the Martinville steeples and the other is clear, definite. But as the road winds and in the sun's reflection they seem to change position. The third, although rising from higher ground in the distance, suddenly appears to be standing by their side, to be one of them.

Further views of them, as the carriage progresses:

Only the Martinville steeples seen; the third not in sight.

The third very dim, quivering.

The Martinville steeples almost blotted out; the third startlingly clear, luminous.

The three steeples apparently side by side, dancing together in the last rays of the sun.

CLOSE-UP. MARCEL'S FACE, ALIVE.

EXT. ALLÉE DES ACACIAS. PARIS. WINTER. 1897. DAY.

Marcel 17 watches a victoria approach.

Odette lies back in it, holding a violet parasol.

Two Men, near Marcel, doff their hats, bow.

She smiles, gently, at them.

ODETTE'S EYES.

THE VICTORIA PASSES.

The Two Men look at each other.

> FIRST MAN
> I was in bed with her the afternoon General MacMahon
> resigned.

EXT. CHAMPS-ÉLYSÉES GARDENS. PARIS. 1897.

*Gilberte 17 whispering with girl friends in the bushes. A girl's voice
laughing, 'Oh Gilberte!'*

MARCEL WATCHING GILBERTE.

SWANN IN FOREGROUND STANDING BY A TREE, WATCHING
MARCEL WATCH GILBERTE.

Marcel is unaware of Swann's presence.

EXT. SWANN'S HOUSE. PARIS.

Gilberte running towards the house and entering.

EXT. MARCEL'S HOUSE. BOULEVARD MALSHERBES. PARIS.
EVENING.

Marcel entering the house.

INT. MARCEL'S HOUSE. THE HALL. 1897.

Marcel 17 passes the open door of his Father's study.

> FATHER
> Ah Marcel. Come here.

Marcel goes into the study.

INT. STUDY.

> FATHER
> Let me introduce you to His Excellency the
> Ambassador, the Marquis de Norpois.

They bow.

The Marquis de Norpois is seventy.

> MARCEL
> Good evening, sir.

> NORPOIS
> Good evening. Your father tells me you wish to pursue
> writing, as a career?

> MARCEL
> I . . . yes, sir. I think so, sir.

> NORPOIS
> Rather than diplomacy?

> MARCEL
> I . . . think so, sir.

> NORPOIS
> You are not inclined to follow in the distinguished
> footsteps of your father?

> FATHER
> Marcel is not yet at the age, of course, where he need
> take a final decision.

> NORPOIS
> A career in writing can bear surprisingly rewarding
> fruits, if I may say so, if, that is, one maintains the
> proper balance of industry, determination, and
> ambition, allied to a clearly defined understanding of

one's own limitations and capabilities, and if one possesses, of course (*with a smile*), talent. The son of a friend of mine, for example – two years ago he published a study dealing with 'The Sense of the Infinite on the Western Shore of Lake Victoria Nyanza', and followed it last spring with a remarkably cutting treatise on 'The Use of the Repeating Rifle in the Bulgarian Army' – written from an entirely different standpoint, of course. He is now, I would say, in a class by himself. I happen to know that his name has been mentioned, and not at all unfavourably, as a possible candidate for the Academy of Moral Sciences.

FATHER

Really?

NORPOIS

Oh yes. I am glad to say that success, usually reserved for agitators and mischief-makers, has certainly crowned his efforts.

(*To Marcel.*)

What have you written?

MARCEL

Sir?

NORPOIS

What have you written?

MARCEL

Nothing . . . I'm afraid . . . that is actually finished.

Father takes a piece of paper from desk.

FATHER

What about this?

MARCEL

What?

FATHER

Your piece. Your prose poem, as you called it. Your piece about steeples.

MARCEL
(*startled*)

Oh no! No . . . that's . . .

FATHER

It's finished, isn't it?

MARCEL

Yes, but it was written years ago. It's . . . juvenile.

NORPOIS

One can often discern a great deal from early efforts.
(*To Father.*)

May I?

FATHER
(*passing paper*)

Please. Please.

NORPOIS
(*glancing at it, murmuring*)

Steeples.

M. Norpois reads. Silence. M. Norpois finishes reading, looks up, clears his throat, hands paper back to Marcel, staring at him.

Father takes paper, puts it back in desk.

FATHER

Shall we go in to dinner?

INT. DINING-ROOM.

The family and Norpois at dinner, with Grandmother.

NORPOIS

You have a chef of the first order, madame. That was a

positive banquet. How rarely does one eat a boeuf en
daube in which the jelly does not taste like glue and the
beef has caught the flavour of the carrots. Admirable!

MOTHER

I am so pleased.

FATHER

Were you at the Foreign Ministry dinner last night? I
couldn't go.

NORPOIS

No. I must confess I renounced it for a party of a very
different sort. I was dining with the beautiful Madame
Swann.

Mother and Father start. Marcel looks at him keenly.

MOTHER

How interesting. Were there many people there?

NORPOIS

Frankly, I would say it was a house which is especially
attractive to gentlemen. There were several married
men there, but their wives (*with a smile*) were all, as it
happened, unwell.

MOTHER

And is Monsieur Swann . . . well, Your Excellency?

NORPOIS
(*winking*)

Oh, he seems to be leading an active enough life by all
accounts, as active as his wife, one gathers, from the way
tongues wag.

Françoise and Footman enter with a pudding.

A Nesselrode pudding! As well! I shall need a slimming
course, madame.

He helps himself.

MARCEL
Was Madame Swann's daughter at the dinner?

NORPOIS
She was indeed. A charming young lady.

MARCEL
I wonder if you could possibly find an opportunity to
introduce me to her.

Mother and Father stare at him.

Norpois looks at him icily, digs into his pudding and mutters:

NORPOIS
Of course, of course.

EXT. CHAMPS-ÉLYSÉES GARDEN. DAY.

Gilberte whispering with girl friends in the bushes.

Marcel watching.

Swann absent.

A girl's voice laughing, 'Oh Gilberte!'

EXT. SWANN'S HOUSE. PARIS. EVENING.

*Gilberte comes out of the house with a young man. They walk
down the street and disappear.*

The camera finds Marcel.

He looks after Gilberte for a moment, turns, and walks away.

EXT. THE PROMENADE. BALBEC. DAY. 1898.

*From outside the Grand Hotel the camera looks along the
promenade and focuses, through the crowds, in the distance, on*

Five Girls, strikingly dressed, quite distinct in their carriage, one pushing a bicycle, two carrying golf clubs.

They approach slowly.

No sound.

INT. DINING-ROOM. BALBEC HOTEL. DAY. 1898.

Very hot afternoon. The curtains are drawn, although not fully, to shield the room from the glare.

Through spaces between the curtains the sea flashes and in one of the spaces Saint-Loup 20, dressed in an almost white, very thin suit, is seen striding from the beach towards the hotel, his monocle dropping from his eye and being replaced.

The camera shifts to look through the foyer to the glass front of the hotel, the bottom half of which is filled with sea, Saint-Loup in foreground striding towards a carriage and pair. He jumps onto the box seat and takes the reins from the groom. The hotel manager rushes out with a letter for him. Saint-Loup opens the letter and, starting the horses at the same time, drives off.

No sound.

EXT. PROMENADE. BALBEC. DAY. 1898.

Close shot.

The Baron de Charlus 51 stands in front of a playbill. Dark suit, dark moustache. His eyes stare piercingly at something.

No sound.

INT. COMPARTMENT OF MOVING TRAIN. DAY. 1898.

Marcel 18 and Grandmother 66.

MARCEL
I really don't see why I couldn't have gone to Venice.

GRANDMOTHER
(*gently*)
The doctor said the air at Balbec would be better for you, you know that.

Marcel grunts.

MARCEL

I need a drink.

She looks at him.

You know I'm ill! Do you want me to have another choking fit? The doctor *ordered* me to have some brandy as soon as the journey started. Anyway, I feel ill now. I *need* some brandy.

GRANDMOTHER
Well, go and have some, then.

MARCEL
It's necessary for my health.

INT. COMPARTMENT. DAY.

Grandmother alone, reading. Marcel enters, drunk.

MARCEL
Charming waiters. Excellent service. Even the ticket collector was a man of . . . great refinement. Witty too.

He staggers.

To be honest . . . to be honest, I thought I would miss Mama in Balbec, but now I know I won't. No. The doctor was absolutely right about the brandy. Absolutely. I feel very much better.

He sits suddenly, looks at Grandmother.

By the way, did you want anything?

GRANDMOTHER

No, no. Why don't you try to get a little sleep?

He closes his eyes.

MARCEL'S BLURRED POINT OF VIEW.

Grandmother looking at him under her veil.

INT. MARCEL'S BEDROOM, GRAND HOTEL, BALBEC. NIGHT.
1898.

*Marcel sits on the bed, looking desolately about the room, which is
curtained and shuttered. A clock ticks heavily. He looks along a
row of bookcases with glass fronts, which glint in the light, and
stares at a long mirror which stands in a corner. He is reflected in
it.*

*He cranes his neck to look up at the high ceilings, shivers, sees
again his reflection in the mirror. He goes to the mirror and turns
its face to the corner.*

*He goes to the wall, hesitates, and then knocks tentatively three
times.*

*A pause, and then three authoritative knocks sound from the next
room. He sits on the bed. The door opens. Grandmother comes in,
dressed in a loose cambric gown.*

GRANDMOTHER

Are you ill?

MARCEL

No. Just tired.

She goes to him, leans over him, touches his forehead.

He embraces her fiercely, kissing her cheek.

She holds him.

GRANDMOTHER

Now stand up.
                    (*He does.*)
And let's get these boots off.

MARCEL

No, no, I'll . . .

GRANDMOTHER

No, no, I'll do it. It's easy for me to do it. Just put your
hand on my shoulder and we'll get these boots off.

*Kneeling, she unbuttons his boots, while he looks down at her
gravely.*

INT. BEDROOM. MORNING.

Sea and sky flashing in glass fronts of bookcases.

An opened trunk, with clothes strewn about it, is on the floor.

*Marcel, with wet face, naked to the waist, moves from wash basin
to towel rack, picks up a clean starched towel, which crackles,
wipes his face, looking out of the window.*

Dazzling sea from window.

He slowly puts the towel back on the rack, gazing out to the sea.

His face, happy.

INT. BEDROOM. MORNING.

Françoise stands, looking down at the trunk.

*She clicks her teeth, begins to fold clothes and put them into
drawers.*

INT. HOTEL DINING-ROOM. LUNCH.

*Marcel and Grandmother are sitting at a table by the windows,
which are closed.*

Grandmother leans over to a side window and opens it. A gust of wind blows in. Newspapers and menus scatter. Ladies clasp their hats, veils fly up. Remonstrances from other guests. Waiters rush to close window.

Marcel looks at Grandmother.

In background, at the dining-room door, an Old Lady 66 appears. She sees Grandmother and her face brightens.

Grandmother however, lowers her eyes, does not respond.

The Old Lady looks away, is escorted to her table.

MARCEL

That lady seemed to know you.

GRANDMOTHER

Yes, she does. She's the Marquise de Villeparisis.

MARCEL

(*staring at Grandmother*)

But she's one of your closest friends! Aren't you going to speak to her?

GRANDMOTHER

One does not go to the seaside to meet people, however pleasant. One goes to the seaside for peace, relaxation, and fresh air. Madame de Villeparisis understands that perfectly.

EXT. THE PROMENADE. DAY.

Marcel stands alone.

In the distance, he sees Five Girls, slowly approaching through the crowds. One pushes a bicycle, two carry golf clubs.

He stares at them.

A call: 'Marcel!' He turns. Grandmother approaches with Mme. de Villeparisis.

GRANDMOTHER

Let me introduce my grandson. Marcel – the Marquise de Villeparisis.

He bows.

MME. DE VILLEPARISIS

How do you do? Your grandmother and I have just collided in a shop doorway. I had no idea she was in Balbec. A delightful surprise.

GRANDMOTHER

You are expecting your nephew to join you from Paris, you say?

MME. DE VILLEPARISIS

I am expecting two nephews. To be exact, one nephew and one great-nephew. One is the uncle of the other (*she chuckles*), but I am the aunt of them both.

The two ladies walk on together.

Marcel follows them, but suddenly pauses and looks back along the promenade.

No sign of the girls.

INT. DINING-ROOM. AFTERNOON.

The curtains are drawn. Marcel sits alone with coffee. From his position he can see through the foyer to the glass front of the hotel.

Against a background of sea, Saint-Loup strides towards a carriage and pair, jumps on the box seat, takes an envelope from the hotel manager, opens it, starts the horses, drives off.

CLOSE-UP. BARON DE CHARLUS IN FRONT OF PLAYBILL.

EXT. THE PROMENADE. DAY.

Marcel, feeling he is being watched, turns.

163

From his point of view sees Charlus in front of the playbill. He wears a dark suit, and slaps the leg of his trousers with a switch, staring at Marcel.

He turns away abruptly to examine the playbill, takes out a notebook, makes a note, looks at his watch, pulls his straw hat over his eyes, looks up and down the front, sighs, walks quickly away.

Marcel stares after him.

EXT. PROMENADE. DAY.

The little band of Girls walking along the front. They keep to an absolutely straight, remorseless course, appearing not to see those in their path. Some people make way for them automatically, some with a slight panic. The Girls ignore them and proceed with an arrogant assurance, occasionally jumping over an obstacle.

One of the Girls suddenly springs onto the platform of the bandstand and jumps over an old man, sitting underneath it in a deck chair. His cap is brushed by her feet. He looks up, terrified. The Girls laugh and applaud.

They draw closer. The sun is bright on the sea.

They are seen against the sea.

A confusion of faces, eyes, colours, hair, moving together, as parts of one unit.

Suddenly one girl's face is precisely focused.

She is dark, wears a polo cap, pushes a bicycle.

She turns her head, looks into the camera.

Albertine. She is eighteen.

EXT. PROMENADE.

Marcel.

The Girls passing.

Albertine looking at him.

She turns away from him.

INT. FOYER. HOTEL.

Mme. de Villeparisis. Charlus. Saint-Loup. Marcel.

MME. DE VILLEPARISIS
The Baron de Charlus.

Charlus, without looking at Marcel, extends his suede-gloved hand, crooks his little finger, forefinger, and thumb, leaving his middle two fingers extended. Marcel takes them.

The Marquis de Saint-Loup-en-Bray.

Saint-Loup's face and body are immobile, his eyes expressionless. He extends his arm abruptly, at full length. Marcel takes his hand.

RIVEBELLE RESTAURANT (NEAR BALBEC). EVENING.

Rivebelle Restaurant possesses a large garden, with tables.

Inside the restaurant a gypsy band plays. All the tables are taken and waiters are moving very quickly in all directions, some arguing with head waiters who respond by prodding them in the ribs on their way. Vast counters of hors d'oeuvres. Two very fat lady cashiers sit behind a bank of flowers.

Saint-Loup and Marcel are at the door with a waiter, who takes Marcel's coat.

SAINT-LOUP
Perhaps you should keep your coat. It's rather draughty in here.

MARCEL
No, no. Not at all.

They pass into the restaurant and move through the crowded tables.

Women look up as they pass.

Saint-Loup bows once or twice.

One Woman turns to another and whispers:

> **WOMAN**
> He remembered me!

Saint-Loup and Marcel sit down and are given menus and beer.

EXT. RIVEBELLE. THE GARDEN.

Night has not quite fallen. The lamps in the restaurant cause a pale green reflection in the windows.

Impression of an aquarium.

INT. RESTAURANT.

> **SAINT-LOUP**
> It isn't very often I meet anyone who's interested in writing, who wants to write, who's concerned about the expression of experience through words.

Saint-Loup waits for Marcel to respond. Marcel does not.

> The world of 'society', to which I unfortunately belong, displays nothing but a carefully cultivated ignorance which over the centuries has become true banality of mind, masquerading behind gesture, behind manner, behind arrogance, as good breeding. It never occurs to them that their posture and pretensions have become atrophied. But in fact they know nothing and are interested in nothing except money and position. They're philistines.

The hors d'oeuvres are served.

They eat.

You looked at me critically, I thought, when I spoke to my groom this evening.

MARCEL

I thought you were a little harsh with him.

SAINT-LOUP

I regard him as my equal. Why should I go out of my way to speak politely to him? You seem to think I should treat him with respect, *as an inferior*. I treat him in the same way I treat my family. You're talking like an aristocrat!

They eat.

MARCEL

These places always make me think of an aquarium. You wonder when the people outside are going to break through the glass and devour the fish.

Saint-Loup stares at him.

THE TABLE. LATER.

They are drinking port.

SAINT-LOUP

My family disapproves of me violently because I'm in love with an actress. She's got more refinement and sensitivity in her little finger than they have in their whole body. However, the fact remains, quite frankly, that she's driving me mad. I dream about her, all the time. Last night I dreamt I was in a house. My sergeant major was the host. I was sitting with him drinking. Suddenly I heard sounds, her sounds . . . you know . . . her sounds. Someone was with her, in her room. I could hear her sounds. But my sergeant major would not allow me to go to her room. He refused absolutely. He was very angry, he said it would be most indiscreet of me, most impolite, most . . . ungentlemanly.

Pause.

What an idiotic dream.

Saint-Loup is sweating.

I won't be a moment.

Saint-Loup rises and forces his way through the packed tables to the door.

Marcel calls a waiter.

MARCEL

A piece of bread, please.

WAITER

Certainly, Monsieur le Baron.

MARCEL

I am not a baron.

WAITER

Sorry, Monsieur le Comte.

Saint-Loup appears at the door with Marcel's coat. He looks swiftly at the packed tables and to where Marcel is sitting at the far end of the red plush bench, which runs round the side of the room. He jumps onto the bench, and from the bench steps on to the narrow ledge which runs behind it.

The staff, stopping their service in midtracks, and the other diners watch as Saint-Loup runs along the ledge, balancing himself with his arms, like a tightrope walker. Discreet applause breaks out. He arrives at his table, jumps down and hands Marcel his coat.

SAINT-LOUP

I thought it was becoming a little chilly.

INT. MARCEL'S BEDROOM. HOTEL. NIGHT.

Marcel alone in the room. A knock at the door.

MARCEL

Who is it?

CHARLUS

It is Charlus. May I come in?

Marcel opens the door. Charlus enters, a book in his hand.

My nephew was telling me that you were often
depressed before going to bed, that you found difficulty
in getting to sleep, and that you admired the work of
Anatole France. I happen to have one of his novels with
me. I thought you might like to read it, that it might
relax you.

MARCEL

How very kind of you. Thank you. But you must think
these . . . moods of mine . . . at night . . . very stupid.

CHARLUS

No, why? You have not, perhaps, any personal merit. So
few have. But for a time at least you have youth and that
is always charming. You have also placed your affection
wisely in your grandmother. It is a legitimate affection, I
mean one that is repaid. That's a rare enough state of
affairs.

Charlus walks up and down the room, thoughtfully.

I have another volume of Anatole France in my room. I
will have it brought for you.

Charlus does not move. They stand in silence.

MARCEL

Please don't bother. One volume will be quite enough.

CHARLUS

That's what I was thinking.

Another silence.

(*abruptly*)

Good night, sir.

He leaves the room.

THE SEA.

Marcel swimming.

Through the froth he sees the little band of Girls walking along the front.

INT. HOTEL. THE LIFT.

Marcel entering the lift.

The lift rises.

Marcel looks through the railings.

On each floor shadowy galleries open out.

A Chambermaid comes along one, carrying a bolster.

Marcel leans forward to look at her.

The lift rises and loses her.

INT. HOTEL. MARCEL'S LANDING.

Marcel leaves the lift.

Françoise is hurrying along the corridor.

FRANÇOISE

The Marquis de Saint-Loup is going to take a photograph of your grandmother. She's so pleased. She's put on her best dress.

Marcel follows Françoise into Grandmother's room.

INT. GRANDMOTHER'S ROOM.

Grandmother is sitting at a mirror trying on hats.

> GRANDMOTHER
>
> Isn't this silly? The Marquis –

> MARCEL
>
> I know. I've heard.

> GRANDMOTHER
>
> Do you mind?

> MARCEL
>
> It seems a quite frivolous and ridiculous idea to me.

> FRANÇOISE
>
> O sir, she's going to wear the hat that Françoise has trimmed for her –

> MARCEL
>
> Which hat?

> FRANÇOISE
>
> The hat she has on.

He does not speak.

> GRANDMOTHER
>
> Don't you like it?

> MARCEL
>
> Most elegant.

> GRANDMOTHER
>
> If you'd rather I didn't –

> MARCEL
>
> Please do as you wish. Although I would have thought at your age . . . Well, I'll leave you to adorn yourself.

He goes out.

Grandmother's face, pained.

She looks at herself in the mirror.

GRANDMOTHER

I look so ill.
> *(She smiles at Françoise.)*

Thank you, Françoise. The hat will disguise it.

EXT. HOTEL.

Saint-Loup with camera. He takes the photograph.

PHOTOGRAPH OF GRANDMOTHER.

Her face, in pain, carefully concealed by the shadow of the brim of her hat.

INT. DINING-ROOM. HOTEL. AFTERNOON.

The dining-room, still, empty.

The whistle of a steamer far away.

CLIFF TOP. BALBEC. LONG SHOT.

The little band of Girls, sitting on the grass with a picnic.

THE ROAD TO HUDIMESNIL. DAY.

The Marquise de Villeparisis' carriage, containing the Marquise, Marcel and Grandmother, travelling downhill.

Marcel sitting, staring rather vacantly ahead.

Suddenly he concentrates, his eyes narrowing.

THE TREES.

Three trees stand alone at the entrance to an avenue.

MARCEL'S FACE.

HIGH SHOT. CARRIAGE ON THE ROAD.

HIS POINT OF VIEW.

The trees, although the carriage is moving away from them, give the impression of following it.

MARCEL'S FACE, ALIVE.

THE TREES.

They follow the carriage.

THE CARRIAGE.

Mme. de Villeparisis and Grandmother regarding gently the passing countryside.

MARCEL'S FACE, INTENSE.

FLASH OF THE STEEPLES AT MARTINVILLE.

THE TREES, WITHDRAWING.

THE TREES ARE NO LONGER IN SIGHT.

MARCEL'S FACE.

He is still looking back.

THE CARRIAGE.

GRANDMOTHER

What are you looking at, Marcel?

MARCEL
(*turning*)

Nothing.

MME. DE VILLEPARISIS
Have I missed something?

MARCEL

No.

CLOSE SHOT. FLOWERS ON CLIFF TOP.

Boats on the horizon.

A butterfly flutters between the flowers.

GISÈLE
(*VO*)
Aren't you eating any sandwiches?

EXT. THE CLIFF TOP. BALBEC. DAY.

*The little band of Girls: Albertine 18, Andrée 20, Gisèle,
Rosemonde and Delphine (all 17), with Marcel, sitting with a
picnic. Hampers, etc. At the edge of the field, bicycles.*

MARCEL
No. I prefer this.

ALBERTINE
What is it exactly?

MARCEL
A chocolate cake.

Silence. They all munch.

ALBERTINE
Don't you actually *like* sandwiches?

MARCEL
Not very much.

Silence.

GISÈLE

What do you think of that, Andrée?

Andrée smiles.

EXT. EDGE OF A WOOD, NEAR BALBEC. DAY.

Albertine sitting with Marcel.

ALBERTINE

What did you normally do, before you met us? Just
mooch about on the beach all day, with all those old
trouts? I mean, don't you like games? We play golf all
the time. Of course, most of the other people who play
golf are perfectly tedious, perfectly boring.

Pause.

I could see you wanted to know us. I could see you were
interested in us. But actually, apart from Andrée . . .
apart from Andrée, the others are extremely stupid. I
suppose you've realized that. They're just children.

ALBERTINE IN PROFILE. HER CHEEKS.

ALBERTINE

But Andrée is really intelligent. Oh yes. Oh, she's quite
intelligent.

ANDRÉE APPROACHES THEM FROM THE WOOD.

Albertine jumps up.

ALBERTINE

Goodness, what's the time? We're supposed to be at tea
with Madame Durieux!

ANDRÉE

There's plenty of time.

ALBERTINE

I'm going.

ANDRÉE

I'm staying. To talk to him.

ALBERTINE

You'll be late.

ANDRÉE

Don't be an idiot.

ALBERTINE

Oh, as you like.
(*To Marcel.*)
I have a note for you.

She takes an envelope from her bag and hands it to him.

Good-bye.

Albertine goes to her bicycle and rides off.

MARCEL AND ANDRÉE.

MARCEL

Do you mind if I open this?

ANDRÉE

Why not?

He tears open the envelope.

CLOSE SHOT. THE LETTER.

It reads: 'I like you'.

MARCEL AND ANDRÉE.

He puts the letter back in the envelope, and into his pocket. He looks up. Andrée smiles at him.

ANDRÉE

She's an orphan, you know.

EXT. THE PROMENADE. BALBEC. DAY.

A line of very old ladies sitting in deck chairs on the promenade.

Camera finds Marcel and Albertine standing together.

ALBERTINE

I'm staying at your hotel tomorrow night. I'm going back to Paris. I'm staying at the hotel, so that I can catch the first train in the morning. You can come and see me in my room, if you like.

MARCEL

Yes. I'd like to.

ALBERTINE

I'm wearing my hair in the way you like. You did say you liked it like this, didn't you?

EXT. CLIFF TOP. DAY.

Andrée smiling at him.

INT. ALBERTINE'S ROOM. HOTEL. NIGHT.

Marcel closing the door, behind him.

Albertine is lying in bed. Her white nightgown leaves her throat bare.

Her hair is undone.

Beyond the bed, through the window, moon on the sea.

ALBERTINE

I went to bed. I had a slight chill.

Marcel stares at her.

MARCEL

You're chilly?

ALBERTINE

No, I'm not chilly. I'm quite warm, thank you. I said I
felt I had a slight chill, so I got into bed.
(*She waves to a chair.*)
Sit down.

He sits slowly on the bed.

ALBERTINE LYING IN BED.

She looks up at him.

He leans towards her, to kiss her.

ALBERTINE

Stop that, or I'll ring the bell!

HIS FACE.

*He pauses, regards her for a moment, and then leans towards her
again, decisively. As his lips touch her turning face he hears the
shrill sound of the bell.*

ALBERTINE'S ARM TUGGING THE BELL.

HEDGE AT TANSONVILLE.

Gilberte looking at him through the hedge.

WINDOW AT MONTJOUVAIN.

*Mlle. Vinteuil running to window to close shutters. Her Friend on
sofa in background.*

FLASH OF YELLOW SCREEN.

Music of Vinteuil.

INT. DRAWING-ROOM. NEW FLAT IN PARIS IN A WING OF
THE DUC DE GUERMANTES' HOUSE. DAY. LATE 1898.

*Grandmother is sitting under a lamp, a book on her lap. She is
reading, but halfheartedly, her eyes continually lifting from the
page, her head slightly nodding.*

She looks heavy, old, ill.

Suddenly she turns towards the camera, smiles with an effort.

INT. DRAWING-ROOM. NEW FLAT. DAY. LATE 1898. A FEW
WEEKS EARLIER THAN PREVIOUS SHOT.

*The room is in a certain amount of disarray, showing evidence of
a recent move.*

*Marcel is standing at the window, looking down on the courtyard.
He is nineteen.*

Françoise and a Footman are fixing a painting to the wall.

OVER MARCEL TO COURTYARD.

*Jupien 49 is passing. He looks up, smiles, lifts his hat, goes
towards his shop.*

>   FRANÇOISE
>   (*VO*)
> He's the only friendly man I've met around here so far.
> The only person of any charm.

>   MARCEL
> Who is it?

>   FRANÇOISE
>   (*VO*)
> Monsieur Jupien. He's a tailor. That's his shop.

EXT. COURTYARD. MARCEL'S POINT OF VIEW.

Jupien enters his shop.

Horses are being led by grooms to stables.

INT. DRAWING-ROOM.

Mother joins Marcel at the window.

> MOTHER
> Isn't it strange? You remember when you were a little
> boy, the magic the name Guermantes had for you? And
> now here you are living so close to them.

Pause.

> MARCEL
> Very strange.

INT. COMBRAY CHURCH, 1893.

The Duchesse 35, turning, smiling.

INT. BOX AT THE OPERA. 1898.

The Duchesse lifting her gloved hand, waving.

The Princesse turns to look down.

INT. THE GUERMANTES' HOUSE. THE HALL. DAY.

*The Duchesse in the hall, at a mirror, adjusting her hat,
smoothing her cuffs. Her hair is golden.*

She leaves the house. The servants bow.

EXT. COURTYARD GATE. THE GUERMANTES' HOUSE.

The Porter opens the gates, bowing, as the Duchesse passes.

*Camera stays with the Duchesse as she walks down the street. Her
eyes suddenly see someone.*

She nods curtly, walks on.

Camera pans to find Marcel, standing, looking after her.

EXT. A BOULEVARD.

The Duchesse walking.

She looks sharply to her right.

HER EYES.

MARCEL. STANDING BY A TREE.

He bows, lifts his hat.

THE DUCHESSE, WALKING.

She nods, curtly. Her face is sullen.

EXT. PASTRY COOK'S SHOP.

Through the window the Duchesse seen pointing to cakes. The Assistant begins to wrap them. The Duchesse's eyes stray to the window.

She stares, turns away, abruptly.

INT. THEATRE. THE STAGE: BACKSTAGE STORAGE AREA. LATE 1898.

The curtain is down. Stagehands are moving scenery. It is the interval.

Saint-Loup and Marcel walk onto the stage.

> SAINT-LOUP
> What did you think?

> MARCEL
> She has a wonderful stage presence.

SAINT-LOUP

She has. It's electric. She's beautiful too, isn't she?

MARCEL

Very striking.

Stagehands continue their work.

Three Journalists appear on the stage, one smoking a cigar.

SAINT-LOUP
(*to Marcel*)

She'll be here in a minute. She's dying to meet you.

Pause.

MARCEL

While we're waiting, I wanted to ask you something.

SAINT-LOUP

Yes?

MARCEL

Your aunt, the Duchesse de Guermantes . . .

SAINT-LOUP

Yes?

MARCEL

I believe she thinks I'm an idiot.

SAINT-LOUP.

What makes you say that?

MARCEL

A rumour . . . that's all.

SAINT-LOUP

Rubbish. Have you met her?

MARCEL

No.

SAINT-LOUP

I'll introduce you.

MARCEL

When?

SAINT-LOUP

When I get the chance.

Saint-Loup walks up and down the stage.

Where is she?

One or two actors and dancers appear in the wings. A man approaches the Journalists in background and questions them. One of the Journalists is heard to say:

JOURNALIST

We're waiting for Monsieur Bouvet.

SAINT-LOUP
(*to Marcel, vaguely*)

How's the writing?

MARCEL

I'm not doing any.

Rachel appears.

SAINT-LOUP

Darling.
(*He kisses her.*)
You were wonderful. This is Marcel. Marcel – Rachel.

They shake hands.

MARCEL

Congratulations.

RACHEL

Did you enjoy it?

MARCEL

Very much.

SAINT-LOUP

You were wonderful.

RACHEL

Oh don't be ridiculous. How could I be wonderful in
such a small part? Next season I'll be playing leads.
Then you can judge.

*During this speech Rachel's gaze has been straying to a male
Dancer, practising on the side of the stage.*

SAINT-LOUP

What are you looking at?

RACHEL

Mmmnn?

SAINT-LOUP

Why are you looking at him?

RACHEL

Who?

SAINT-LOUP

That damn dancer.

RACHEL

Was I?

*Stagehands, in moving scenery, press Saint-Loup, Rachel and
Marcel close to the group of Journalists, who listen with interest to
the conversation.*

Why shouldn't I? Look how beautifully made he is. And
look at his hands.

*The Dancer is dressed as a Watteau page, his eyelids stiff with
paint, his cheeks plastered with rouge. Hearing Rachel's remarks,
he very delicately repeats the movements of his hands.*

184

How exquisite.

SAINT-LOUP

If you don't stop this I'll leave at once, do you
understand?
>   (*To Marcel.*)
You shouldn't stand about in the cigar smoke like this.
It'll make you ill.

RACHEL
>   (*to Saint-Loup*)
Oh, go then, for goodness' sake!

SAINT-LOUP

If I go I won't come back.

RACHEL

Good.

SAINT-LOUP
>   (*whispering*)
I promised you that necklace, if you remember –

RACHEL

Don't try to blackmail me! I'm not a moneygrubber.
Keep your necklace.

SAINT-LOUP

You want me to leave you then? Is that what you want?

RACHEL

Isn't he wonderful with his hands?

Marcel coughs.

SAINT-LOUP
>   (*to Journalist*)
Would you mind putting out your cigar, sir? The smoke
is bad for my friend.

RACHEL
(*to Dancer*)

Do they do those tricks with women too, those lovely hands? They're girl's hands. I'm sure I could have a wonderful time with you and a girl I know.

CLOSE-UP. THE DANCER.

He is smiling.

THE STAGE.

Rachel walks slowly into the wings.

JOURNALIST

There's no rule against smoking, as far as I know. He's not forced to stay here, is he?

SAINT-LOUP
(*politely*)

I'm afraid you are not very civil, sir.

Saint-Loup raises his arm and hits the Journalist with extreme force across the face. The Journalist staggers back. His Colleagues turn away. One rubs his eyes, as if dust had entered it. The other looks at his watch.

SECOND JOURNALIST

Good gracious, the curtain's going up in a minute. We shan't get to our seats.

Saint-Loup strides out. Marcel follows him.

QUICK SHOT.

The Dancer, moving his hands.

EXT. STAGE DOOR OF THE THEATRE. EVENING.

Marcel comes out of the stage door.

He sees Saint-Loup walking up the street.

A Man approaches Saint-Loup, who stops. The Man begins to speak rapidly to him.

Saint-Loup suddenly hits him a number of times, knocking him down. He turns, sees Marcel, joins him. They walk in the opposite direction.

SAINT-LOUP

Damn filth! He made a proposition to me! Can you imagine it? In broad daylight! They don't even wait for night to fall now, the scum!

INT. THE FLAT. DAY.

Grandmother sitting under lamp with book.

She turns to camera, smiles.

GRANDMOTHER

Hullo, Marcel.

EXT. STREET. DAY. 1899.

Marcel 19 walking towards the house of Mme. de Villeparisis.

INT. MME. DE VILLEPARISIS' DRAWING-ROOM. DAY. 1899.

The drawing-room is hung with yellow silk, sofas upholstered in Beauvais tapestry. Many portraits.

Mme. de Villeparisis is seated at a desk dressed in a cap of black lace, spectacles and an apron.

On the desk are paintbrushes, a palette and an unfinished watercolour, and in glasses, saucers and cups are moss roses, zinnias and maidenhair ferns.

She is painting. Some people stand around the desk, watching, including Marcel; various others are about the room, talking.

A Butler is serving tea and cakes.

> **MME DE VILLEPARISIS**
> Yes, I remember Monsieur Molé very well. He was
> extraordinarily pompous. I can see him now coming
> downstairs to dinner in his own house with his hat in his
> hand.

> **AN HISTORIAN**
> Was that a common habit at the time, madame?

> **MME. DE VILLEPARISIS**
> Not at all. It was just a habit Monsieur Molé had, that's
> all. I never saw my father carry his hat in the house,
> except of course when the King came, because the King
> being at home wherever he is, the master of the house is
> a visitor in his own drawing-room.

*The Footman at the door announces: 'The Duchesse de
Guermantes'.*

The Duchesse 41 walks across the room to Mme. de Villeparisis.

> How are you, Oriane?
> > (*To the small group.*)
> Let me introduce my niece, the Duchesse de
> Guermantes.

The Duchesse bows very quickly and coldly to them.

Footman at the door announces: 'The Comte d'Argencourt'.

THE DUCHESSE DE GUERMANTES.

*She sits alone on a sofa. She wears a straw hat trimmed with
cornflowers and a blue striped silk skirt.*

With the point of her sunshade she traces circles on the carpet.

Her eyes then inspect each sofa and swiftly its occupant.

MARCEL.

He stands alone, watching her.

AT THE DOOR OF THE ROOM.

Two Young Men are at the door. They are both tall, slender, goldenhaired. The Footman, who is also young, announces: 'The Prince de Foix'.

The Prince passes into the room.

The Footman and the other Young Man suddenly stare at each other in recognition.

The Footman's eyes are wide. The Young Man quickly closes his.

> FOOTMAN
> (*in a low voice*)
> Your name, sir?

> YOUNG MAN
> (*in a lower voice*)
> The Duc de Châtellerault.

The Footman turns to the room and announces with pride: 'His Royal Highness, the Duc de Châtellerault'.

THE DUCHESSE ON THE SOFA.

The Prince and the Duc kiss her hand and sit on either side of her, laying their silk hats on the floor by their feet.

The Historian looks at the hats.

> HISTORIAN
> I don't think you should leave your hats on the floor, gentlemen. They might be trodden on.

CLOSE-UP. THE PRINCE DE FOIX.

He stares at the Historian, his eyes piercing, very cold.

THE HISTORIAN.

He flushes, stammers, turns away.

THE SOFA.

> PRINCE DU FOIX
> (*to the Duchesse*)
> Who is that person? The person who just addressed me.

> DUCHESSE
> I haven't the slightest idea.

She turns to Châtellerault, who is sitting with his eyes closed.

> You look dreadfully pale, Châtellerault. Are you ill?

> CHÂTELLERAULT
> (*without opening his eyes*)
> Hay fever.

MME. DE VILLEPARISIS, PAINTING.

The Butler brings to her a card on a tray. She looks at it.

> MME. DE VILLEPARISIS
> The Queen of Sweden! Good gracious. I had no idea
> she knew I was back in Paris.

Footman at door announces: 'Her Majesty, the Queen of Sweden'.

Enter the Duc de Guermantes. He roars with laughter.

General laughter.

The Duc approaches Mme. de Villeparisis, greeting people as he walks, shaking hands.

He kisses Mme. de Villeparisis' hand.

> DUC
> I thought you'd be amused.

MME. DE VILLEPARISIS
(*unamused*)

What an idiotic joke.

The Duc laughs.

DUC

I knew it would amuse you.

He sees Marcel.

Ah, my neighbour! How do you do?

DUCHESSE

We met the Queen last night as a matter of fact at
Blanche Lord's. She's grown absolutely enormous.

DUC

Oriane said she looked like a frog.

DUCHESSE

A frog in an 'interesting condition'.

Laughter.

MARCEL, UNSMILING.

THE ROOM.

Footman announces: 'The Baron de Charlus'.

The camera glimpses Charlus through the now packed gathering.

Marcel turns to find M. de Norpois beside him.

NORPOIS

Writing anything these days?

Norpois is greeted by someone else and turns away.

Mme. de Villeparisis leans towards the Duchesse.

MME. DE VILLEPARISIS

I think you should know that I am expecting Madame
Swann to visit me this afternoon.

DUCHESSE

On really? Thank you for telling me.

The Duchesse turns abruptly to look for the first time at Marcel.

Good afternoon. How are you?

MARCEL

Thank you, madame. I am quite well.

*Footman's voice announcing: 'The Prince von Faffenheim-
Munsterburg-Weinigen'.*

The Duchesse regards Marcel.

DUCHESSE

I see you sometimes in the morning. It's so good for
one, a walk.

Footman announces: 'Madame Charles Swann'.

The Duchesse looks at her watch.

Gracious, I must fly.

She stands, and moves swiftly away.

*Marcel wanders through the now very crowded room, carefully
stepping over the long skirts of the ladies and avoiding the crowd
of hats that litter the carpet.*

Around him an intense chatter of conversation; indecipherable.

He glimpses Charlus talking to Odette on a sofa.

*He turns to see the Duc de Châtellerault and the Prince de Foix
sitting erect and silent.*

INT. MARCEL'S BEDROOM. COMBRAY. 1888.

The magic lantern.

The image of Geneviève de Brabant floats over the walls and ceiling.

INT. MME. DE VILLEPARISIS' DRAWING-ROOM.

Marcel draws near to Mme. de Villeparisis, still painting, watched by a circle of admirers.

He is tapped on the shoulder. He turns. It is Charlus.

>   CHARLUS
> As I see you've taken to going into society you must do
> me the pleasure of coming to see me. But it's a little
> complicated. I am seldom at home. You will have to
> write to me. I am just going. Will you walk a short way
> with me?

>   MARCEL
> Certainly.

>   CHARLUS
> Wait for me.

Charlus turns away.

Mme. de Villeparisis has overheard these remarks. She beckons Marcel to her, speaks quietly.

>   MME. DE VILLEPARISIS
> You are leaving with my nephew?

>   MARCEL
> Yes, he has asked me to walk home with him.

>   MME. DE VILLEPARISIS
> Don't wait for him. He's busy talking. He's certain to
> have forgotten what he said to you. Go now quickly
> while his back is turned.

INT. MME. DE VILLEPARISIS' HOUSE. THE STAIRCASE.

Marcel descending the staircase alone.

Charlus' voice from the top of the stairs.

> CHARLUS
> (*VO*)
> So this is how you wait for me, is it?

Marcel turns to see Charlus staring down at him.

EXT. STREET.

Marcel and Charlus come out of the house.

> CHARLUS
> We'll walk a little way, until I find a cab that suits me.

They walk.

> What in heaven's name were you doing at that idiot tea
> party? It's a complete waste of your time. I know I was
> there myself, but for me it was not a social gathering –
> simply a family visit.

Charlus waves him on. They continue walking.

> What nonsense the newspapers talk about that fellow
> Dreyfus. How can one charge Dreyfus with betraying
> his country? He's a Jew, not a Frenchman. The only
> sensible charge against him would be one of infringing
> the laws of hospitality.

*Charlus pauses in his step to stare at another passing cab. The driver
stops. Charlus waves him on. Marcel looks at him questioningly.*

> I didn't like the colour of his lamps.

They walk.

> I will ask you a simple question. Are you worth my
> trouble or not?

MARCEL

I am very grateful . . . that you should take an interest in me.

Charlus clasps his arm.

CHARLUS

Your words touch me.

They walk arm in arm.

I think I can help you. I do not, as a rule, care to talk about myself, but you may possibly have heard – it was referred to in a leading article in *The Times*, which made a considerable impression – that the Emperor of Austria, who has always honoured me with his friendship, said the other day in an interview that if the Comte de Chambord had been advised by a man as thoroughly conversant with the undercurrents of European politics as myself he would be King of France today.

Charlus looks at Marcel. Marcel looks at Charlus.

The fact is, I have within me an invaluable secret record which it has taken me over thirty years to collect. I could hand it over to a deserving young man in a few months. I have but one passion left, to seek to redeem the mistakes of my life by conferring the benefit of my knowledge on a soul that is still virgin. But if you are to be that young man, I would have to see you often, very often, every day.

Charlus stops walking, and looks into Marcel's eyes, still clasping his arm.

He abruptly drops Marcel's arm and continues walking. Marcel follows.

A cab passes.

In it Marcel sees the Comte d'Argencourt, looking at them.

Charlus continues speaking as if there had been no pause.

> For the time being, you must keep out of society. Parties
> like the one we've just left will warp your intellect and
> character. And be very careful in choosing your friends.
> Keep mistresses if you like, that doesn't concern me,
> > (*he squeezes his arm*)
> you young rascal, but your choice of men friends is more
> important. My nephew Saint-Loup is a suitable companion
> for you. At least he's a man, not one of those effeminate
> creatures who abound today, little whores who so casually
> bring their innocent victims to the gallows.

A cab approaches, zigzagging along the street.

*The young Cabman is driving it from inside the cab, sprawling
across the cushions.*

Charlus stops the cab.

CABMAN
(*drunkenly*)

Which way are you going?

CHARLUS

Yours.

CABMAN

I'm driving it from down here. It's up to you.

CHARLUS

Put the hood up.

The Cabman staggers to put up the hood.

CHARLUS
(*to Marcel*)

I give you a few days to think about my offer. Consider
it most seriously.

He bows quickly and goes to the cab.

He helps the Cabman to put up the hood, climbs in with him, and takes the reins.

CHARLUS
I'll drive.

The horse trots off.

INT. MARCEL'S FLAT. GRANDMOTHER'S ROOM. DAY. 1899.

Mother is helping Grandmother into her cloak.

MOTHER
A walk will do you good.

GRANDMOTHER
Yes.

MOTHER
The doctor said it would be good for you. It's a lovely day.

GRANDMOTHER
Yes. Yes, it is.

The door opens. Marcel comes in.

MARCEL
Oh, come on. I've been waiting for you for hours.

GRANDMOTHER
Yes, yes. I'm coming. It is a lovely day.

MARCEL
It'll probably be pouring with rain by the time we get there.

MOTHER
No, no, it won't.
(*To Grandmother.*)

It'll be good for you. The air will do you good.

EXT. AVENUE GABRIEL. DAY.

A cab stops. Marcel and Grandmother get out. They walk slowly along the treelined path.

MARCEL
Not a bad day, is it?

Grandmother, without speaking, suddenly turns away and heads for a public lavatory; a pavilion covered with green trellis.

The female attendant, known as La Marquise, is sitting outside talking to a Park Keeper. She stands, takes Grandmother inside. Marcel climbs the steps and stands, waiting.

La Marquise returns and sits again.

LA MARQUISE
What was I saying?

PARK KEEPER
About the magistrate.

LA MARQUISE
That's right. For the last eight years that man has been here every day at the stroke of three. Always a perfect gentleman. Stays half an hour, reads his papers, goes away satisfied. It's like a haven for him, my little place, my little piece of Paris. One day he didn't come. I thought he must have died. But the next day there he was again, right on the stroke of three. 'I hope nothing happened to you yesterday', I said. But he told me nothing had happened to him, it was just that his wife had died. I said to him: 'You just keep coming here, the same as before, and it'll be a little distraction for you in your sorrow'.

Pause.

I choose my customers. I don't let everybody come into my little parlours.

She turns to Marcel.

You wouldn't like me to open a little place for you?

MARCEL

No, thank you.

LA MARQUISE

You're quite welcome, as my guest. But, of course, not having to pay for a thing won't make you want to do anything if you've got nothing to do.

Grandmother comes out, slowly. She gives La Marquise some money.

Thank you, madame. Have a nice walk.

EXT. THE AVENUE.

Marcel and Grandmother walking, slowly.

GRANDMOTHER

I heard what she was saying. Could anything be more like the Guermantes, the Verdurins? Exactly the same.

Grandmother has spoken with great difficulty, wincing, clenching her teeth. Her hat is crooked, her cloak stained. She looks dazed. Marcel looks at her closely. He speaks cheerfully.

MARCEL

It's getting cold. I suggest we go home.

GRANDMOTHER

Yes.

MARCEL

We'll just find a cab and be home in next to no time.

GRANDMOTHER

Yes.

She smiles and grips his hand.

He leads her to a bench.

MARCEL

You sit down here. I'll find the cab.

GRANDMOTHER

Yes.

She sits, but does not let go of his hand, looking up at him. He gently loosens her grip.

MARCEL

I'll look for the cab.

GRANDMOTHER

Yes.

INT. FLAT. MARCEL'S ROOM. NIGHT.

He is in bed.

The door opens. Mother enters. She goes to the bed, looks down at him, her face drained.

MOTHER

I'm sorry . . . to disturb your sleep.

He looks up at her.

MARCEL

I wasn't asleep.

He gets out of bed.

INT. GRANDMOTHER'S BEDROOM. NIGHT.

Dr Cottard, Marcel's Father, Françoise, are in the room.

Marcel and Mother enter.

Grandmother, in the bed, is having convulsions.

The oxygen cylinder is at work.

The blankets heave. Her hands keep trying to thrust them aside, impotently. Her hair is wild.

She suddenly groans violently and lurches into a sitting position. Both eyes are closed, but one eyelid is not completely down.

She lurches forward again.

The chink of her left eye, filmy, dim. She groans.

Abruptly she is still.

Both her eyes open, very clear.

INT. MARCEL'S ROOM. HIS WRITING DESK. 1900.

Hands opening two envelopes.

The first is an invitation to Marcel to dinner from the Duchesse de Guermantes.

The second is a note from Charlus asking Marcel to visit him the same night, at eleven o'clock.

EXT. COURTYARD. NIGHT.

Marcel walking across the courtyard towards the brightly lit Guermantes' house.

Carriages arriving through the gates.

INT. THE GUERMANTES' DRAWING-ROOM. 1900. (SILENT.)

Marcel is being introduced by the Duc to a group of ladies. They all have bare bosoms, to which are attached sprays of mimosa, roses, garlands of orchids. They appear to respond to Marcel seductively, coyly, mischievously.

INT. THE GUERMANTES' DINING-ROOM. (SILENT.)

Dinner being served.

Various shots of the diners.

The Duc looking with a slight smile at a young lady, who is aware of his look.

The Duchesse says something dryly. Everyone laughs.

The Duc glances with irritation at the Duchesse, gestures to a waiter for more meat.

Marcel, bosoms heaving on either side of him.

EXT. THE GUERMANTES' GARDEN. NIGHT. (SILENT.)

The guests sipping orange juice and liqueurs, sitting, walking.

Musicians play.

The Duc talking to the young lady.

Marcel alone on a bench. The Duchesse comes to sit next to him. She wears a very wide dress. He stands for her to sit, sits again on the end of the bench and nearly falls off.

INT. BARON DE CHARLUS' HOUSE. THE BARON'S ROOM. NIGHT.

Charlus, in a Chinese dressing gown, throat bare, is lying on a sofa.

The Valet shows Marcel into the room and withdraws.

A tall hat, its top flashing in the light, sits on a cape on a chair.

Charlus stares at Marcel in silence.

MARCEL

Good evening.

No reply. The stare is implacable.

May I sit down?

Silence.

CHARLUS

Take the Louis Quatorze chair.

Marcel sits abruptly in a Directoire chair beside him.

Ah! So that is what you call a Louis Quatorze chair! I can see you have been well educated. One of these days you'll take Madame de Villeparisis' lap for a lavatory and goodness knows what you'll do in it.

Pause.

Sir, this interview which I have condescended to grant you will mark the end of our relationship.

He stretches an arm along the back of the sofa.

Since I was everything and you were nothing, since I, if I may state it plainly, am a prodigious personage and you in comparison a microbe, it was naturally I who took the first steps towards you. You have made an imbecilic reply to what it is not for me to describe as an act of greatness. In short, you have lied about me to others. You have repeated calumnies against me to others. Therefore these are the last words we shall exchange on this earth.

Pause.

MARCEL

Never, sir. I have never spoken about you to anyone.

CHARLUS

You left unanswered the proposal I made to you here in Paris. The idea did not attract you. There is no more to be said about that. But that you did not take the trouble to write to me shows that you lack not only breeding, good manners, sensibility, but common or garden intelligence. Instead, you prove yourself despicable in speaking of me disrespectfully to the world at large.

MARCEL

Sir, I swear to you that I have said nothing to anyone that could insult you.

CHARLUS
(*with extreme violence*)
Insult me? Who says that I am insulted? Do you suppose it is within your power to insult me? You evidently do not realize to whom you are speaking. Do you imagine that the envenomed spittle of five hundred little gentlemen of your type, heaped one upon the other, would succeed in slobbering so much as the tips of my august toes?

Marcel stares at him, jumps up, seizes the Baron's silk hat, throws it down, tramples it, picks it up, wrenches off the brim, tears the crown in two.

What in heaven's name are you doing? Have you gone mad?

Marcel rushes to the door and opens it.

Two Footmen are standing outside. They move slowly away.

Marcel walks quickly past them, followed by Charlus, who bars his way.

There, there, don't be childish. Come back for a minute. He that loveth well chasteneth well. I have chastened you well because I love you well.

He draws Marcel back into the room.

CHARLUS
(*to Footman*)
Take away the hat and bring me a new one.

Charlus and Marcel stand as the Footman collects the pieces of the hat together.

MARCEL

I would like to know the name of your informer, sir.

CHARLUS

I have given a promise of secrecy to my *informant*. I do not intend to betray that promise.

MARCEL

You insult me, sir. I have already sworn to you that I have said nothing.

CHARLUS
(*thunderously*)

Are you calling me a liar?

MARCEL

You have been misinformed.

CHARLUS

It is quite possible. Generally speaking, a remark repeated at second hand is rarely true. But true or false, the remark has done its work.

MARCEL

I had better go.

CHARLUS

I agree. Or, if you feel too tired, I have plenty of beds here.

MARCEL

Thank you, I am not too tired.

CHARLUS

It is true that my affection for you is dead. Nothing can revive it. As Victor Hugo's Boaz said: 'I am widowed, alone, and the dark gathers o'er me.'

INT. CHARLUS' HOUSE. DRAWING ROOM.

Charlus and Marcel walking through the green room.

Music is heard from another floor. A Beethoven romance.

Charlus points at two portraits.

> CHARLUS
> My uncles. The King of Poland and the King of
> England.

EXT. CHARLUS' HOUSE. THE FRONT DOOR.

The carriage waits. Charlus and Marcel look up at the night sky.

> CHARLUS
> What a superb moon. I think I shall take a walk in the
> Bois.

Marcel does not respond to this.

> It would be pleasant to walk in the Bois under the moon
> with someone like yourself. For you're charming, really,
> quite charming. When I met you first I must confess I
> found you quite insignificant.

He takes Marcel to his carriage. Marcel gets in.

> Remember this. Affection is precious. Do not neglect it.
> Thank you for coming. Good night.

CHARLUS AT FRONT DOOR. NIGHT.

His face. Impassive.

Sound of carriage departing.

EXT. THE GUERMANTES' COURTYARD. DAY.

*Charlus, in a dark suit, looking at something, his face curiously
soft.*

INT. WINDOW OF MARCEL'S FLAT. DAY.

The shutters are ajar.

Through the shutters Charlus can be seen looking at Jupien, who has just come out of his shop.

Jupien, aware of Charlus' gaze, returns it.

Charlus turns his head to look carelessly around the courtyard, his gaze regularly returning to Jupien. His gaze is searching. Jupien puts his hand on his hip, sticks out his buttocks, inclines his head to one side, holds the pose.

Charlus casually approaches him. They stand close to each other for a moment in silence.

>   CHARLUS
> Do you by any chance have a light?

>   JUPIEN
> Of course.

>   CHARLUS
> Unfortunately I've left my cigars at home.

>   JUPIEN
> Come inside. I have cigars.

They go into the shop. The door shuts.

EXT. THE EMPTY COURTYARD.

Marcel comes out of his door.

He strolls round the courtyard, keeping close to the walls, apparently deep in thought.

When he reaches the shop next to Jupien's he casually opens the door and goes in.

INT. VACANT PREMISES OF SHOP.

Marcel stands quite still in the gloom by a partition, on the other side of which is Jupien's shop.

Violent inarticulate sexual sounds emerge from behind the partition.

Gasps. A sudden silence.

Sound of running water.

Voices:

> **JUPIEN**
> No, I don't want any money. It was my pleasure.

Water.

> Why do you shave your chin like that? A nice beard is so becoming.

> **CHARLUS**
> A nice beard is disgusting. Listen. You don't know anything about the man who sells chestnuts round the corner, not the one on the left, he's a horror, but the other one, a big dark fellow?

> **JUPIEN**
> You're heartless.

A scrape of furniture, a squeal from Jupien, sudden silence.

> **JUPIEN**
> (*short of breath*)
> You're very naughty. You're a big baby.

Marcel climbs a ladder and peers down through a ventilator into the other shop.

Charlus is moving away from Jupien. He sits and lights a cigar.

CHARLUS

Do you know any ticket collectors, by any chance? I often need entertainment on my homeward journeys. You see, it falls to my lot, now and then, like the caliph who used to roam the streets of Baghdad in the guise of a common merchant, to condescend to follow some curious little person whose profile may have taken my fancy. He takes a tram. I follow. He takes a train. I follow. But more often than not I find myself at the end of the line at eleven o'clock at night with nothing to show for it. That's why I should like to get to know a ticket collector or a sleeping car attendant, to console me on my way home.

He looks sharply at Jupien.

You could be my agent! A brilliant idea. You could render me great service.

JUPIEN

Could I?

CHARLUS

Indisputably. You're a man of sensitivity and perspicacity. It shines out of your face.

JUPIEN

How sweet of you to say so.

INT. MARCEL'S BEDROOM. PARIS. DUSK. 1900.

Marcel 20 is in bed. Albertine 20 sits in a chair by the bed.

ALBERTINE

And are you well?

MARCEL

Fairly well. I get bouts, from time to time.

ALBERTINE

But you have to rest, like this?

MARCEL

Yes.

ALBERTINE

My poor boy.

She looks at watch.

I can't stay long.

MARCEL

You've only just come.

ALBERTINE

Yes, but I can't be late.

MARCEL

Where are you going?

ALBERTINE

Oh, I have to see some friends.

Pause.

I like your room. It's nice.
(*She looks at him.*)
I thought you might have grown a moustache.

MARCEL

I prefer to be clean shaven.

ALBERTINE

Moustaches can be nice.

Pause.

Do you ever think about Balbec, the sea?

MARCEL

Sometimes.

Pause.

The last time we saw each other you were in bed and I was sitting on the bed.

ALBERTINE

That's right.

MARCEL

Well, I think you should come and sit on the bed now and that will make a proper symmetry.

ALBERTINE

A proper what?

MARCEL
(*patting bed*)

Sit here.

ALBERTINE
(*slowly doing so*)

Here?

MARCEL

Now I can see you.

ALBERTINE

You could see me as easily as before.

MARCEL

I can see your eyes better now.

Pause.

You'd be more comfortable, though, if you lay down.

ALBERTINE

Do you think so?

MARCEL

Try it.

ALBERTINE
I have to go soon, you know.

She lies down by him, on her front, half over him.

Sound of the door opening.

Albertine jumps off the bed, falls into her chair.

Françoise comes in, carrying a lamp. She stops.

MARCEL
The lamp already! Early, isn't it?

FRANÇOISE
Do you want me to put it out?

Albertine giggles.

MARCEL
No. Leave it.

Françoise puts lamp down and leaves.

Albertine slowly stands, sits on bed, lies by his side.

I don't think I can resist the temptation to kiss you.

ALBERTINE
It would be a pity if you did.

He draws her towards him.

EXT. BEACH. BALBEC. DAY. 1898.

Albertine outlined against the sea and sky, laughing.

INT. MARCEL'S BEDROOM. DUSK. 1900.

Marcel drawing Albertine towards him.

Her cheeks, smooth and flushed, come closer to his eye and show a coarser grain.

Their lips meet. Darkness.

After a long kiss he whispers:

> MARCEL
> Why didn't you let me kiss you at Balbec?

> ALBERTINE
> (*whispering*)
> I didn't know you properly.

MARCEL AND ALBERTINE KISSING.

She leans over him, crushing him.

The camera concentrates on their heads only.

Suddenly he clutches her. They are still.

ANOTHER VIEW OF THE BED.

They lie together.

Albertine's face is docile, relaxed, abstracted.

> MARCEL
> Do you have to go?

> ALBERTINE
> No, no. I have plenty of time.

She regards him.

> What lovely hair you have, and eyes. You're a sweet
> boy.

INT. DUC DE GUERMANTES' HOUSE. FIRST LANDING. DAY.
1900.

The Duc de Guermantes is standing at the door of the library.

> DUC
> Marcel! How nice of you to look in.

They shake hands.

Oriane will be here in a moment.

They walk into the library.

INT. LIBRARY. DAY.

DUC
She's changing. We're dining with Madame de Saint-
Euverte, and then we're going to a rather grand party at
my cousin's – the Prince de Guermantes. And then we
have to be back here by midnight to change again for a
very important fancy dress ball given by the Marquise
d'Arpajon. I'm going as Louis XI and Oriane as Isabel
of Bavaria. Charles, have you met this young man?

Marcel turns to Swann at the far end of the library.

Swann comes towards him. He is fifty-two. His face is haggard.

Swann looks doubtfully at Marcel. They shake hands.

SWANN
How do you do?

MARCEL
I'm amazed that you remember me, sir.

SWANN
Of course I do. Of course I do. Are your people well?

MARCEL
They are, thank you.

SWANN
Good, good.

*Swann wears a pearl grey frockcoat, white gloves stitched in black
and carries a grey very wide hat, lined with green leather.*

DUC

Charles, you're an expert. I want your opinion of this.

He leads them to a painting.

What do you think of it? I've just swapped it for a couple of Monets. I think it might be a Vermeer. What do you think?

SWANN

Difficult to say.

DUC

Oh come on, we all know you're an expert. You're writing a book about Vermeer, aren't you?

SWANN

Oh, hardly a book . . . Just an article, about one painting.

MARCEL

View of Delft?

SWANN

Yes.

MARCEL

That patch of yellow wall.

SWANN

Yes.

DUC

Patch? What patch?

Swann suddenly recognizes Marcel.

Marcel turns to the Duc.

MARCEL
(*to the Duc*)
I think it's the most beautiful painting in the world.

DUC

I've probably seen it. But anyway, Charles,
(*he points to the painting on the wall*)
what would you say this was?

SWANN

A bad joke.

DUC

Oh, would you?

The Duchesse comes in. She wears a gown of red satin, the skirt bordered with spangles, an ostrich feather in her hair.

DUCHESSE

Charles! Marcel! How delightful. What a pity we have to
go out. Dining out is such a bore. There are evenings
when one would sooner die. But perhaps dying is an
even greater bore, who knows?
(*She looks at Swann's hat*)
How nice to have one's hat lined with green leather. But
with you, Charles, everything is always charming,
whether it's what you wear or what you say, what you
read or what you do. Which reminds me. Basin and I
are thinking of spending next spring in Italy and Sicily.
Will you come with us? It would make such a difference
to us. I'm not thinking only of the pleasure of seeing you
but of all the things you could explain to us there.
Admit it. You know everything.

SWANN

I'm afraid it won't be possible.

DUC

What a pity.

DUCHESSE

I'd like to know how, ten months before the time, you
can know that a thing will be impossible.

SWANN

I'm not very well.

DUCHESS

Yes, you do look a little pale. But I'm not asking you to
come next week, but next year!

A Footman enters.

FOOTMAN

The carriage is at the door, Your Grace.

DUC

Come on, Oriane. We'll be late.

INT. THE GUERMANTES' HOUSE. THE STAIRS.

They all walk down the stairs.

DUCHESSE

Charles, give me in one word the reason you won't
come to Italy.

SWANN
(*gently*)

Because by next spring I shall have been dead for some
time. According to the doctors I have only three or four
months to live.

The Footman opens the door. She pauses.

DUCHESSE

What's that?

EXT. THE GUERMANTES' COURTYARD. THE CARRIAGE.

The Duchesse, Swann and Marcel on the steps.

The Duc at the carriage.

DUCHESSE

You're joking.

SWANN

It would be a joke in charming taste. I'm sorry . . . but
since you asked me . . . but you'll be late, I mustn't
keep you.

DUCHESSE

Being late is not of any importance.

DUC

Oriane, you know perfectly well that Madame de Saint-
Euverte insists on dining at eight o'clock sharp. I'm
sorry, Charles, but it's ten to eight already and Oriane is
notorious for being late.

DUCHESSE
(*to Swann*)

I can't believe what you're saying. But we must talk
about it quietly. Come to luncheon, please, any day you
like. And we'll talk.

She puts her foot on the step of the carriage.

DUC

Oriane, what on earth are you doing? You're wearing
black shoes! With a red dress! Go upstairs and put some
red ones on, for goodness' sake!

DUCHESSE

But Basin, you say we're late.

DUC

What does it matter whether we're late or not? Anyway
we're not late. The point is you can't possibly go into
that house in a red dress and black shoes.

The Duchesse goes into the house.

(*To Swann and Marcel.*)
A red dress with black shoes.

SWANN

I thought they went rather well together.

DUC

I don't say you're wrong, but it's really far preferable to
match the dress, I'm quite convinced of that. I'm dying
of hunger. I had a terrible lunch. As for you, Charles,
don't believe a word those doctors tell you. You'll live
to bury us all.

MARCEL LOOKING AT SWANN.

SWANN LOOKS AT MARCEL, BRIEFLY.

INT. BALLROOM. BALBEC CASINO. 1901. (SILENT SHOT.)

Albertine and Andrée dancing together.

INT. FOYER. GRAND HOTEL. BALBEC. 1901.

Marcel 21 and the Manager are waiting for the lift.

Albertine's voice over:

ALBERTINE
(*softly*)

Oh, how heavenly.

INT. MARCEL'S BEDROOM. BALBEC HOTEL. 1901. DAY. HIGH
SHOT.

The door shuts. Marcel is alone.

He bends to unbutton his boots.

He stops, suddenly rigid, remains bent.

CLOSE-UP. MARCEL.

His face, overcome with grief.

On the soundtrack, three knocks are heard, on the wall.

INT. MARCEL'S HOTEL BEDROOM. THE FOLLOWING NIGHT.

Marcel, in a dressing gown, sits still in a chair by the window.

Dawn is growing over the sea.

The bed is disturbed.

He sits still.

There is a soft knock at the door. He looks up.

The door opens. His Mother comes in.

Her hair, greying, is dishevelled.

She wears Grandmother's dressing gown and for a moment is indistinguishable from her.

Marcel stares at her in astonishment.

> MOTHER
> Why are you looking at me like that?
> *(Gently.)*
> Ah. Yes. I look like your grandmother.

She goes towards him.

> Why are you sitting in that chair? What's the matter? What is it?

She takes him in her arms. He weeps.

INT. MARCEL'S HOTEL BEDROOM. MORNING. THE DOOR.

The door opens. Françoise

> FRANÇOISE
> Mademoiselle Albertine is here to see you.

INT. THE ROOM.

Marcel is at the window, looking out.

Included in the shot is the framed photograph of Grandmother, standing on a cabinet.

He turns.

> FRANÇOISE
> Mademoiselle Albertine's here.

> MARCEL
> Tell her I can't see her.

Françoise goes out.

Marcel stares at the photograph.

INT. HOTEL BEDROOM. DAY.

Albertine and Marcel sitting.

> ALBERTINE
> Would you like us to meet every day?

> MARCEL
> No. I can't. I don't feel . . . very bright. But we'll see each other . . . from time to time.

> ALBERTINE
> I'll come any time you want. I'll stay with you as long as you like.

INT. MARCEL'S HOTEL BEDROOM. ANOTHER DAY.

Albertine, in a different dress, on the bed in Marcel's arms. She looks at her watch, jumps up, goes to mirror, combs her hair.

> ALBERTINE
> I must go.

MARCEL

What? Why?

ALBERTINE

I have to be somewhere at five o'clock.

MARCEL

Where?

ALBERTINE

I have to pay a call on a friend of my aunt's. At
Infreville.

MARCEL

But you didn't mention this when you came.

ALBERTINE

I didn't want to upset you. She's at home every day at
five o'clock. I can't be late.

MARCEL

But if she's at home every day why do you have to go
today?

ALBERTINE

She expects me. My aunt expects me to go.

MARCEL

But what difference does a day make?

ALBERTINE

Well . . . as a matter of fact, I've arranged to meet some
of my girl friends there. It'll be less boring.

MARCEL

Oh. So you prefer this boring lady and your friends to
me?

ALBERTINE

I've said I'll give the girls a lift. Otherwise they can't get
back.

MARCEL

There are trains from Infreville up till ten o'clock at night.

ALBERTINE

Yes, but she might ask them to stay for dinner.

Pause.

MARCEL

All right. Listen. I feel some fresh air will do me good. I'll come with you, just for the ride. I won't come into the house. I'll just go with you to the door.

Albertine stares at him, still.

I really feel like some fresh air.

ALBERTINE

Let's go in the other direction. It's prettier.

MARCEL

The other direction? But you were going to see your aunt's friend.

ALBERTINE

Oh, I can't be bothered.

MARCEL

Don't be silly. You must go. She's expecting you.

ALBERTINE

She won't notice whether I'm there or not. I can go tomorrow, next week, the week after, it doesn't matter.

MARCEL

And your friends?

ALBERTINE

They can walk back. It'll do them good.

He studies her.

> MARCEL

I'm not coming with you.

> ALBERTINE

Why not?

> MARCEL

You don't want me to come with you.

> ALBERTINE

How can you say that?

> MARCEL

Because you're a liar.

> ALBERTINE

I am not! Really, it's too bad. I alter all my plans, so that I can spend a nice long evening with you alone and all you can do is insult me. You're cruel. I don't want to see you again. Ever.

> MARCEL

That would be wise.

Albertine looks at her watch.

> ALBERTINE

In that case I'll go to see my aunt's friend.

She leaves the room.

EXT. PARIS STREET. NIGHT. 1880.

Swann, in foreground, looks towards Odette's house, which is dark and silent.

EXT. BALBEC BEACH. NIGHT. 1901.

Moonlight. The camera moves through the dunes. Two shapes, lying in a dune, embracing.

ALBERTINE
(*VO*)

Oh my dear, my dear.

EXT. PROMENADE. BALBEC. DAY. 1901.

Marcel walking towards the Casino.

Dr Cottard calls to him.

COTTARD

Hullo!

Marcel stops.

You remember me? I'm Doctor Cottard. I treated your grandmother. To no avail, I'm afraid. Well, well.

MARCEL
(*shaking hands*)

Yes, of course.

COTTARD

I'm just on my way to the Verdurins'. They've got a house for the summer near here. La Raspelière. Why don't you come with me? They'd be delighted to see you.

MARCEL

I'm afraid I'm meeting some friends in the Casino.

COTTARD

Ah. Well, I'll come in with you for a bit, if I may. My train is not till six.

They walk towards the Casino.

You must come to La Raspelière sometime soon. The Verdurins have a remarkable position in society, you know. They entertain all the very best people. Do you know, they say Madame Verdurin is worth at least thirty-five million? Thirty-five million, what do you think of that? And of course she's done so much for the arts, a very great deal. You're a writer yourself, aren't you? That's why she'd be delighted to meet you.

INT. CASINO. BALBEC. BALLROOM.

There are no men in the room.

A few girls sit at tables, drinking. A girl is playing a waltz on a piano.

About half a dozen girls are dancing together.

Albertine and Andrée dance together.

Marcel and Cottard stand watching at the door.

> MARCEL
> They dance well together, don't they? Girls?

> COTTARD
> Parents are very rash to allow their daughters to form such habits. I'd never let mine come here.
> (*Indicating Albertine and Andrée.*)
> Look at those two. It's not sufficiently known that women derive most excitement from their breasts. Theirs are completely touching. Look at them.

Albertine and Andrée dancing close together.

Andrée whispers to Albertine. Albertine laughs. They ease the contact.

INT. BALLROOM.

Marcel sitting at a table with Andrée by the mirrored wall. At the next table Albertine, with Gisèle and Rosemonde. Albertine has her back to the room.

Andrée turns her head sharply as two women walk into the room and sit. Marcel follows her gaze.

MARCEL

What are you looking at?

ANDRÉE

Those women.

MARCEL

Which?

ANDRÉE

Over there. Do you know who they are?

MARCEL

No.

ANDRÉE

Léa, the actress. And her friend. They live together
quite openly. It's a scandal.

MARCEL

Oh . . . You've no sympathy with that kind of thing,
then?

ANDRÉE

Me? I loathe that kind of thing. I'm like Albertine in
that. We both loathe that kind of thing.

Léa talks quietly to her friend, who listens gravely.

THE BACK OF ALBERTINE'S HEAD.

Gisèle and Rosemonde whispering.

In the mirror beyond them, Albertine's face, glimpsed.

INT. MARCEL'S HOTEL. SITTING ROOM. DAY.

Marcel and Albertine enter the room.

He closes the door. She speaks at once.

ALBERTINE

What have you got against me?

Marcel walks to the window, turns from it, sits, looks at her gravely.

MARCEL

Do you really want me to tell you the truth?

ALBERTINE

Yes, I do.

He speaks quietly.

MARCEL

I admire Andrée . . . greatly. I always have. There you are. That's the truth. You and I can be friends, I hope, but nothing more. Once, I was on the point of falling in love with you, but that time . . . can't be recaptured. I'm sorry to be so frank. The truth is always unpleasant – for someone. I love Andrée.

ALBERTINE

I see. I don't mind your frankness. I see. But I'd just like to know what I've done.

MARCEL

Done? You haven't done anything. I've just explained to you –

ALBERTINE

Yes, I have. Or you think I have.

MARCEL

Why can't you listen?

ALBERTINE

Why can't you tell me?

Silence.

MARCEL

I've heard reports.

She gazes at him.

Reports . . . about your way of life.

ALBERTINE

My way of life?

MARCEL

I have a profound disgust for women . . . tainted with
that vice.

Pause.

You see, I have heard that your . . . accomplice . . . is
Andrée, and since Andrée is the woman I love, you can
understand my grief.

Albertine looks at him steadily.

ALBERTINE

Who told you this rubbish?

MARCEL

I can't tell you.

ALBERTINE

Andrée and I both detest that sort of thing. We find it
revolting.

MARCEL

You're saying it's not true?

ALBERTINE

If it were true I would tell you. I would be quite honest
with you. Why not? But I'm telling you it's absolutely
untrue.

MARCEL

Do you swear it?

ALBERTINE

I swear it.

She walks to him and sits by him on the sofa.

(*softly*)

I swear it.

She takes his hand.

You are silly.

She strokes his hand.

All those stories about Andrée . . .

She touches his face.

You are silly. I'm your Albertine.

She strokes his face.

Aren't you glad I'm here . . . sitting next to you?

MARCEL

Yes.

She attempts to kiss him. His mouth is shut.

She passes her tongue over his lips.

ALBERTINE

Open you mouth. Open your mouth, you great bear.

She forces his mouth open, kisses him, forcing him down on the sofa.

INT. ROOM IN SANATORIUM. 1917. DAY.

Marcel 37 sitting at his desk, motionless as an owl. The desk is empty.

Over this shot Grandmother's voice.

GRANDMOTHER
(*VO*)
How's your work getting on?

Pause.

(*gently*)
Oh I'm sorry, I won't ask you again.

EXT. BEACH. BALBEC. DAY. 1901.

Marcel and Mother sitting in deck chairs.

MOTHER
I think you should know that Albertine's aunt believes
you are going to marry Albertine.

MARCEL
Oh?

MOTHER
You're spending a great deal of money on her. They
naturally think it would be a very good marriage, from
her point of view.

Pause.

MARCEL
What do you think of her yourself?

MOTHER
Albertine? Well, it's not I that will be marrying her, is it?
I don't think your grandmother would have liked me to
influence you. But if she can make you happy . .

MARCEL
She bores me. I have no intention of marrying her.

MOTHER
In that case I should see less of her.

EXT. DONCIÈRES STATION. PLATFORM. DAY.

Saint-Loup 23 is standing on the platform.

He is dressed in uniform and has with him a small dog, on a lead.

The little train draws in.

Marcel, leaning out of a carriage, waves.

The train stops. Marcel jumps out. They shake hands.

> SAINT-LOUP
> I just got your telegram. Good to see you.

> MARCEL
> I thought it might be nice to meet, if only for five minutes.

> SAINT-LOUP
> Brilliant idea!

> MARCEL
> (*turning to carriage*)
> Albertine, come out and meet Robert.

Albertine steps down from the train.

> MARCEL
> Mademoiselle Albertine Simonet. The Marquis de Saint-Loup.

Saint-Loup bows.

> ALBERTINE
> Oh, what a lovely little dog. What's his name?

> SAINT-LOUP
> She's a bitch. Pepi.

> ALBERTINE
> Hullo, Pepi.

MARCEL

We're on our way to the Verdurins'. Pity you can't come with us.

SAINT-LOUP

I'm afraid even if I could I wouldn't. I find that sort of atmosphere maddening.

Albertine is playing with the dog.

The lead tightens about Saint-Loup's legs.

Albertine's body brushes against Saint-Loup.

ALBERTINE

Sorry! Your dog is so enchanting. Come here, Pepi.

MARCEL

What do you mean?

ALBERTINE

Look! Your little dog has left hairs on your lovely uniform. Isn't that terrible? Look at your leg. You naughty little dog!

SAINT-LOUP

They'll brush off.
>> (*To Marcel.*)
They're a sect.
>> (*With a smile.*)
A naughty little sect. They're all butter to those who belong, contemptuous of those who don't. They're not for me.

Station Master blows his whistle.

MARCEL

We must get in.

ALBERTINE

Good-bye, little dog. What did you say her name was?

SAINT-LOUP

Pepi.

They all shake hands.

EXT. ROAD TO LA RASPELIÈRE.

Charlus and Morel in a chauffeur-driven car.

They sit expressionless.

Morel is twenty-one, very handsome.

INT. THE DRAWING-ROOM. LA RASPELIÈRE. SUNSET.

The drawing-room is very large. Displays of fresh grasses, poppies, wild flowers alternate with a similar theme painted on the walls. Huge windows look down over the terraces.

MME. VERDURIN
We have a really brilliant musician coming tonight. My husband and I discovered him. His name's Morel. He has a great future. Unfortunately an old friend of his family has apparently latched on to him. So we'll have to put up with him. Someone called the Baron de Charlus.

Mme. Verdurin 59 turns to join a group consisting of the Marquis and Marquise de Cambremer, Mme. Cottard, M. Verdurin and Albertine.

Albertine is exquisitely dressed.

Brichot 64, Cottard 57 and Marcel stand apart.

Brichot is half blind.

BRICHOT
(*to Cottard*)
By the way, did you hear the news? Dechambre's dead.

COTTARD
That's right. He is. Liver.

234

(*To Marcel.*)

Dechambre was Madame Verdurin's favourite pianist. Quite a young man too.

BRICHOT

Not as young as all that. He used to play Vinteuil's sonata for Swann, years ago, don't you remember?

COTTARD

Did he? I can't remember that.

BRICHOT

Poor Swann.

COTTARD

What's the matter with Swann?

BRICHOT

He's dead, my dear fellow. He died about two months ago.

COTTARD

Did he really? Nobody told me. My goodness, they're all dying like flies.

M. Verdurin 61 joins them.

BRICHOT
(*to Verdurin*)

Terrible news about Dechambre.

VERDURIN

Yes, but it's no use crying over spilt milk; talking about him won't bring him back to life, will it? And for heaven's sake don't start talking about Dechambre to Madame Verdurin. She's quite morbidly sensitive. When she heard he was dead she almost cried.

COTTARD

Did she really?

Cottard looks across to the Cambremers.

> (*To Verdurin.*)
> Did you say those two were a marquis and marquise?

VERDURIN
Yes, yes, what does it matter?
> (*To Marcel.*)
> We've rented this house from them for the summer.
> They're ghastly bores, but we had to invite them once.
> Courtesy.

COTTARD
(*murmuring*)
A marquis and marquise.
> (*To Marcel.*)
> Would you believe it? You meet everyone here, you
> know.

A Footman opens the door.

FOOTMAN
Monsieur Morel and the Baron de Charlus.

The Verdurins walk towards Morel and Charlus.

Marcel and Morel catch each other's eye.

A flash of recognition.

ALBERTINE ALONE BY THE WINDOWS.

In background at the far end of the room Morel is introducing the Verdurins to Charlus.

Albertine is looking at Morel.

She turns away to gaze out of the window.

AT THE DOOR OF THE DINING-ROOM.

Mme. Verdurin whispering to her husband.

> MME. VERDURIN

Shall I offer my arm to the Baron?

> VERDURIN

No, surely not? Cambremer is a marquis, Charlus a
baron. A marquis is higher than a baron. Isn't it?
Anyway, I'm sure I'm right. Cambremer must be on
your right at the table. Go in with him.

INT. DINING-ROOM.

*From the dining table the camera sees Mme. Verdurin on the arm
of the Marquis de Cambremer 55 lead the procession into the room.*

*A great fish sits on the sideboard. M. de Cambremer stares at it as
he passes.*

> M. DE CAMBREMER

I say, that looks a fine animal.

The guests take their places.

*Mme. Verdurin sits at the head of the table, M. de Cambremer to
her right, Marcel to her left.*

To Marcel's left, Mme. Cottard, Brichot, Morel and Charlus.

*To M. de Cambremer's right, Albertine, Cottard, Mme. de
Cambremer.*

M. Verdurin at the foot of the table.

> (*To Mme. Verdurin.*)

I feel so at home here, you know.

> MME. VERDURIN

You must notice a good many changes, I should think.
There were some horrid little plush chairs in this room,
which I must confess I packed off at once to the attic –

*She picks up a piece of bread, bites into it, and mutters into her
bread:*

– even that's too good for them.

MME. DE CAMBREMER 50, HEARING THIS REMARK,
STIFFENS.

She is very plump.

> COTTARD
> (*to Mme. de Cambremer*)
> Fine house, this, don't you think?

> MME. DE CAMBREMER
> We own it.

MOREL LOOKING ACROSS THE TABLE AT ALBERTINE.

ALBERTINE LOOKING ACROSS THE TABLE AT MOREL.

MARCEL LOOKING AT ALBERTINE LOOKING AT MOREL.

> COTTARD
> (*VO, to Marcel*)
> When you come to a relatively high altitude such as this,
> do you find the change increases your tendency to
> choking fits?

> MARCEL
> No.

THE TABLE.

The fish is being served.

> M. DE CAMBREMER
> (*turning*)
> Choking fits? Who has choking fits?

> MARCEL
> I do. Sometimes.

M. DE CAMBREMER
Really? Do you? You know, I can't tell you how amused
I am to hear that. You see, my sister has them too. She's
had choking fits for years. I must tell her I met a fellow
sufferer. She'll be so amused.

CHARLUS AND MOREL.

Morel is looking at Albertine.

Charlus is looking at Morel.

VERDURIN
(*VO, to Charlus, whispering*)
Of course, I realized from the first words we exchanged
that you were one of us.

Charlus lifts his eyebrows, looks at M. Verdurin.

CHARLUS
I beg your pardon?

M. VERDURIN AND CHARLUS.

VERDURIN
I mean, I can understand how little such things mean to
you.

CHARLUS
I don't quite follow you.

VERDURIN
I'm referring to the fact that we gave precedence to the
Marquis. That the Marquis is seated to Madam
Verdurin's right. I myself attach no significance
whatever to titles of nobility, but of course you do
understand that as Monsieur Cambremer is a marquis
and you are only a baron –

CHARLUS

Pardon me. I am also Duc de Brabant, Damoiseau de
Montargis, Prince d'Oléron, de Carency, de Viareggio
and des Dunes. However, please do not distress
yourself. It is not of the slightest importance, here.

INT. DRAWING-ROOM. AFTER DINNER.

The Cambremers whispering.

MME. DE CAMBREMER

They've destroyed the house, totally desecrated it. But
I'm not in the least surprised. You can't expect good
taste from retired tradespeople, which is what I would
say they are.

M. DE CAMBREMER

I quite like the chandeliers.

MME. DE CAMBREMER

I think we should put up the rent.

INT. DRAWING ROOM.

Morel playing the violin, accompanied by Charlus on the piano.

The music stops. Calls of 'Sublime!' etc.

Mme. Cottard 53 is asleep in a chair.

Charlus turns to Marcel.

CHARLUS

He plays like a god, don't you think?

MME. VERDURIN
(*to Morel*)

Please let us have some more.

MOREL

No, sorry. I have to go soon.

CLOSE-UP. ALBERTINE, SITTING.

THE ROOM.

> COTTARD
> (*to Mme. Cottard*)
> Léontine, you're snoring.

> MME. COTTARD
> (*faintly*)
> I am listening to Monsieur Swann, my dear.

> MME. VERDURIN
> She's in touch with spirits, doctor, and rather dubious spirits at that.

> COTTARD
> Swann!
> > (*He shouts.*)
> Léontine! Pull yourself together!

> MME. COTTARD
> (*murmuring*)
> My bath is nice and hot.
> > (*She sits up abruptly.*)
> Oh good lord, what is it, what have I been saying? I was thinking about my hat, in another minute I should have been asleep, it's that wretched fire.

> COTTARD
> (*shouting*)
> There's no fire in sight! We're in the middle of summer.
> > (*To the gathering.*)
> She looks like an old beetroot!

MOREL SIPPING A DRINK.

He is sitting in a chair next to Albertine. They are looking in different directions.

THE ROOM.

Charlus and Marcel are looking towards Morel.

> CHARLUS
>
> I shall make him great.

Mme. Verdurin approaches Morel.

> MME. VERDURIN
>
> My Mozart! My young Mozart! Would you like to stay
> the night? We have some lovely rooms facing the sea.

> CHARLUS
> (*moving to her*)
>
> Impossible. He must get back to his own bed like a good
> little boy, obedient and well behaved.

Mme. Verdurin looks down at Albertine.

> MME. VERDURIN
>
> What a pretty dress you're wearing.

> ALBERTINE
>
> Thank you, madame.

> MME. VERDURIN
>
> Would you like to stay the night? I can show you a room
> I think you'd adore.

> MARCEL
> (*moving forward*)
>
> I'm afraid it's not possible. Mademoiselle Simonet's
> aunt is expecting her.

> MME. VERDURIN
>
> What a pity.

EXT. LA RASPELIÈRE. CLIFF TOP. NIGHT.

*Sound of the sea. In the distance the lights of the house. The door
is open. The carriages are being brought to the front of the house.*

The guests stand in the moonlight. Their distant voices. Sound of the sea.

EXT. THE HOUSE.

Charlus is talking to the Verdurins and Mme. de Cambremer.

Marcel stands with Albertine, Morel in background, his back to them. M. de Cambremer turns to Marcel.

>   M. DE CAMBREMER
> You must come to see us soon. You could discuss your
> attacks with my sister. I'm sure she'll be most amused.

INT. CARRIAGE. THE LITTLE TRAIN FROM LA RASPELIÈRE.
NIGHT.

Marcel and Albertine alone.

>   ALBERTINE
>   (*yawning*)
> What a lovely house. I really did enjoy myself.

>   MARCEL
> A waste of time.

>   ALBERTINE
> I had a lovely time.

Pause.

>   MARCEL
> What did you think of Morel's playing?

>   ALBERTINE
> Oh . . . he's a beautiful player.

>   MARCEL
>   (*sharply*)
> His father was my uncle's valet.

ALBERTINE

Was he? Well, he's a beautiful player.

MARCEL

How could you behave so disgracefully with Saint-Loup?

ALBERTINE

Saint-Loup? What do you mean?

MARCEL

Rubbing against him, flirting with him. What did you think you were doing?

ALBERTINE

Oh, I did that deliberately. I didn't want to give him the impression that you and I were . . . close friends. But anyway, I wasn't flirting with him, I was flirting with his dog.

MARCEL

Didn't you hear him say? The dog was a bitch.

ALBERTINE

Oh.

Silence.

Albertine looks out of the window.

MARCEL

I must finish with all this. I must have done with it.

He looks at the back of Albertine's head and mutters:

Waste of time.

Pause.

For instance, there was one thing I did want to ask them, but of course one never gets the chance.

ALBERTINE

What?

MARCEL

You wouldn't be interested.

Slight pause.

About a composer. Used to be a protégé of theirs. He
wrote a sonata. I want to find out if he's written
anything else.

ALBERTINE

What composer?

MARCEL

If I told you his name was Vinteuil, would you be any
the wiser?

ALBERTINE

Vinteuil? How funny.

He looks at her.

Do you remember once I told you I had a friend, older
than me, who has been a sister, a mother to me, with
whom I spent the happiest years of my life at Trieste?

MARCEL
(*slowly*)

No. I don't remember.

ALBERTINE

Oh yes. In fact I'm to join her in a few weeks at
Cherbourg, we're going on a cruise together. Well, this
woman is the dearest, most intimate friend of Vinteuil's
daughter. In fact, I know Vinteuil's daughter almost as
well as I know her friend. I always call them my two big
sisters.

Marcel does not comment. The train runs on.

Silence.

INT. MARCEL'S ROOM. HOTEL.

Mother sitting. Marcel standing.

> MARCEL
>
> I know what I'm going to say will distress you. I must go
> back to Paris. I want to take Albertine with me, to stay,
> as my guest, in our flat. It is absolutely necessary – and
> please don't let's argue about it, because I am quite
> clear in my own mind, and because I shan't change my
> mind again, and because otherwise I couldn't go on
> living – it is absolutely necessary that I marry Albertine.

MOTHER'S FACE.

MLLE. VINTEUIL RUNNING TO THE WINDOW TO CLOSE
SHUTTERS.

ODETTE PLAYING VINTEUIL'S SONATA. SWANN LISTENING.

EXT. FIELD. DAY.

A riderless horse gallops away from the camera.

INT. LIBRARY. MARCEL'S PARIS FLAT. NIGHT. 1902.

Tapestries hang on the walls.

Albertine is asleep in bed.

Marcel stands watching her.

INT. KITCHEN.

A bunch of syringa lying on the kitchen table.

INT. THE LIBRARY. (ALBERTINE'S ROOM.) NIGHT.

Albertine, in nightdress, standing at the open window.

INT. MARCEL'S FLAT. CORRIDOR. MORNING.

Françoise walking along corridor with tray.

She stops at library door and knocks.

> FRANÇOISE
> Mademoiselle Simonet, your coffee.

INT. TWO ADJOINING BATHROOMS. FROSTED GLASS.

The shape of Albertine seen through the glass drying herself.

She is humming.

Marcel in the other bathroom listening.

He smiles.

INT. MARCEL'S ROOM. MORNING.

He is in bed. Albertine enters.

> ALBERTINE
> Good morning.

She gets on the bed. They kiss.

> What lovely skin. You've shaved.

> MARCEL
> I did, yes – then got back into bed.

> ALBERTINE
> You're lazy. Did you sleep badly?

> MARCEL
> Very.

ALBERTINE

Are you feeling ill?

MARCEL

No. But not well either. I'll stay in bed today.

ALBERTINE

My poor boy.

MARCEL

Andrée will be here soon, won't she, to take you out?

ALBERTINE

Yes.

MARCEL

Where will you go?

ALBERTINE

Oh, I don't know. Why don't you come with us? Or I
can tell her to go home and we can go out by ourselves.

MARCEL

Andrée is a very good friend . . . to both of us.

ALBERTINE

I didn't say she wasn't.

MARCEL

I trust her.

Pause.

Anyway I'm not well enough to go out.

ALBERTINE

Will you work then, if we leave you alone? Will you try?

MARCEL

Yes, yes.

ALBERTINE

I'll bring you paper and pencils and put them on the

248

bed for you, so you won't have to get up. Or if you like,
I'll stay here with you.

MARCEL

How can I work if you're with me?

ALBERTINE

Would I distract you?

She laughs.

Sometimes I feel I never want to go out at all, never
want to leave you. Never.

She nuzzles him.

But if you ever want me to go you'll tell me, won't you?
You'll tell me quite simply? And I'll go.

He stares at her uncertainly. She smiles.

That is, if your parents don't ask me to go first.

MARCEL

My parents are perfectly happy for you to stay here, as
my friend. They don't mind your staying here . . . at all.

ALBERTINE

I don't mind either.

MARCEL

I might even marry you.

ALBERTINE

No, no. There are so many other prettier, more
intelligent girls than me . . . for you.

The doorbell rings.

That's Andrée.

INT. ALBERTINE'S BEDROOM. EVENING.

Albertine sleeping on the bed.

Marcel watches her.

He gets onto the bed and lies behind her, very close.

THEIR HEADS.

Albertine, eyes closed. Her eyelids flutter.

Marcel, eyes open, moving gently against her.

INT. MARCEL'S ROOM. AFTERNOON.

The door is open. Through the door we see Albertine and Andrée walking down the corridor. Albertine goes into her room.

Andrée enters Marcel's room, closes the door.

A pile of notebooks lie unopened on the bed.

> ANDRÉE
> We had a very pleasant time.

> MARCEL
> Where did you go?

> ANDRÉE
> Versailles.

> MARCEL
> Did you meet anyone?

> ANDRÉE
> Albertine met an old friend.

> MARCEL
> Who?

> ANDRÉE
> An old school friend. I can't remember her name.

MARCEL

What was she like?

ANDRÉE

Mousy. Rather plain, actually.

MARCEL

What did they talk about?

ANDRÉE

Paintings. All rather schoolgirlish.

Pause.

MARCEL

And that's all?

ANDRÉE

Absolutely.

ALBERTINE IN BED, LOOKING UP, HAIR OVER PILLOW.

ALBERTINE

I was so ignorant before I met you, wasn't I? I'm really quite intelligent now. Aren't I? It's all due to you. I owe everything to you.

VIEW OF COURTYARD FROM WINDOW OF ALBERTINE'S ROOM. DAY.

Marcel walking across courtyard with a bunch of syringa.

Sharp sound of sudden movement in room. Rustle of skirt.

INT. STAIRWAY.

Marcel climbing stairs, carrying flowers. He looks up.

Andrée comes out of the door of the flat.

MARCEL

What, are you back already?

ANDRÉE

We've just got in. Albertine wanted to write a letter, so I've left her alone.

MARCEL

A letter? To whom?

ANDRÉE

Her aunt.

MARCEL

A pity you've closed the door. I've forgotten my key. Is Françoise in?

ANDRÉE

She's out shopping. That's syringa, isn't it?

MARCEL

Yes.

ANDRÉE

Albertine hates syringa. It's the scent, it's so strong.

MARCEL

Does she? I didn't know that.

ANDRÉE

The scent is overpowering. Well, good-bye.

She descends.

Marcel rings the bell.

The door is opened immediately, by Albertine.

The hall is dark.

ALBERTINE

Syringa! Oh!

She runs down the hall.

MARCEL
I'll take them into the kitchen.

INT. KITCHEN.

Marcel puts syringa on table, goes back into hall.

ALBERTINE
(*VO*)
I'm in your room.

He goes in.

INT. MARCEL'S BEDROOM.

She is lying on the bed.

MARCEL
I'm sorry. I didn't realize you hated syringa.

ALBERTINE
It's their scent, that's all. It's so strong. It's probably all over you. Don't come too near me until it wears off.

INT. MARCEL'S ROOM. MORNING.

He is in bed. Françoise with coffee. She gives it to him, stands, mutters.

MARCEL
What?

She moves about the room, tidying.

FRANÇOISE
She'll land you in trouble, that one.

MARCEL
What do you mean?

FRANÇOISE
I've been with your family forty years.

MARCEL

What are you talking about?

FRANÇOISE

You're breaking your parents' hearts.

MARCEL

How dare you? My parents are perfectly happy, perfectly happy. My mother says so in all her letters.

FRANÇOISE

You are bringing this house into dangerous disrepute.

MARCEL

That's enough!

INT. ALBERTINE'S ROOM. NIGHT.

Albertine is sleeping, murmuring.

Marcel, beside her, strains to catch the words.

ALBERTINE

Oh, darling.

He frowns.

INT. SITTING ROOM. EVENING.

Marcel is looking at Albertine's sketches.

MARCEL

They're excellent.

ALBERTINE

They're not, no. If only I'd had drawing lessons.

He looks at her.

MARCEL

You had drawing lessons, at Balbec.

ALBERTINE

Did I?

MARCEL

One evening. You couldn't see me. You said you had a
drawing lesson.

ALBERTINE

Oh, so I did. She was such a bad teacher I'd forgotten
all about it. She was hopeless.

Pause.

MARCEL

Oh, I've been meaning to ask you something – not that
it's of the slightest importance . . .

ALBERTINE

What?

MARCEL

Have you ever met Léa?

ALBERTINE

Léa?

MARCEL

The actress.

ALBERTINE

No, I don't think so. Why?

MARCEL

What do you know about her? What kind of woman is
she?

ALBERTINE

Perfectly respectable, as far as I know.

MARCEL

That's not what I've been led to understand.

                      ALBERTINE

I know nothing about it.

Pause.

                      MARCEL

You don't trust me, do you? Why? You know I love you.

                      ALBERTINE

I trust only you. You know that. And you know I love
you.

Pause.

                      MARCEL

I've decided it's too dangerous for you to go riding. You
could easily have an accident.

She looks at him with a slight smile.

                      ALBERTINE

If I died, would you commit suicide?

INT. MARCEL'S BEDROOM. NIGHT.

*Albertine in dressing gown. Marcel takes off her gown, opens her
nightdress, looks at her breasts, bends to take off her shoes.*

Smiling, she helps him take off her nightdress.

Briefly, we glimpse her naked body.

She lies on the bed.

CLOSE-UP. ALBERTINE'S HEAD AND SHOULDERS.

Her arms are folded behind her head.

CLOSE-UP. MARCEL LOOKING DOWN AT HER.

> MARCEL
> (*softly*)

Oh darling.

INT. ALBERTINE'S BEDROOM. NIGHT.

Albertine in nightdress standing by open window.

INT. SITTING ROOM. MORNING.

Marcel and Albertine at window.

Street cries of traders.

> ALBERTINE

Oh listen! those cries! Aren't they wonderful! Oysters!
I've been longing for oysters! Mussels! I must have some
mussels.

> MARCEL

If they're not as fresh as the ones at Balbec, they'd make
you very ill.

> ALBERTINE

Listen! Onions, cabbages, carrots, orange, all the things
I want to eat. Françoise can cook us a dish of creamed
carrots, can't she, with onions? We'll be eating all the
sounds we hear, won't we, all the sounds will be sitting
on a plate. Will you tell her?

> MARCEL

Yes, yes.

> ALBERTINE

I'd also like an ice, from Rebattets. I might look in and
buy one.

MARCEL

You don't need to go to Rebattets. I can order one for
you from the Ritz.

Pause.

ALBERTINE

Why? Are you going out?

MARCEL

I may, I may not.

Pause.

ALBERTINE

Well, if you do order me an ice, I'd like one of those
old-fashioned ones, the ones that are shaped like
temples, churches, things like that, monuments. A
raspberry or vanilla monument. I shall make its pink
granite crumble and melt deep down in my throat. Isn't
that well put? My lips will destroy pillar after pillar.
Venetian strawberry churches will be demolished by my
tongue. I'll swallow them up, so cool, cool, cool.

INT. THE CORRIDOR. NIGHT.

The corridor is dark.

*Marcel's door opens. He walks up the corridor to the door of
Albertine's room. He stands still, listening.*

Silence.

EXT. BALBEC BEACH. DAY.

Albertine outlined against the sea and sky, laughing.

INT. SITTING ROOM. EVENING.

Marcel and Albertine at the table with coffee.

Silence.

MARCEL

You seem depressed.

ALBERTINE

I couldn't be happier.

MARCEL

You don't feel imprisoned?

ALBERTINE

I told you, I couldn't be happier.

Pause.

I might possibly look in at the Verdurins' tomorrow. I
don't really want to, but I might.

MARCEL

Why?

ALBERTINE

I told you Andrée and I met Madame Verdurin by
accident the other day, didn't I?

MARCEL

No. You didn't.

ALBERTINE

Didn't I? I thought I had. Anyway, she insisted that I go
to see them one day for tea. I don't really want to, but I
suppose it would be a change. She asked Andrée too.

INT. MARCEL'S ROOM. EVENING.

Marcel on telephone.

MARCEL

Andrée.

ANDRÉE
(*VO*)

Oh. Hullo.

MARCEL

You and Albertine are supposed to go to the Verdurins'
tomorrow afternoon?

ANDRÉE

That's right.

MARCEL

Why?

ANDRÉE

Why?

MARCEL

Why does she want to go there?

ANDRÉE

Madame Verdurin asked us for tea, that's all. It's quite
innocent.

MARCEL

Are you sure –

Françoise comes in, opens a drawer, puts some shirts in.

He waits.

ANDRÉE

Hullo?

MARCEL

Yes . . . yes . . . I'm sorry . . .

Françoise goes out.

Are you sure there won't be someone there she wants to
meet?

                    ANDRÉE
I can't think who.

                    MARCEL
I may come with you.

Pause.

                    ANDRÉE
Ah.

INT. ALBERTINE'S ROOM. EVENING.

Marcel enters.

                    MARCEL
I may come with you.

                    ALBERTINE
Where?

                    MARCEL
To the Verdurins. Tomorrow. For tea.

                    ALBERTINE
Oh. Yes, why not, if you'd like to. There's an awful mist
about today, though. It'll probably clear by tomorrow. It
would be so much nicer if you were there, of course.
But I don't think I'll go, actually. I must get a white
scarf to wear with this dress. I'll probably do that
instead.

INT. SITTING ROOM. FOLLOWING EVENING.

Marcel and Albertine with coffee.

Silence.

                    MARCEL
Did you find the scarf you wanted?

ALBERTINE

No.

Pause.

MARCEL

I'm feeling better tonight. I think I'll look in at the Guermantes', or Madame de Villeparisis'. I haven't been out for ages. Would you like to come?

ALBERTINE

No. thanks. My hair's all wrong today.

He goes to the door.

MARCEL

Well I'll have a little walk. You'll be here when I come back?

She looks at him.

ALBERTINE

Of course.

MOREL TUNING HIS VIOLIN.

CHARLUS GREETING GUESTS.

THE VERDURINS STANDING GRIMLY.

EXT. STREET. EVENING. LONG SHOT.

Marcel, walking in the distance.

He is hailed and joined by Charlus.

They walk along together.

Over this:

ALBERTINE

I might possibly look in at the Verdurins' tomorrow. I don't really want to, but I might.

CHARLUS AND MARCEL WALKING. TWO SHOT.

CHARLUS

I assure you, tonight will prove to be a quite memorable
and even historic occasion. Do you know what you're in
for?

MARCEL

No. What?

CHARLUS

The first performance of a new work by Vinteuil, played
by Morel. I'm delighted you're coming. I would
naturally have sent you an invitation but I understood
you were ill. Are you better?

MARCEL

Thank you, yes. A new work? By Vinteuil?

CHARLUS

Yes, a septet.

MARCEL

But he's been dead for years.

CHARLUS

Indeed. But it transpires that he left illegible, quite
indecipherable manuscripts everywhere, no more than
scribblings. And can you guess who has been working
on them, for years, trying to make sense of them?
Mademoiselle Vinteuil's infamous friend, with his
daughter at her side. First they kill him by their
shamelessness and now they insist on saving his work
and thereby keeping him alive. It's a superb work and
Morel will play it superbly. I believe the two
disreputable ladies were at the rehearsal this afternoon.
Morel said they were expected.

*The camera pans to Marcel and remains on him for the rest of
Charlus' speech.*

I haven't seen the rascal since this morning, when he came into my room and tried to pull me out of bed. Pure wickedness. He knows how I hate being seen first thing in the morning. After all, I'm no longer five and twenty, they won't choose me to be Queen of the May, will they? But I must confess the boy seems to grow more beautiful every day, wicked or not.

MARCEL

Mademoiselle Vinteuil, and her friend . . . were expected at the Verdurins' this afternoon.

CHARLUS

They were expected.

He stops.

I shall confide something to you. You are a writer –

MARCEL

No I'm not –

CHARLUS

You will be. You wish to be. You are interested therefore in the complex and mysterious tissues of human nature. Also I trust you, I've no idea why. I happened, by accident, you see, to open a letter addressed to Morel the other day. It was from the actress Léa, who as all the world knows, is a particularly notorious lesbian. Its indelicacy prevents me from repeating it in full, but it contained phrases – to Morel, remember – such as 'You naughty little girl' and 'Of course you're one of us, you pretty sweetheart'. And the letter also made quite clear that other women, friends of Léa's, were most attracted to Morel. Lesbians, the lot of them. Now I have always known that Morel was 'one of us'. Oh, he's had women, women by the mile, he has women now, when he feels like it, and I couldn't care less, but these are not women. Do you follow me? When

Léa refers to him, as 'one of us', what can she possibly
mean? I thought he was one of *us*. I mean we know that
Morel is – ambidextrous. Do you think he is also a
lesbian?

MARCEL

I don't know.

CHARLUS
(*wickedly*)
I mean, how on earth can a man be a lesbian? In other
words, what do they *do*?

MARCEL

I don't know.

CHARLUS

I'm not surprised you can't help me. You are totally
inexperienced in these matters.

Charlus moves on, followed by Marcel.

Have you heard that my nephew, Saint-Loup, is to
marry Swann's daughter, Gilberte? A match that would
have pleased Swann greatly, had he been alive to witness
it, poor man.

They reach the door of the Verdurins' house.

I must tell you that I have issued the invitations for
tonight myself. Madame Verdurin can ask her grocer
and milliner and butcher acquaintances, not to mention
the lavatory woman from the Champs-Élysées, to the
next party. Tonight the cream of society will hear Morel
play.

He looks sharply at Marcel.

What's the matter with you? You look ill. Are you
feeling ill?

MARCEL

No. I'm perfectly all right.

They go into the house.

The camera holds on the door closing.

ALBERTINE
(*VO*)

I don't really want to, but I might.

INT. CONCERT ROOM. THE VERDURINS' HOUSE. EVENING.

The Verdurins standing alone, their faces grim.

In background Charlus is welcoming the guests.

The guests approach Charlus immediately on entering the room.
They ignore the Verdurins.

DUCHESS DE GUERMANTES

Mémé, how lovely to see you. We do find you in the
most unlikely houses these days. Where is this Mother
Verdurin? I don't need to speak to her, do I?

THE VERDURINS.

MME. VERDURIN

I am the hostess. This is my house. He seems to have
forgotten that. I will not stand for it.

The voice of the Duchesse floats over.

DUCHESSE

I do hope she won't put my name in the newspapers
tomorrow. Nobody will ever speak to me again.

*Laughter from the gathering and further greetings from and to
Charlus.*

Marcel approaches the Verdurins.

MARCEL

Excuse me, isn't Mademoiselle Vinteuil supposed to be here? With one of her friends?

In background the Queen of Naples approaches Charlus.

Other guests curtsey and bow to her.

She is sixty.

MME. VERDURIN

She sent a telegram. They were obliged to remain in the country.
(*To M. Verdurin.*)
Morel must know the truth about the man. We owe it to him. You must speak to him. He must be warned. It is our duty.

VERDURIN

I agree. But after the performance.

MME. VERDURIN

I have devoted my life to art, to music. We must save him from that monster.

MARCEL
(*to Mme. Verdurin*)
Will the actress Léa be here tonight, by any chance?

She looks at him sharply.

MME. VERDURIN

Certainly not!

THE QUEEN OF NAPLES WITH CHARLUS.

QUEEN OF NAPLES

May I meet our hostess?

CHARLUS

Our hostess! But of course, of course. Madame
Verdurin!

He moves to her.

Her Majesty the Queen of Naples desires me to present
you to her.

MME. VERDURIN

Oh!

Charlus leads the Verdurins to the Queen.

CHARLUS

May I have the honour, Ma'am, to present Madame
Verdurin, our hostess this evening. Monsieur Verdurin.

The Verdurins curtsey and bow, murmuring, 'Your Majesty'.

QUEEN OF NAPLES

It is so kind of you to invite me to your beautiful house
and on such an auspicious occasion. I am quite
delighted to meet you.

MME. VERDURIN

You overwhelm me, M'am. I hope you may enjoy your
visit to my temple of music, as I venture to call it.

QUEEN OF NAPLES

It is such a very pretty temple.

*The musicians have mounted the platform and are tuning their
instruments.*

*Charlus coughs loudly at the assembly, who take their seats. He
leads the Queen to a chair.*

MME. VERDURIN
(*to Verdurin*)

How simple and unaffected! That's the true blood royal.
What a difference from the rest of these upstarts. I

268

expect if the truth were known, half these precious
duchesses are on the books of the police.

The musicians are silent, about to begin.

The music begins.

The camera moves along the seated gathering.

Ladies nod their heads vacantly in supposed time to the music.

*Others turn to look at others, greeting them with smiles and
waves.*

Others use their fans constantly.

A Man whispers to a Lady.

MAN

I keep forgetting the name of this composer. Who is it?

CHARLUS

Ssshh!

MARCEL, LISTENING.

*Over all shots of Marcel the music is quite clear, pure, no
extraneous sounds.*

His face is revitalized, unanxious, totally concentrated.

THE AUDIENCE.

*In all shots of the audience at this stage, the sound of the music is
dominated by those of fans, feet shifting, yawns, coughs, and these
sounds are at the forefront over shots of Charlus, sitting tensely,
trying to concentrate, glaring furiously at the audience; Mme.
Verdurin, sitting stiffly; the Queen of Naples, listening intently.*

MOREL PLAYING.

A lock of hair falls onto his forehead.

MARCEL, LISTENING.

(NOTE: *The septet continues over the following shots, which are now all silent, the music quite pure, no extraneous sounds.*

During the course of this sequence, the music will cross-fade to the climax of the third movement of the septet.)

MARCEL.

THE MUSICIANS.

THE AUDIENCE.

MARCEL.

YELLOW SCREEN.

THE MUSICIANS.

THE AUDIENCE.

MARCEL.

YELLOW SCREEN.

In this shot of the yellow screen the music reaches its sustained climax.

MARCEL.

Applause around him.

He sits still, joyous.

THE PROUST SCREENPLAY

FLASH OF THE STEEPLES AT MARTINVILLE. SILENT.

M. VINTEUIL WALKING TOWARD CAMERA. SILENT.

In background Mlle. Vinteuil and Friend playing the piano.

INT. CONCERT ROOM.

A queue of guests waits to speak to Charlus.

The Verdurins stand apart, with Brichot.

Two Ladies are looking at some Impressionist paintings.

> LADY
> What ghastly paintings.

The Duchesse de Guermantes with Charlus.

> DUCHESSE
> Honestly, Mémé, you are remarkable. If you were to
> stage an opera in a stable or bathroom it would still be
> perfectly charming.

Laughter.

> Has there ever been a *Monsieur* Verdurin, by the way?

THE VERDURINS WITH BRICHOT.

> MME. VERDURIN
> The man is obscene.
> (*To Brichot.*)
> Take him out of the room to smoke a cigarette with you,
> so that my husband can warn our young man of the
> abyss that yawns at his feet.

CHARLUS AT DOOR OF ROOM.

The last guest has gone.

*He turns from the door and walks the length of the room to Mme.
Verdurin.*

CHARLUS

There. Are you satisfied? You have every reason to be.
You have had the Queen of Naples, the Princess of
Taormina, the brother of the King of Bavaria, the three
premier peers, countless duchesses, including my own
sister-in-law, Oriane de Guermantes. If Vinteuil is
Mahomet, we may say we have brought to him some of
the least movable of mountains.

Mme. Verdurin points to a fan on a chair.

MME. VERDURIN

The Queen of Naples has left her fan.

CHARLUS

So she has. One would know it anywhere. It is uniquely
hideous. Didn't Charlie play divinely? Where is he? I
meant to present him to the Queen. And you yourself,
my dear lady, played your part. Your name will not go
unrecorded. The Duchesse de Duras was enchanted.
She even asked me to tell you so. But where is Charlie? I
haven't congratulated him.

BRICHOT

He's with the other musicians. Come and smoke a
cigarette, Baron, for a few minutes. I would say you
deserved one.

CHARLUS

I agree with you.

He walks with Brichot towards an outer room.

What an immensely successful evening. He played like a
god, didn't you think? Did you notice when that
exquisite lock of hair came loose and fell onto his
forehead? The Princess of Taormina, confronted by the

message of the miraculous lock, suddenly realized it was music they were playing and not poker.

Charlus and Brichot pass into the other room.

INT. ANOTHER ROOM.

M. Verdurin and Morel are standing in a corner. Morel is pale.

> VERDURIN
>
> If you like, we can go and ask my wife what she thinks. I give you my word of honour, I've said nothing to her about it. We shall see how she looks at it. You know very well she's a lady of the soundest judgement.

INT. CONCERT ROOM.

M. Verdurin opens the door carefully, sees that Charlus is not there, leads Morel to Mme. Verdurin.

> VERDURIN
> (*to Mme. Verdurin*)
> He would like to ask your advice about something.

> MME. VERDURIN
>
> I agree with my husband. You cannot tolerate this situation for another moment.

> VERDURIN
> (*stammering*)
> What . . . what do you mean? Tolerate what?

> MME. VERDURIN
>
> I guessed what you were saying to him.
> (*To Morel.*)
> It is quite out of the question for you to endure any longer this degrading promiscuity with a tainted person whom nobody will have in her house. You are the talk of the Conservatoire. Another month of this life and your artistic future will be shattered.

MOREL

But I am . . . amazed . . . I . . . I've never heard anyone
utter a word.

MME. VERDURIN

Then you are unique. His reputation is black. Blacker
than black. I know for a fact he's been in prison. The
police are watching him day and night. Even financially
he can be of no use to you. He's the prey of every filthy
blackmailer in Paris.

MOREL

I should never . . . have suspected it.

MME. VERDURIN

People are beginning to point you out, did you know
that? It is essential that you wipe out this stain before it
marks you for the rest of your life, before your life and
your career are totally ruined!

MOREL

Yes, yes.

MME. VERDURIN

He pretends to be your friend but he talks of you with
contempt. The other day someone said to him: 'We
greatly admire your friend Morel'. Do you know what
he said? 'How can you call him my friend? We are not of
the same class, you must call him my creature.'
Someone said he also used the word 'servant', but I
can't vouch for that. But what he did say, what he
undoubtedly went on to say, was that your uncle was a
footman, a flunkey.

MOREL

What!

Charlus and Brichot return.

CHARLUS

Charlie! Well, how do you feel after your triumph? How does it feel to be covered in glory?

MOREL

Leave me alone! Don't come near me! I know all about you! I'm not the first person you've tried to corrupt!

Charlus stands still, paralysed.

Silence.

MOREL

Pervert!

Charlus looks at the others. No one moves.

CHARLUS
(*almost soundless*)

What has happened?

The Verdurins go through an arch into an outer room.

Morel, trembling, goes quickly to platform to pack his violin.

Charlus stands still, looking at nothing.

Morel suddenly notices the Queen of Naples, standing at the door of the room. She has clearly overheard the preceding scene.

INT. THE OUTER ROOM.

The Verdurins. They stand looking out of the window.

MME. VERDURIN
(*smirking*)

I think Charlus should sit down. He's tottering, he'll be on the floor in a minute.

Morel comes through the arch.

MOREL

Isn't that lady the Queen of Naples?

They turn to look.

MME. VERDURIN

It is.

The Queen can be seen talking quietly to Charlus.

MOREL

The Baron was going to introduce me . . .

MME. VERDURIN

I'll introduce you. She's charming.

They move into the room and stand in front of the Queen. Mme. Verdurin curtseys.

I am Madame Verdurin, Your Majesty. Your Majesty does not remember me.

QUEEN OF NAPLES
(*distantly*)

Quite well.

The Queen picks up her fan and offers Charlus her arm.

You look ill, my dear cousin. Lean on my arm. It once held the rabble at bay at Gaeta. It will serve as a rampart for you, now.

Charlus takes her arm.

They both walk slowly from the room.

The Verdurins and Morel stare after them.

Marcel watches.

EXT. MARCEL'S FLAT. NIGHT.

Marcel stands on the pavement looking up.

A light shines from his flat.

INT. SITTING ROOM. NIGHT.

Albertine reading. Marcel enters, in his fur coat.

> MARCEL
>
> Hullo. You're still up.

> ALBERTINE
>
> Yes.

> MARCEL
>
> Guess where I've just been. To the Verdurins'.

She throws down the book.

> ALBERTINE
>
> I thought as much.

Pause.

> MARCEL
>
> Why does that annoy you so much?

> ALBERTINE
>
> Annoy me? What do you mean? Why should I care
> where you've been? It's all the same to me. Was
> Mademoiselle Vinteuil there?

He sits down.

Pause.

> How was the septet?

> MARCEL
>
> How do you know about the septet?

> ALBERTINE
>
> Everyone knows. It's not a secret.

> MARCEL
>
> I didn't know.

Pause.

ALBERTINE

Did Morel play well?

MARCEL

Have you had any contact with Morel?

ALBERTINE

Contact? Of course not. I hardly know him.

MARCEL

Then how did you hear about the septet?

ALBERTINE

I think it must have been Andrée who told me. She
knows Morel quite well.

Pause.

MARCEL

The septet was wonderful. It gave me a happiness I have
felt . . . rarely.

Pause.

Léa was there. The actress.

ALBERTINE

How odd.

MARCEL

She's a friend of Morel.

ALBERTINE

Is she?

MARCEL

She sent you her best wishes.

ALBERTINE

Did she? How odd. I hardly know her. We went to see
her act once last year and went round to her dressing
room afterwards, to say hullo. That's all.

Pause.

MARCEL

Who went?

ALBERTINE

Oh, a few of us.

Pause.

MARCEL

You knew that Mademoiselle Vinteuil was expected at
the Verdurins' this afternoon, didn't you?

ALBERTINE

Oh, these questions!
         (*Shrugging.*)
Yes, I knew that.

MARCEL

Can you swear to me that it was not in order to renew
your relations with her that you wanted to go there?

ALBERTINE

I never had any relations with her.

MARCEL

Can you swear to me that the pleasure of seeing her
again had nothing to do with your wanting to be there?

ALBERTINE

No, I can't swear that. It would have given me great
pleasure to see her again.

MARCEL

Listen . . . this evening I learned that what you had told
me about Mademoiselle Vinteuil –

ALBERTINE

Was a lie. Yes. Yes, I did lie when I pretended to know
her and her friend well, when I called them my two big

sisters. But you see I thought you found me so boring, I thought if I told you I knew the family and knew about Vinteuil's music, you'd think better of me, you'd find me more interesting. When I lie to you, it is always out of affection for you! I've only met them about twice, in fact. I invented the story because I'm out of my depth with all these smart people you know – I haven't any money in the world – I'm absolutely poor . . .

He studies her.

MARCEL

That's silly. I have money. If you want to, you can give a dinner party for the Verdurins, for instance, any time you like.

ALBERTINE

Oh God! Thank you for nothing. A dinner party for those bores?
(*Murmurs swiftly.*)
I'd much rather you left me alone for once in a way so that I can go and get myself –

She stops abruptly.

MARCEL

What did you say?

ALBERTINE

Nothing . . . the Verdurins . . . the dinner.

MARCEL

No. You were saying something else. You stopped. Why did you stop?

ALBERTINE

Because I felt my request was unfair.

MARCEL

What request?

ALBERTINE

To be able to give a dinner party.

MARCEL

You didn't request it.

ALBERTINE

It's not right to take advantage of the fact that you have money. It's wrong.

Pause.

MARCEL

I didn't understand what you were saying. I didn't catch exactly what you said. You wanted to get –

ALBERTINE

Oh leave me alone, please!

MARCEL

But why? Why can't you finish . . . ?

ALBERTINE

I didn't know what I was saying. I was going to say – words I heard once, in the street. I don't even know what they mean. Just came into my head. It means nothing. I don't know what I meant.

Marcel looks at her in bewilderment.

I'm just so upset that you went to the Verdurins' without telling me. You've deceived me and insulted me. I think I'll go to bed.

She goes.

He sits still.

Silence.

The camera remains on him for some moments.

IMAGE OF ALBERTINE.

She stops talking abruptly.

MARCEL IN CHAIR.

He closes his eyes, clenches them in pain.

INT. ALBERTINE'S BEDROOM.

She is looking at herself in a mirror.

Marcel comes in.

> MARCEL
>
> Albertine, I think we should part. I want you to leave, first thing in the morning.

> ALBERTINE
>
> In the morning?

> MARCEL
>
> We have been happy. Now we're unhappy. It's quite simple.

> ALBERTINE
>
> I'm not unhappy.

> MARCEL
>
> Never see me again. It's best.

> ALBERTINE
>
> You are the only person I care for.

> MARCEL
>
> I've always wanted to go to Venice. Now I shall go. Alone.

Silence.

> How many times have you lied to me?

Pause.

ALBERTINE

Well, I should have told you, when we were speaking
about Léa just now, that I once took a three-week trip
with her, it was before I knew you, but it was quite
innocent, she behaved perfectly properly, she was just
quite fond of me, that's all, as a daughter. I didn't tell
you because I thought it might upset you, but absolutely
nothing happened, nothing at all, I swear to you.

She looks about the room.

I can't believe I shall never see this room again. It seems
impossible.

MARCEL

You were unhappy here.

ALBERTINE

No. It's now I shall be unhappy.

MARCEL

Where will you go?

ALBERTINE

I don't know. I shall have to think. Back to my aunt's, I
suppose.

Pause.

MARCEL

Would you like us . . . to try again . . . for a few more
weeks?

ALBERTINE

Yes. I would.

MARCEL

A few more weeks.

ALBERTINE

Yes. I think we should.

INT. MARCEL'S BEDROOM.

Marcel alone in his room, sitting still.

Suddenly the sound of a window being opened violently, from Albertine's room.

He looks round sharply.

INT. CORRIDOR. NIGHT.

The corridor is dark.

Marcel's door opens. He walks down the corridor to stand outside Albertine's room, he listens.

Silence.

INT. MARCEL'S BEDROOM. MORNING.

Marcel in bed. Françoise comes in.

> FRANÇOISE
> I didn't know what to do. Mademoiselle Albertine asked me for her trunks – at seven o'clock this morning. You were asleep. I didn't want to wake you. You say never to wake you. She packed. She's gone. She left.

He stares at her.

> MARCEL
> You were quite right not to wake me.

MARCEL'S EYES.

THE EYES OF GILBERTE AT TANSONVILLE.

THE EYES OF THE DUCHESSE DE GUERMANTES IN THE STREET.

THE EYES OF ODETTE IN THE AVENUE DES ACACIAS.

THE EYES OF MOTHER IN THE BEDROOM AT COMBRAY.

THE EYES OF MARCEL IN THE LAVATORY AT COMBRAY.

THE EYES OF MARCEL.

INT. MARCEL'S BEDROOM. PARIS. 1902.

Françoise handing him a telegram.

He opens it, reads it.

He lets it drop.

Françoise picks it up, reads it.

She gasps and puts her hand to her mouth.

She looks at Marcel.

She puts the telegram on the table and slowly leaves the room.

The camera stays on Marcel who remains still, his face blank.

EXT. FIELD. DAY.

A riderless horse gallops away from the camera.

The camera pulls back slightly to reveal the suggestion of the broken body of a girl.

INT. MARCEL'S FLAT. THE HALL. DAY.

The empty hall.

INT. THE DINING ROOM. EVENING.

The empty dining room.

INT. MARCEL'S ROOM. NIGHT.

Marcel sitting, his face blank.

INT. THE HALL. NIGHT.

The door of Albertine's room is ajar.

The hall is empty.

Silence.

INT. MARCEL'S ROOM. DAY.

Marcel sitting, his face blank.

CLOSE-UP. ANDRÉE.

Marcel's VO.

> MARCEL
> (*VO*)
> Now that she's dead . . . I can ask you quite frankly . . .
> You like women, don't you?

Andrée smiles.

> ANDRÉE
> Yes. I do.

INT. MARCEL'S ROOM. TWO SHOT. DAY. 1902.

> MARCEL
> You knew Mademoiselle Vinteuil . . . well, didn't you?

> ANDRÉE
> No, not her, actually. Her friend.

Pause.

> MARCEL
> I have known for years, of course, of the things you used
> to do with Albertine.

> ANDRÉE
> I never did anything with Albertine.

INT. MARCEL'S ROOM. NIGHT.

Marcel and Andrée sit in different positions in the room. Andrée wears a different dress.

> MARCEL
>
> I find you very attractive. Perhaps because of the things you did with Albertine. I want what she had.

> ANDRÉE
>
> That's impossible. You're a man.

Pause.

> She was so passionate. Remember that day you lost your key, when you brought home syringa? You nearly caught us. It was so dangerous, we knew you would be home any minute, but she needed it, she had to have it. I pretended she hated the scent of syringa, do you remember? She was behind the door. She said the same thing, to keep you away from her, so that you wouldn't smell me on her.

INT. MARCEL'S ROOM. DAY.

Marcel and Andrée sitting.

> ANDRÉE
>
> You *want* me to say it, don't you? But I won't say things which aren't true. Albertine detested that sort of thing. I can swear it. I can swear that I never did that sort of thing with Albertine.

INT. MARCEL'S ROOM. NIGHT.

Marcel and Andrée sitting.

> ANDRÉE
>
> She and Morel understood each other at once. He procured girls for her. He would seduce the girl first,

and then, when the girl was absolutely under his control, he'd hand her over to Albertine, and they'd both enjoy the girl together.

Pause.

Léa had her many times at the baths at Balbec, last summer in Balbec. I remember once being with her and some laundresses – oh quite young – by the banks of a river near Balbec. I remember one girl – very sweet she was too – doing something to Albertine – I can't possibly tell you what – and she cried out: 'Oh how heavenly'. 'Oh how heavenly' . . . quivering, naked, on the grass.

INT. MARCEL'S ROOM. DAY.

Marcel and Andrée sitting.

> ANDRÉE
> The people who have told you these stories about Albertine were lying to you . . . can't you understand that?

> MARCEL
> No one has told me any stories.

INT. MARCEL'S ROOM. NIGHT.

> ANDRÉE
> She hoped that you would rescue her, that you would marry her. She loved you. She felt in her heart her obsession was a sort of criminal lunacy. I think she might quite possibly have killed herself out of despair.

LARGE PROFILE. SWANN.

Swann's VO.

SWANN
(*VO*)

To think I have wasted years of my life, that I have
longed for death, that the greatest love I have ever
known has been for a woman who did not appeal to me,
who was not my type.

EXT. GRAND CANAL. VENICE. DAY. 1903.

Wintry. desolate.

Marcel in a gondola approaching a palazzo.

MOTHER FRAMED IN A WINDOW.

She is sitting on a balcony of the palazzo reading.

She looks up from her book to see Marcel in the gondola.

THE GONDOLA ARRIVING AT THE LANDING.

*Marcel steps out of the gondola, looks up to see his mother. His
face is expressionless.*

CLOSE-UP. MOTHER.

She looks down with an expression of helpless love.

EXT. SAINT MARK'S SQUARE. DAY.

The square is desolate.

Marcel and Mother sitting among empty tables outside a café.

Mother is reading. She glances from her book at Marcel.

EXT. VENICE. EVENING.

Gondola swaying near Saint Mark's Church.

INT. SAINT MARK'S CHURCH.

Sound of two pairs of feet walking over the cobbles. They stop.

The camera pans up to the blue fresco of the church.

EXT. PARIS STREET. 1915.

Searchlights in the sky, air raid sirens.

The camera pans down to a rather derelict street.

There is a general blackout.

Marcel 35 walks alone into the street.

Lights glint through the shutters of what appears to be a small hotel.

He walks towards it, stops.

The door of the hotel has suddenly opened. An officer comes out.

In the flash of light Marcel recognizes Saint-Loup 37. Saint-Loup hesitates a moment, and then strides away.

INT. HOTEL FOYER.

Marcel enters.

A Man at the desk in evening clothes is whispering to the Manager.

> MANAGER
> Impossible, sir. Next week perhaps. I'll see what I can do.

In an anteroom Marcel notices a group of young soldiers lounging about, playing dice, and also one or two young civilians.

The Man in evening clothes turns from the desk, glances quickly at Marcel, leaves the hotel.

Marcel walks slowly to the desk.

From outside, gunfire in the distance.

> MARCEL

I'd like a room, until the raid's over.

> MANAGER

Yes, yes. We can do that. Is there . . . anything else I
can get you, sir?

> MARCEL

A bottle of champagne.

> MANAGER

Ah.

INT. HOTEL. LANDING.

*The Manager, carrying a tray with a bottle of champagne, leads
Marcel to a room.*

They go in.

INT. ROOM.

The room is very bare.

The Manager opens the bottle and pours a glass.

Marcel sits down.

> MARCEL

Thank you.

> MANAGER

When you're . . . ready for anything else, sir, just ring,
and I'll be up to see what you require.

He goes out.

Marcel sits drinking.

Gunfire in the distance.

He suddenly notices an object lying on the floor by the foot of the bed. He goes to it, picks it up.

It is a Croix de Guerre.

The gunfire stops. In the silence Marcel becomes aware of faint cries from somewhere in the hotel.

He puts the Croix de Guerre in his pocket and goes out of the room.

INT. LANDING.

Marcel walks in the direction of the cries.

STAIRS TO THE NEXT FLOOR.

Marcel reaches the top of the stairs.

The cries are nearer.

He walks towards a room at the end of the corridor.

A VOICE
Have mercy, have mercy, you're killing me!

ANOTHER VOICE
Mercy? For a filthy old bastard like you?

Cracks of a whip. Shouts of pain.

Marcel notices a small oval-shaped window looking into the room, the curtain half-pulled.

He looks in.

THE ROOM FROM MARCEL'S POINT OF VIEW.

Charlus 68, chained to the bed, naked, being beaten by a Young Man with a whip.

The door opens. Jupien 66 comes in.

JUPIEN

Everything all right, Baron?

CHARLUS

Can we have a word?

JUPIEN

Go downstairs, Maurice.

MAURICE

Yes, Monsieur Jupien.

Maurice bows shyly to Charlus and goes out.

CHARLUS

He hasn't got his heart in it, that fellow. I know he's
doing his best but he's simply not brutal enough,
nowhere near brutal enough. He doesn't mean it, you
see! He's pretending.

JUPIEN

Oh, I'm so sorry. I have a butcher's assistant downstairs.
An absolute thug. He nearly killed a defrocked priest up
here the other day. Would you like him?

CHARLUS

He sounds a better bet.

JUPIEN

Shall I unchain you while I look for him?

CLOSE-UP. CHARLUS.

CHARLUS
(*heavily*)

No. Leave me chained.

EXT. CORRIDOR.

Jupien comes out of the room.

Marcel lets himself be seen. Jupien stares at him.

Marcel glances in at Charlus again, and then walks down the stairs in silence.

Jupien follows.

> JUPIEN
> I'm . . . very surprised to see you here, sir.

> MARCEL
> I came in to shelter from the raid.

INT. MARCEL'S HOTEL ROOM.

Marcel and Jupien enter.

Marcel pours himself another glass of champagne. Jupien stands looking at him.

> MARCEL
> You own this . . . hotel, I take it?

> JUPIEN
> Yes, but I don't want you to misjudge me. The profit's very small. I have to let rooms to respectable people as well, sometimes. The running costs are high. Equipment, overheads, labour, et cetera. No, you see, I took this house for the Baron, to amuse him in his old age. I'm fond of him. As for the lads, the Baron enjoys their companionship, as much as anything else. He often plays cards with them. I must get my thug for him. Actually he's not a thug. He's a sweet young thing who sends most of the money he earns here home to his mother.

> MARCEL
> I think you should have this. It was lying on the floor in this room.

He hands Jupien the Croix de Guerre.

                        JUPIEN
My goodness. A Croix de Guerre.

                        MARCEL
Perhaps you might return it to its owner.

                        JUPIEN
Yes, yes. Of course.

EXT. PARK AT TANSONVILLE. DAY. 1915.

The pond, seen through a gap in the hedge.

A fishing line rests by the side of the pond, the float bobbing in the water.

Marcel and Gilberte appear and walk to the side of the pond. They are both aged thirty-five and both dressed in mourning.

                        GILBERTE
Two days after Robert was killed I received a package, sent anonymously. It contained his Croix de Guerre. There was no note of explanation, nothing. The package was posted in Paris.

Pause.

Isn't that strange?

                        MARCEL
Yes.

                        GILBERTE
He never mentioned, in any letter, that it had been lost, or stolen.

INT. DRAWING-ROOM. SWANN'S HOUSE AT TANSONVILLE. EVENING.

Marcel and Gilberte stand by the windows.

GILBERTE

I loved him. But we had grown unhappy. He had
another woman, or other women, I don't know.

MARCEL

Other women?

GILBERTE

Yes. He had some secret life, which he never confessed
to me, but I know he found it irresistible.

EXT. PARK. TANSONVILLE. MORNING.

Marcel and Gilberte walking.

GILBERTE

Do you remember your childhood at Combray?

MARCEL

Not really.

GILBERTE

How long is it since you've been back?

MARCEL

Oh, a very long time. It's changed.

GILBERTE

The war has changed everything.

MARCEL

No, it's nothing to do with the war.

GILBERTE

But are you saying that these paths, these woods, the
village, excite nothing in you?

MARCEL

Nothing. They mean nothing to me. It's all dead. I
remember almost nothing of it.

Pause.

I remember seeing you, through the hedge. I adored
you.

GILBERTE

Did you? I wish you'd told me at the time. I thought
you were delicious.

Marcel stares at her.

MARCEL

What?

GILBERTE

I longed for you. Of course I was quite precocious, I
suppose, then. I used to go to some ruins – at
Roussainville – with some girls and boys, from the
village, in the dark. We were quite wicked. I longed for
you to come there. I remember, that moment through
the hedge, I tried to let you know how much I wanted
you, but I don't think you understood.

He laughs.

Why are you laughing?

MARCEL

Because I didn't understand. I've understood very little.
I've been too . . . preoccupied . . . with other matters
. . . To be honest, I have wasted my life.

INT. SANATORIUM. MARCEL'S ROOM. DAY. 1917.

The sanatorium is in a large château by the side of a lake.

Marcel sits still, alone, in the large room. He is thirty-seven.

He wears his coat.

He is motionless as an owl.

INT. SANATORIUM. CORRIDOR.

A doctor in a white coat passes the camera in foreground.

At the very end of the long corridor we see Marcel standing.

INT. SANATORIUM. MARCEL'S ROOM.

Marcel sitting still.

Birds wheel at the window.

He does not hear them.

EXT. SANATORIUM. THE LAKE.

Marcel sitting on a bench with his back to the lake. In the distance figures in white coats.

EXT. COUNTRYSIDE. DAY. 1921.

A train, still.

A railwayman walks along the side of the train, tapping the wheels with a hammer. The sound echoes.

INT. RAILWAY CARRIAGE.

Marcel alone. He is forty-one.

A line of trees in background.

A window is open but the sound of the hammer is not heard.

INT. MARCEL'S FLAT. 1921.

His hands opening an envelope.

He takes out a card.

It is an invitation to an afternoon party given by the Prince and Princesse de Guermantes.

He puts the invitation on his desk.

FLASH OF THE PRINCESSE DE GUERMANTES AT HER BOX AT THE OPERA.

EXT. PRINCE DE GUERMANTES' HOUSE. AVENUE DU BOIS.

Marcel walking towards it.

Carriages, cars, crowds of chauffeurs.

A car is driving towards the house. Marcel steps in front of it. The chauffeur shouts. Marcel steps back, trips over uneven paving stones.

He sways, recovers balance, puts his foot back on the lower paving stone.

Very dim quick flash of Venice.

Marcel's face.

EXT. PRINCE DE GUERMANTES' HOUSE.

Marcel stands still.

He sways back again and forward.

He remains still.

He sways back again and forward.

In background chauffeurs regarding him curiously, with amusement.

Marcel sways back.

Blue glow.

Chauffeurs.

Blue fresco in Saint Mark's Church.

Marcel's face.

INT. PRINCE DE GUERMANTES' HOUSE.

The doors of the Guermantes' house have been opened.

Camera follows Marcel into the house and up the stairs.

Sound of music from behind closed doors.

A Butler on the landing comes forward.

BUTLER
The Princess has given orders for the doors to be kept shut until the music has ended. Will you wait in the library, sir?

INT. THE LIBRARY.

Marcel enters the library and sits down.

He is alone apart from a Waiter who stands at the table with refreshments.

The Waiter inadvertently knocks a spoon against a plate.

Open countryside, a line of trees, seen from a railway carriage.

Sound of a hammer tapping a wheel.

The Waiter with the spoon.

Sound of hammer over.

The train in the clearing.

Railwayman tapping wheel.

Marcel in carriage. No sound.

Marcel in library. Sound of hammer.

Marcel looks down at the table by him. On it are some petits fours and a glass of orange juice.

He drinks, wipes mouth with starched napkin.

The napkin crackles.

Flash of blue sky seen through a window.

Marcel with napkin at his mouth.

Full still frame of the sea and sky seen from a high window, a starched towel being placed on a towel rack in the foreground.

Marcel and the Waiter, still.

Water pipes in the library.

Shrill noise of water running through pipes.

Flash of silver cutlery glittering on table.

Marcel's face.

The dining-room at Balbec. Empty. Sunset.

The tables are laid. In the distance sounds of a steamer.

Marcel in library.

Sounds of a steamer over.

INT. DRAWING-ROOM. PRINCE DE GUERMANTES' HOUSE. 1921.

The drawing-room doors open.

Camera enters with Marcel, who hesitates.

Hundreds of faces, some of which turn towards him, grotesquely made up, grotesquely old.

He walks into the room. Voices. Faces. The wigs and make-up, combined with the extreme age of those who with difficulty stand, sit, gesture, laugh, give the impression of grotesque fancy dress.

IMAGE OF VENICE APPEARS ON THE SCREEN AND
IMMEDIATELY FADES.

THE DUCHESSE DE GUERMANTES 63 AND MARCEL.

> DUCHESSE
>
> It's years, years, years. How many years? When was it
> exactly? Where have you been? You haven't changed a
> bit, have you? Well, just a little perhaps. I'm very long in
> the tooth, aren't I? Well, of course I'm no chicken.

SEA AND SKY AND THE WINDOW AT BALBEC APPEAR ON THE
SCREEN AND IMMEDIATELY FADE.

DUCHESSE AND MARCEL.

A very old bent man passes.

> MARCEL
>
> Who is that?

> DUCHESSE
>
> The Comte d'Argencourt. Do you remember him? Had
> a terrible reputation. Mostly with footmen.

> MARCEL
> (*looking after d'Argencourt*)
> I can't believe it.

> DUCHESSE
>
> Well, he's changed, of course. Do you know you're
> probably my only friend here, my truest friend? You met
> everyone at my house, didn't you? You met Swann first
> at my house.

> MARCEL
> I knew him a little, when I was a child.

DUCHESSE

His daughter's here somewhere, Gilberte. Do you know her?

MARCEL

Not very well.

DUCHESSE

She never loved Robert, you know, never. She's a bitch.

THE COUNTRYSIDE AND LINE OF TREES FROM TRAIN WINDOW APPEAR ON THE SCREEN AND IMMEDIATELY FADE.

DUCHESSE AND MARCEL.

MARCEL

Where is the Princess?

DUCHESSE
(*pointing*)

She's there, over there.

Marcel looks in the direction of her finger and sees Mme. Verdurin, who is eighty-one.

The camera focuses on Mme. Verdurin, momentarily.

MARCEL

That's not the Princess.

DUCHESSE

Oh yes it is. She was once called Verdurin. My darling cousin is dead. Mother Verdurin is the new Princess, my new cousin. Can you believe it? The Prince found her money very useful.

THE BALBEC DINING-ROOM AT SUNSET APPEARS ON THE SCREEN AND IMMEDIATELY FADES.

M. DE CAMBREMER AND MARCEL.

M. de Cambremer is seventy-five, his face pock-marked and distorted.

> **M. DE CAMBREMER**
> Someone told me you've been in a sanatorium for years, my dear fellow. Do you still suffer from choking fits? I mean has there been any improvement?

> **MARCEL**
> Not much.

> **M. DE CAMBREMER**
> They become much less frequent with age though, surely? And after all you're getting on.
> (*Absently.*)
> My sister suffers much less from them, now.

MARCEL ALONE.

He looks closely at people in the room and the camera pans over limping crooked men, half-paralysed women, bodies trembling, faces caked with make-up.

SUDDEN CLOSE-UP OF THE VICOMTESSE DE SAINT-FIACRE.

She is a cocaine addict. Her face is haggard. She grins permanently.

> **VICOMTESSE**
> (*into camera*)
> Hullo.

MARCEL

He gazes at a group of people who from a distance appear to be young.

He draws nearer and sees that the faces are actually wrinkled and greasy, the eyes tiny behind pouches of flesh.

Brichot passes, totally blind. He is eighty-four.

ODETTE SITTING ON SOFA SURROUNDED BY YOUNG MEN.

She is sixty-four, but remains beautiful.

MOREL ENTERS THE ROOM.

He is forty-one.

He is greeted warmly.

The Princesse de Guermantes (Mme. Verdurin) calls across the room.

> PRINCESSE DE GUERMANTES
> Ah here's the great musician, the great man!

Morel goes towards her and the Prince de Guermantes, who is seventy-five.

MME. DE CAMBREMER 70 AND THE DUCHESSE DE GUERMANTES.

Marcel in background.

> MME. DE CAMBREMER
> What has become of the Marquise d'Arpajon?

> DUCHESSE DE GUERMANTES
> She died.

> MME. DE CAMBREMER
> No no, you're confusing her with the Comtesse d'Arpajon.

> DUCHESSE DE GUERMANTES
> Certainly not. The Marquise is dead too. About a year ago.

> MME. DE CAMBREMER
> But I was at a musical party at her house about a year ago.

DUCHESSE DE GUERMANTES
Well she's quite dead, I can promise you. I'm not
surprised you haven't heard. She died in a quite
unremarkable way.

GILBERTE 4I AND MARCEL.

GILBERTE
I can't understand what you're doing at a party like this.
Why don't we dine together tonight in a restaurant?

MARCEL
Yes, of course . . . if you won't find it compromising to
dine alone with a young man.

Gilberte laughs.

One or two other people turn smiling at this remark.

An old man.

CLOSE SHOT. THE PRINCESSE DE GUERMANTES.

She laughs wildly and adjusts her monocle.

GILBERTE
(*VO*)
She's my aunt now, you know.

MARCEL AND GILBERTE.

GILBERTE
I must tell you, I have a great friend now who knew you
once, I believe. Her name's Andrée.

MARCEL
Yes, I knew her.

GILBERTE
She's here somewhere, with her husband. Oh no, there
she is, over there, talking to Morel.

Morel and Andrée 43 across the room talking.

MARCEL AND RACHEL.

Rachel 44 looks much older than she actually is.

> RACHEL
>
> No, I can see you don't remember me.

> MARCEL
>
> Yes yes, I do.

> RACHEL
>
> Who am I then?

> MARCEL
>
> I . . .

> RACHEL
>
> I'll tell you. We met backstage once in a theatre with a friend of yours. He was madly in love with me. Do you remember?

> MARCEL
>
> Oh yes. Yes I do.

> RACHEL
>
> He adored me.

THE DUC DE GUERMANTES SITTING WITH ODETTE ON A SOFA.

The Duc appears to be as handsome and majestic as ever. His hair is white. He is seventy-five.

Young men are talking to Odette.

Occasionally the Duc speaks. Odette turns sharply to him and then back smiling to the young men.

THE DUCHESSE AND MARCEL.

DUCHESSE
You've met Rachel. Do you know she's the greatest actress in Paris? Oh by the way, my husband is having another affair at the age of seventy-five! Remarkable isn't it? But we're still quite fond of each other.

GILBERTE AND MARCEL.

GILBERTE
The duc de Guermantes is a great admirer of my mother. He is in her house all the time. She doesn't age at all, does she?

MARCEL
No, not at all.

GILBERTE
People have always fallen in love with my mother.

THE DUC DE GUERMANTES WALKING TO THE DOOR.

Now he is standing, we realize his age.

He finds great difficulty in walking, gropes along, wipes his brow, totters.

ODETTE AND MARCEL.

ODETTE
Sit down by me. I'm delighted to meet you. You knew my first husband well, didn't you?

MARCEL
Your *first* husband?

ODETTE
Charles Swann. I'm Madame de Forcheville now. But Monsieur de Forcheville is dead too, now. But you did know Charles.

MARCEL

Yes, in my childhood, a little.

ODETTE

I know you're a writer. Oh the things I could tell you,
the material I could give you. Are you interested in love,
I mean do you write about it? But what else is there to
write about? All my lovers have been so ridden with
jealousy. Charles was unbelievably jealous. But he was
so intelligent. I could never love a man who was
unintelligent. I never loved Monsieur de Forcheville. He
was quite commonplace, really. But I adored Charles,
and we were so happy, most of the time. Charles always
intended to write himself, you know, but

(*she giggles*)

I think he was too much in love with me to find the
time.

MARCEL STANDING ALONE.

*Gilberte approaches Marcel with a Young Girl of sixteen. She is
very lovely.*

GILBERTE

This is my daughter.

Mlle. de Saint-Loup smiles and inclines her head.

Marcel gazes at her.

Suddenly all the sounds in the room die.

Mlle. de Saint-Loup speaks silently, smiling.

*Over this shot we hear the garden gate bell at Combray, 'resilient,
ferruginous, interminable, fresh and shrill'.*

The bell continues over the following shots:

The vast room, the multitude of people, talking.

No sound.

Mlle. de Saint-Loup smiling.

The trees at Hudimesnil.

The steeples at Martinville.

Flash of yellow screen.

The river Vivonne at Combray.

The roofs of Combray.

The garden at Combray in the evening.

The bell at the garden gate.

Swann opening the garden gate and departing.

Marcel as a child looking out of his bedroom window.

The bell ceases.

Vermeer's View of Delft.

Camera moves in swiftly to the patch of yellow wall in the painting.

Yellow screen.

MARCEL
(*VO*)

It was time to begin.

Victory

AUTHOR'S NOTE

I wrote *Victory* in 1982, working with the director, Richard
Lester. The finance for the film was never found.

Harold Pinter

A boat becalmed, far out to sea. The mast slowly sways. Heat haze. Red sun.

Gulls encircle the boat, screeching.

Screeching violins. A ladies' orchestra. Bare arms. White dresses. Crimson sashes.

A wall of foliage. Bamboo spears pierce the foliage, quiver, stay pointed.

Camera pans up to see, through leaves, impassive native faces.

An island. Moonlight. Silence.

Figures of men seen from a distance at the door of a low, thatched house. The door is kicked open. The sound reverberates in the night. Explosion of shrieking birds.

Driving rain. Leashed, barking dogs leading men with rifles through jungle.

One of the men suddenly turns in panic, raises gun to shoot.

Champagne cork popping.

Two men standing on a jetty. Champagne is poured into glasses. In background a freighter leaving. Natives waving, cheering. The freighter whistles.

A cylinder gramophone playing in a room. Rosalia Chalier singing.

Moonlight.

A girl's figure in a sarong passes, carrying a bowl of water.

In background a mosquito net canopy over bed. A man's body on the bed.

313

The girl parts the netting, places the bowl on the bed, kneels on the bed, looks down at the man.

The gramophone hissing.

A creek. Night. Crackle of fire. Two figures seated in foreground.

Fire burning.

Beyond the fire two Venezuelan Indians poking long knives into fish. They eat.

The two foreground figures remain still.

One of these raises a hand and wipes it on a silken handkerchief.

High up on a hillside two figures in the grass. Bright sunlight.

A girl's stifled scream.

EXT. SURABAYA HARBOUR. DAY.

1900.

A large mail boat approaching the harbour.

The captain, Davidson, on the prow, looking towards the port. Small boats coming from the port. Boatmen shouting.

EXT. SURABAYA HARBOUR.

The mail boat at anchor. From quayside Davidson seen in a sampan approaching the shore. Dozens of sampans and other small boats with painted wooden roofs and striped sails.

EXT. QUAYSIDE.

Davidson steps on to the quayside and hails a dogcart taxi.

Hubbub.

On the quayside Malays, Chinese, Negroes, Arabs, Javanese, some Europeans. Native carriers with bamboo poles over their shoulders, baskets hanging front and back.

Stalls along the quayside: cloth, hardware, fruit, food-stalls, etc.

EXT. HOTEL GROUNDS. AFTERNOON.

*Davidson walking towards Schomberg's Hotel through the hushed
garden.*

*Another building glimpsed through the trees – the concert hall.
Torn, fluttering bills stuck to tree trunks. Davidson stops to look
at one of them: 'Concerts Every Night'.*

EXT. HOTEL VERANDA.

*Davidson walks along the veranda. The screens are down.
Silence.*

No one in sight.

He enters the hotel.

INT. HOTEL LOBBY.

*Empty. Blinds down. Davidson walks towards calico curtains
and passes through.*

INT. HOTEL ROOM.

*Davidson stands in the darkened room. At the back of the room a
shrouded billiard table.*

*Davidson discerns, in the dim light, a form lying across two
chairs.*

It suddenly sits up and stands. Schomberg.

SCHOMBERG

Yes? You desire?

DAVIDSON

Mr Schomberg?

Schomberg pulls a bell.

SCHOMBERG

What is it you desire?

DAVIDSON

Just got into port. Come to pick up Mr Heyst. We sail
again at midnight.

SCHOMBERG

He's not here.

A Chinese servant enters.

Take the gentleman's order.

DAVIDSON

Nothing, thank you.

The servant withdraws.

I'd like to see Mr Heyst. He's expecting me.

SCHOMBERG

He's not here.

DAVIDSON

But I left him here – three weeks ago. He *has* been
staying here?

SCHOMBERG

Yes.

Pause.

DAVIDSON

Well, do you know where he is?

SCHOMBERG

He has left this hotel.
                              (*Shouts.*)
Boy!

Schomberg leaves the room. Davidson stands still.

The servant enters, waits.

DAVIDSON

A citron, thank you.

The servant goes.

Davidson perches on the billiard table, looks about the room.

Through calico curtains he sees Mrs Schomberg go into the lobby. She goes to a chair behind a raised counter and sits, without moving.

Davidson watches her and then goes through the curtain into the lobby.

INT. HOTEL LOBBY.

Mrs Schomberg does not look at him. Davidson examines a large poster on the wall: 'Concerts Every Night. Ladies' Orchestra. Zangiacomo's Eastern Tour. Eighteen Performers'.

The servant comes in, gives Davidson his drink, goes.

DAVIDSON

Is the orchestra still here?

MRS SCHOMBERG

No. They have gone.

DAVIDSON

Were they good?

Silence.

Italian, were they?

MRS SCHOMBERG

He's German. He calls himself Zangiacomo – for business. He dyes his hair and his beard black – for business.

DAVIDSON

Oh.

317

VICTORY

Pause.

MRS SCHOMBERG

One of the girls was English.

DAVIDSON

Oh really?
                    (*He drinks.*)
Where did they go from here?

MRS SCHOMBERG

I don't know. She didn't go with them.

DAVIDSON

Oh? Why not?

MRS SCHOMBERG

She ran away.

DAVIDSON
                    (*lightly*)
Who with?

MRS SCHOMBERG

That friend of yours.

Davidson stares at her.

DAVIDSON

Eh?

MRS SCHOMBERG

Your friend.

DAVIDSON

My friend?

She is silent.

She ran away with Heyst? But that's ... He could never
do such a thing. It's ... impossible. He's a gentleman.

She swiftly throws him a piece of paper, twisted.

318

MRS SCHOMBERG

He left you a note.

He unfolds it and reads it.
(*Whispers.*)
I helped them. I tied her things in my shawl and threw
them into the compound. I did it.

*Through this, various growing sounds: footsteps and voices on the
veranda. Pings of a bell.*

Say nothing –

Schomberg comes in. He glares at them.

SCHOMBERG
(*to Mrs Schomberg*)
There are customers! What are you doing! Where are
the boys? Do something!

*She slips from behind the counter and goes into an inner room.
Schomberg and Davidson look at each other.*

DAVIDSON
So you can't help me? You've no idea where my friend
Heyst is?

SCHOMBERG
He's a pigdog. He's a criminal.

DAVIDSON
Has he run off with your cash box?

SCHOMBERG
He's run off with a whore.

DAVIDSON
Good Lord.

SCHOMBERG
A girl from the orchestra. This is a respectable hotel. Do
you know what it cost me to build my concert hall?

Seven hundred and thirty-four guilders. He's ruined the reputation of this hotel. It's an atrocity! He's a public danger. Everyone knows he killed Morrison. He was always a swindler, a ruffian, a spy, an imposter, a Schweinhund! I tell you – I will be revenged.

DAVIDSON

But where has he taken her?

SCHOMBERG

Where do you think? He's taken her to his island, where he thinks nobody can get at him.

EXT. HOTEL GARDEN. LATE AFTERNOON.

Davidson leaving hotel garden. In background the concert hall.

The garden still.

Over this, sound of ladies' orchestra.

EXT. HOTEL GARDEN. NIGHT.

Earlier.

The concert hall illuminated. The orchestra playing. Japanese lanterns in the trees.

Impression through screens: the orchestra in white muslin dresses and crimson sashes. Bare arms. Men drinking, smoking, etc. Violins.

The music 'murdering silence'.

INT. HOTEL. HEYST'S BEDROOM. NIGHT.

Heyst lying on bed, awake, under mosquito net. Music rasping from garden.

VICTORY

INT. HOTEL DINING-ROOM. DAY.

Heyst eating, alone.

Schomberg telling story on the veranda. Loud laughter from the veranda.

EXT. SURABAYA HARBOUR. DAY.

Heyst walking along the quayside. He passes a street market. The girls from the orchestra at various stalls, examining trinkets, etc.

Mrs Zangiacomo ushers them along.

Heyst approaches a small house.

INT. DOCTOR'S SURGERY. DAY.

Doctor examining Heyst with stethoscope. He completes the examination.

> DOCTOR
> All correct, I would say. Shipshape.

> HEYST
> Ah.

> DOCTOR
> But you were right to come, however. Eighteen months is a long time. Never know what the body can get up to. No doctor on your island, Heyst?

> HEYST
> Nothing on my island. Some natives on the west coast. We have no social intercourse.

> DOCTOR
> Must be a funny life.

> HEYST
> It suits me.

Heyst begins to put on his shirt.

> DOCTOR
> What happened to that partner of yours? Morrison.

> HEYST
> Dead. Died in Sussex. Went back to England. Died of a
> cold.

> DOCTOR
> Did he? Poor chap.

EXT. NICARAGUAN CREEK.

One year earlier.

*Pedro, carrying bags, Ricardo, carrying cash box and Jones
walking along beach to small boat. They climb into it. Pedro picks
up oars and begins to row. The boat moves away from the beach.*

EXT. HOTEL VERANDA. NIGHT.

*Heyst lying on easy chair on veranda, eyes closed. Music
screeching from concert hall. He opens his eyes abruptly. Stares at
concert hall.*

*Stands, walks across the garden towards it. Pushes calico curtain.
Goes in.*

INT. HOTEL CONCERT HALL.

Fiddles and a grand piano. 'An instrumental uproar'.

Zangiacomo conducting. Mrs Zangiacomo at the piano.

Dutch and Eurasian businessmen drinking Jenever and beer.

Heyst sits, grimacing.

Music comes to an end. Applause.

The women come down from the platform and join men at the tables.

Some sit together at the empty tables, to be joined by men.

*Mrs Zangiacomo and Lena remain on the platform. Lena is a
slim, frail girl of nineteen. Mrs Zangiacomo arranging music at
the piano. Lena motionless. Mrs Zangiacomo suddenly goes across
to Lena, bends over her, pinches her arm. Lena jumps up quickly
and goes down into the hall, where she stands, uncertain.*

Mrs Zangiacomo passes her roughly.

Men and women moving about. Lena remains standing.

Heyst gets up and goes to her.

HEYST

Excuse me. That woman did something to you. She
pinched you, didn't she? I saw it.

She looks at him, speaks nervously.

LENA

And what are you going to do about it if she did?

HEYST

I don't know. What would you like me to do?
Command me.

LENA

Command you?
                    (*She studies him.*)
Who are you?

HEYST

I am staying in this hotel – for a few days.

LENA

She pinched me because I didn't get down here quick
enough.

HEYST

Well, as you are down here now, won't you sit down?

They sit.

> Do you sing as well as play?

LENA

> Never sang a note in my life. Never had any reason to.

Pause.

HEYST

> You are English?

LENA

> What do you think?

HEYST

> How do you come to be here, with this ... orchestra?

LENA

> Bad luck.

INT. HOTEL KITCHEN. NIGHT.

*Steaming saucepans, vats, etc. The ladies of the orchestra cooking
for themselves.*

*Schomberg comes in, looks about, sees Lena in a corner of the
kitchen stirring a saucepan, goes towards her. He touches her arm.
Lena throws his hand away from her. The other women observe
this and turn away.*

SCHOMBERG
(*whispering*)

> Listen to me. Listen. You're adorable, adorable. You're
> a thing –

LENA

> Stop it!

SCHOMBERG
(*whispering*)

> A thing of beauty. Put your trust in me. I'm in the prime

of my life. Look at me. Listen. I'll sell this hotel, we'll buy another one, somewhere else, just you and me –

She breaks away from him and leaves the kitchen.

INT. HOTEL. SCHOMBERG'S BEDROOM. NIGHT.

Mrs Schomberg sitting at dressing-table in her night clothes, looking into a mirror.

Schomberg comes in. He stands, looking at her reflection in the mirror. She does not meet his gaze.

INT. HOTEL. WOMEN'S BEDROOM. EVENING.

Two ladies of the orchestra doing their hair. Lena lying on her bed, crying into the pillow.

The women speak in broken English.

> FIRST WOMAN
> Stop that crying, you stupid bitch!

> LENA
> I'm ill. Tell them I'm ill.

> SECOND WOMAN
> Cry-babies make me sick.

First Woman leans over Lena.

> FIRST WOMAN
> There's nothing special about you, my darling.

Mrs Zangiacomo appears at the door. She claps her hands. The two women leave the room.

Lena looks up.

> LENA
> I'm not well.

Mrs Zangiacomo goes to the bed, yanks Lena off the bed.

Lena falls to the floor, clutching the bedclothes. Mrs Zangiacomo pulls her to her feet.

MRS ZANGIACOMO
If I have any more of this, we'll kick you out and leave you in this place to rot.

INT. HOTEL CONCERT HALL. NIGHT.

It is the interval. Scene as before. The camera moves through men and women drinking and laughing, to find Heyst and Lena at the corner table.

LENA
My dad was a musician. My mum ran away. He taught me the violin. He was a drunk. He had a paralytic stroke. They put him in a home for incurables. I had seven shillings and sixpence in my purse when I left him in that home.
> (*She looks at him.*)

What country . . . do you come from?

HEYST
I am a Swede.

LENA
Oh. But what are you –

HEYST
I live on an island. I came ashore . . . on some business. I'm returning shortly.

LENA
Oh, are you? Listen, what is the name of this place? This town we're in?

HEYST
Surabaya.

LENA

You see, what happens is, we just come off a steamer,
we go to a hotel, we're locked up, we get on another
steamer, we go somewhere else, I never know where I
am. And no one cares if I make a hole in the water the
next chance I get or not. Who lives with you, on this
island?

HEYST

No one. I like solitude.
                    (*Pause.*)
Have you thought of going to the British Consul?

LENA

What's that?

HEYST

He represents the British government. He might be able
to send you home.

LENA

There's no home to go to.
                    (*Heyst looks at her.*)
What did you mean by saying 'command me'?

HEYST

Precisely that.

They sit looking at each other.

*The Zangiacomos go back to the platform, followed by the other
girls. Lena stands and follows them.*

THE ORCHESTRA.

Lena playing the violin.

EXT. HOTEL GARDEN. MIDNIGHT.

Heyst walking backwards and forwards under the black shadows of the trees. The Japanese lanterns are extinguished. They swing gently. He stops. He sees something white flitting between the trees. It disappears.

Suddenly Lena is in his arms, clinging to him.

LENA

I saw you. I saw you. I had to come to you.

HEYST
(*holding her*)

Calm, calm.

She becomes still in his arms.

It will be all right.

LENA

I knew it would be all right the first time you spoke to me. You spotted something in me, didn't you? In my face. It isn't a bad face, is it? I'm not twenty yet. All these men – they pester me all the time –

He takes his arms away.

What is it? What's the matter? I don't lead them on. I don't look at them. Did I look at you? I did not. You began it.

HEYST

Yes. I began it.

Pause.

LENA

I am dead tired.

He holds her.

HEYST

I shall steal you ... from here.

Her body stills. She looks up at him.

I shall take you with me. Will you come?

                    LENA
Yes. Yes.
                    (*Pause.*)
I will.
                    (*Pause.*)
Will you . . . take care of me?

                    HEYST
Yes.

Pause.

                    LENA
What will I ever talk to you about?

                    HEYST
Your voice is enough. I am in love with it, whatever it
says.

                    LENA
What is it called, your island?

                    HEYST
Samburan.

INT. HOTEL. HEYST'S BEDROOM. NIGHT.

He goes into the room, stands, looks at his face in the mirror.

INT. HOTEL LOBBY. DAY.

Long shot.

*Mrs Schomberg at counter. Lena standing by counter with a
newspaper.*

Lena murmurs.

Schomberg comes in.

Lena reads the newspaper.

Mrs Schomberg motionless.

Schomberg passes through.

EXT. SURABAYA HARBOUR. DAY.

Long shot.

Heyst talking to a Javanese boatman.

EXT. HOTEL GARDEN. DAY.

The ladies of the orchestra walking towards the concert hall.

Heyst approaches, stops.

Lena looks at him, then away.

The other ladies look at him.

INT. HOTEL BILLIARD ROOM. NIGHT.

A clock ticking.

Zangiacomo stands with Lena. She holds a lamp. He holds her other hand. She watches him tensely. He strokes her hand.

ZANGIACOMO
(*softly*)

You're a good girl. A good girl. Go to bed.

She withdraws her hand.

INT. HOTEL LANDING. NIGHT.

An unseen presence in foreground, breathing.

Lena, with the lamp, appears at the bottom of the flight of stairs and climbs them.

She reaches the top. A hand suddenly pulls her into an alcove.

SCHOMBERG

Ssh! No sound. I burn for you. I burn. You understand?
Yes, you understand. That man, that Swede, is after
you, isn't he? He talks to you. What does he talk about?

LENA

Nothing.

SCHOMBERG

He's a fool. Don't waste your time. He knows nothing
of women. He's a hermit. He lives on a derelict island.
He's a man of shadow. I am a man of substance. I know
about women. God, your body.

>   (*He strokes her upper arm.*)

Your body. You will stay when the others go. I'll send
my hag away. You provoke me, don't you? You
deliberately provoke me.

He reaches for her breast. She breaks away. Her dress rips.

INT. HOTEL. SCHOMBERGS' BEDROOM. NIGHT.

Mrs Schomberg in bed. Sound of running footsteps.

Schomberg comes in, looks at her. He undresses and gets into bed.

SCHOMBERG

Put the light out.

She does so.

EXT. HOTEL GARDEN. NIGHT.

Whispers. Shadows. A bundle thrown out of the window.

EXT. SURABAYA HARBOUR. DAWN.

A boat sailing away.

VICTORY

INT. HOTEL DINING-ROOM. MORNING.

The orchestra ladies, with Mrs Zangiacomo, at breakfast. They sit at one big table. One chair is empty.

In background Zangiacomo in the lobby.

ZANGIACOMO

Schomberg! Schomberg!

SCHOMBERG
(*VO*)

What are you shouting for? What is it?

ZANGIACOMO

What have you done with her?

SCHOMBERG
(*VO*)

What, what?

He comes into the shot.

Who?

The ladies look at each other in foreground. One giggles. Mrs Zangiacomo glares.

ZANGIACOMO

Where is she? My youngest! My youngest child! She's nowhere. She's not in her room. She's nowhere.

SCHOMBERG

Who, for God's sake?

ZANGIACOMO

Lena, you fool!

SCHOMBERG

Lena?

ZANGIACOMO

Where is she? She has disappeared.

VICTORY

Schomberg turns, goes out of shot, followed by Zangiacomo.

INT. HOTEL STAIRS.

Schomberg rushing up the stairs, followed by Zangiacomo.

INT. LENA'S ROOM.

Schomberg bursts in, followed by Zangiacomo.

Four beds. A violin sits on one bed.

ZANGIACOMO
I told you, she'd disappeared, idiot! What have you done with her?

SCHOMBERG
Me? Nothing! Nothing! What –

Chinese Servant appears at the door.

SCHOMBERG
(*to servant*)
What is it?

SERVANT
Mr Heyst has gone.

He goes.

Schomberg and Zangiacomo look at each other.

SCHOMBERG
Heyst!

ZANGIACOMO
Heyst, Heyst. Yes. Yes, of course. This is your fault. It is your fault.

Schomberg goes out, followed by Zangiacomo.

EXT. HOTEL VERANDA.

Schomberg comes along it with Zangiacomo. The ladies stand in background. Chinese servants gathering in the garden.

> SCHOMBERG
> (*shouting*)
>
> Heyst! Ruffian!

He turns to the ladies and the servants.

> When did he go? Who saw him? Did anybody see them?

> ZANGIACOMO
>
> It is your fault!

Zangiacomo attacks him, hitting him in the stomach, going for his throat. They stagger into the garden, fall, roll over, Zangiacomo lunging wildly at Schomberg.

EXT. HOTEL GARDEN.

Schomberg and Zangiacomo grappling on the grass. Ladies on the veranda. One screams. Servants climb up trees and sit watching. Schomberg picks Zangiacomo up, throws him to the ground and falls on him. Zangiacomo lies still, breath crushed.

INT. HOTEL LOBBY.

Mrs Schomberg sitting at her counter, still.

EXT. SAMBURAN ISLAND. DAY.

Lena and Heyst standing on the shore.

Behind them a boat going away.

VICTORY

CHANG STANDS, LOOKING AT THEM.

THE ISLAND — HER POINT OF VIEW.

*One long bungalow. Smaller bungalows across the clearing.
Decay. Trees encroaching on the bungalows. Jungle.*

LENA'S FACE.

EXT. SURABAYA HARBOUR. DAY.

A mail boat at anchor.

*Schomberg's launch among other hotel launches alongside it.
Painted on Schomberg's launch: 'Schomberg's Hotel'. Boatmen
shouting: 'Imperial Hotel', 'Hotel Splendide', etc.*

EXT. JONES'S FACE.

He is leaning over the rail. He looks down at Schomberg.

> JONES
> Mr Schomberg?

> SCHOMBERG
> At your service, sir.

> JONES
> I would like to take rooms at your hotel.

> SCHOMBERG
> Certainly, sir.

Jones withdraws.

SCHOMBERG'S LAUNCH.

*Jones and Ricardo climbing into the launch, followed by Pedro
with luggage.*

*Jones has a long, thin face and a long, thin body. He wears a
white suit.*

335

Ricardo is thick-set, muscular, pock-marked.

Pedro is hairy, flat-nosed, squat and brown-skinned.

JONES
(*of Ricardo*)
My friend must have the room next to mine.

SCHOMBERG
Certainly, sir.

Schomberg looks at Pedro.

JONES
Pedro needs a mat to sleep on. Any grog-shop will do.

Schomberg steers the launch towards the shore. Jones leans back, closes his eyes.

Schomberg catches Ricardo's gaze. Ricardo grins at him.

EXT. QUAY.

Jones and Ricardo driving away in a carriage.

Schomberg walking towards another carriage, followed by Pedro with bags, very close behind him, muttering to himself in an unknown language.

The carriage drives away.

EXT. HOTEL VERANDA. DAY.

Jones reclining. Ricardo sitting, shuffling a pack of cards.

INT. HOTEL LOBBY.

Schomberg comes in, looks at the two men on the veranda, collects the registration book, comes out to veranda.

EXT. HOTEL VERANDA.

SCHOMBERG

I have found your man a place.
(*They look at him.*)
May I have your names, please? For my book.

JONES

Our names? Ah. Yes. My name is Jones. A gentleman –
at large. This is Ricardo. Martin Ricardo. Secretary. Put
us down as tourists.

EXT. SAMBURAN ISLAND. DAY.

Heyst and Lena standing. Chang at a distance.

HEYST

This is Chang. He's the whole establishment.

LENA

Oh.

Chang impassive.

HEYST

This is the house. The sun's too heavy to stand about.
You'd better go in.

*He takes her to the steps of the bungalow. She leaves him, crosses
the veranda, goes in.*

*He turns back. Chang is pushing a truck along rusty rails. It
carries Heyst's bag and Lena's bundle. He stops the truck and
takes them out.*
(*Pointing to bundle.*)
Put that in the bedroom. Bring another bed from that
small house – for me. I will sleep at the end of the big
room.

Chang nods.

VICTORY

INT. HEYST'S BUNGALOW. MAIN ROOM. DAY.

Lena is standing in the room. Shutters closed. Slices of light. She looks about: a painting on the wall of a white-haired man sitting at a desk, heavy furniture, dozens of books.

Chang comes in with bundle. He goes into the bedroom, comes out, goes out of the house.

She goes into the bedroom.

INT. BEDROOM.

Bare. A large chest. Piles of books. Bed with mosquito netting. She looks about.

Heyst's voice.

> HEYST
> (*VO*)
>
Where are you?

> LENA

I'm in here.

He comes into the bedroom.

I'm sorry. This is your room.

> HEYST

No. Yours.

> LENA

Mine?

> HEYST

You have it.

> LENA

No. No, no. I can't. I can't take your bed. I don't want to.

338

HEYST

You're not taking it. I'm giving it to you.

LENA

But where will you –

Heyst puts his finger to her mouth.

HEYST

Not another word. Have you said good day to my
father?

LENA
(*startled*)

What?

He laughs.

HEYST

In here.

INT. HEYST'S BUNGALOW. MAIN ROOM. DAY.

They come into the other room. He points to the painting.

HEYST

That's him.

LENA

Oh. He looks very gloomy.

HEYST

He was. And this is his furniture, and these are his
books. So when he died, you see, I brought him to live
with me here, at Samburan.

LENA

And now you've brought me.

Pause.

HEYST

Yes.

LENA

You've saved me.

Pause.

HEYST

There's only Chang – and me. It could become a prison for you.

LENA

No.

She suddenly sees cylinder gramophone and drops to her knees to examine it.

What's this?

HEYST

A gramophone. We can listen to music.

LENA

What music?

He looks at her gravely.

HEYST

Zangiacomo's Ladies' Orchestra.

She stares at him, and suddenly laughs.

CHANG STANDING IN THE CLEARING, LOOKING TOWARDS THE HOUSE.

EXT. HOTEL VERANDA. NIGHT.

Men standing with drinks. Ricardo walks on to the veranda.

RICARDO

Any of you gentlemen care for a game of écarté?

MAN

Splendid idea.

SECOND MAN

Very good idea.

Ricardo turns, looks into the shadows.

RICARDO

And you, sir, would you like to join us in a game?

Jones comes out of the shadows.

JONES

What a good idea.

SCHOMBERG, HALF HIDDEN BEHIND LOBBY DOOR, LOOKING OUT ON TO THE VERANDA.

Jones and Ricardo settling down to play cards with the two men.

EXT. SAMBURAN. MORNING.

Heyst on veranda, looking towards the sea. He listens. Light footsteps in the room behind him.

Lena comes out. He does not turn to her.

HEYST

Where have you been?

LENA

I've been doing my hair.

HEYST

I was wondering when you would come out.

LENA

I wasn't very far. You could have called. And anyway I wasn't so long . . . doing my hair.

HEYST

Too long for me, apparently.

Pause.

LENA

Well, you were thinking of me, anyhow. I'm glad. Do you know, it seems to me that if you were to stop thinking of me I should not be in the world at all.

HEYST

What on earth do you mean?

LENA

What I said – just what I said. You understand what I said.

HEYST

No, I don't.

LENA

I can only be what you think I am.

HEYST

Nonsense.

She puts her hand on his arm.

LENA

Don't forget we're alone. There's no one else here to think anything of me. Except Chang. And not even you know what he thinks. Do you? And don't forget I don't even know where we are, what this place is.

HEYST
(*briskly*)

There was a coal mine here. I was Number One. The manager. A friend I once had – it was his idea to start the mine. I agreed to help him. The business went bankrupt. I stayed. Come.
            (*He takes her hand.*)
Breakfast.

They go into the house.

INT. HEYST'S BUNGALOW. MAIN ROOM.

Breakfast is laid on the table.

LENA

Is that why you were impatient for me to come? You
were hungry?

HEYST

Famished.

He picks up a small bell and rings it.

INT. HOTEL LOBBY. NIGHT.

*Suddenly the door kicked open. Pedro enters with tray, on which
are empty glasses. Schomberg is sitting in the room, still. Pedro
puts tray down, waves his hand at it, mutters.*

Schomberg pours drink into glasses.

Pedro takes the tray, kicks door open, lurches out.

EXT. HOTEL GARDEN. NIGHT.

*Pedro with tray going towards concert hall. He goes in through
curtains.*

INT. HOTEL CONCERT HALL.

*A long trestle-table covered with a green cloth. Candlelight.
Twenty to thirty men around the table. Jones the banker. Ricardo
the croupier. Baccarat being played. Pedro silently serves the
drinks.*

INT. HOTEL LOBBY. NIGHT.

*Mrs Schomberg on the stairway, looks into the darkened billiard
room.*

MRS SCHOMBERG
(*whispering*)

Come to bed.

SCHOMBERG

Shut up!

She goes.

EXT. HOTEL GARDEN. NIGHT.

Shapes of men leaving the hotel grounds.

Candlelight going out in the concert hall.

Jones and Ricardo walking towards the hotel. Ricardo giggling.

INT. HOTEL BILLIARD ROOM.

Schomberg in the shadows. Door into lobby ajar. A chink of light. The figures of Ricardo and Jones pass through and go up the stairs.

Schomberg listens to the shutting of doors above.

Silence.

INT. HOTEL. JONES'S BEDROOM. NIGHT.

Jones lying on bed, fully dressed, staring at the ceiling.

INT. HOTEL. RICARDO'S ROOM.

Ricardo lying on bed, naked.

The door opens, Jones enters, closes door.

Ricardo does not move.

Jones goes to the window and looks out.

Silence.

VICTORY

INT. HOTEL BILLIARD ROOM.

Schomberg sitting in the shadows, licking his lips.

EXT. SAMBURAN. DAY.

Chang, in clearing, looking up.

CHANG'S POINT OF VIEW: THE MOUNTAIN RIDGE.

Two white specks moving, high up on the mountain ridge. They disappear.

EXT. FOREST.

Heyst and Lena walking under enormous trees festooned with creepers. Great splashes of light.

They emerge on to the highest point on the island. Rocks.

She looks out to sea.

THE SEA AND HORIZON. HEAT HAZE.

EXT. LENA AND HEYST.

She shuts her eyes.

> LENA
> It makes my head swim.

> HEYST
> Too big?

> LENA
> Too lonely. All that water. All that light.

> HEYST
> Come into the shade.

They sit under a tree.

LENA

How could you . . . how could you live here alone?
Before I came. And you were coming back here, weren't
you? Alone. Before you found me.

HEYST

Oh, yes.

LENA

But why?

Pause.

HEYST

Temperament.
> (*She looks at him, intently.*)

Well . . . Princess of Samburan . . . you're gazing at me.
What do you see?

LENA

You liked living here alone?

HEYST

Yes.

LENA

Then I don't understand why you . . . burdened yourself
. . . with me.

HEYST

You're not a burden.
> (*Pause.*)

You were being persecuted. You were . . . cornered.
> (*Pause.*)

Oddly, it was because of a cornered man that I found
myself here in the first place. He was in terrible debt. I
was able to help him. He was excessively grateful. He
decided I had saved his life, that I was his true, his only,
friend. He started the mine here. He implored me to
become its manager. It was absurd. I knew nothing

346

about coal and I suspected he didn't either. Anyway, I
gave in. I ran the mine, which naturally collapsed before
the year was out. And so that was the end of his dream.

LENA

What was his name?

HEYST

Morrison.

(*She starts, stares at him.*)

What is it?

LENA

What?

HEYST

What is it? You look –

LENA

Nothing. No, nothing. I – What name did you say?

HEYST

Name? Morrison. What of it?

LENA

He was your friend?

HEYST

Yes, yes.

LENA

Your partner?

HEYST

My partner, yes.

LENA

And he's dead?

HEYST

Yes, as I told you –

LENA

You never told me.

HEYST

Didn't I? I thought I had. But what is this? Have you
heard the name before?
(*She sits still, biting her lip.*)
Did you ever know anybody of that name?
(*She shakes her head.*)
Well, what is this mystery?

LENA

I've heard the name. But I didn't know ... that it was
your partner he was talking about.

HEYST

Talking? Who?

LENA

He was talking of you. But I didn't know it.

HEYST

Who was talking of me?

LENA

In that hotel. That man Schomberg, talking to my boss
and – sometimes – to others. It was impossible not to
hear what he said. He was so loud. He used to shout.

Heyst laughs.

HEYST

And what did he shout about?

Pause.

LENA

He used to talk of a Swede.

HEYST

He talked of a Swede? And what did he say of this Swede?

LENA

That he had had a partner called Morrison. That the
Swede first got all he wanted out of him, tricked him,
swindled him, then kicked him out to die – that he as
good as murdered him.

He stares at her.

HEYST

And you believed it?

LENA

I didn't know who he was talking about. I remember
him saying that everybody in these parts knew the story.

HEYST

Well, well.

(*Pause.*)

Can you remember any more? I've often heard of the
moral advantages of seeing yourself as others see you.
Let us go further. Can you recall anything else that
everybody knows – everybody but me?

LENA

Don't laugh!

HEYST

Laugh? I am not laughing, I assure you. The
abominable idiot!

He stands, walks away, stops.

Tell me – would you have gone with me if you had
known of whom he was speaking?

LENA

It was stupid of me to listen, stupid of me to remember
. . . and to repeat it to you.

HEYST

Schomberg! The man is an animal.

349

(*Pause.*)

Why should I care? I have never cared. It has never
mattered to me what anyone said or believed, from the
beginning of the world till the crack of doom. I have
lived a life of hard indifference. Do you understand? I
have simply been moving on, while others were going
somewhere. No aims, no attachments, no friends, no
acts. I leave all that to others. Let *them* live, as they call
it. But abuse and kill Morrison? No. He was an
innocent. I respected his innocence. I respected his
dreams.

Pause.

LENA

You are not a murderer.

HEYST

But you believed it?

LENA

I didn't know you.

HEYST

But just now – when you heard the name – you were
moved – you were shocked –

LENA

Because of the name. That was all. Because of the
name.

Pause.

HEYST

I feel disgust . . . at myself . . . as if I had fallen into a
filthy hole.

LENA

I can't believe anything bad of you.

He stands, clenched, moves away violently, and then suddenly swerves back, sits by her, takes her in his arms and kisses her.

She averts her face, lifts her arm against him.

He pulls her arm away. She resists. He seizes her roughly. Her dress rips. He embraces her fiercely.

EXT. HILLSIDE. DAY.

Long shot.

Two figures descending. Lena walks ahead of Heyst, apart from him.

As they draw nearer we see that Lena is in pain. Her dress is torn. She stumbles. Heyst is walking slowly. He stops. She continues, and then slowly stops. She stands for a moment with her back to him. He is still. She turns, looks at him. He walks to her.

> HEYST
> *(quietly)*
> Please ... forgive me.

INT. HOTEL BILLIARD ROOM. AFTERNOON.

Ricardo sitting with pack of cards, shuffling. He looks up.

> RICARDO
> Take one! Come on, man. Take one. Quick.

Schomberg comes into the shot, takes a card from the pack.

> Look at it.
> *(Schomberg does so.)*
> King of Hearts. Right?

> SCHOMBERG
> Yes.

> RICARDO
> I can make you take any card I like nine times out of ten.

351

Schomberg sits at the table. Ricardo shuffles the cards in a number of elaborate ways.

SCHOMBERG

You're fond of cards?

RICARDO

Fond of cards?
(*He laughs.*)
Yes, you might say that. Picked it up at sea. Playing for tobacco. We'd keep a game going right through the night, round a chest, under a slush lamp. That was gambling for you!

SCHOMBERG

You were a sailor?

RICARDO

Bred to the sea from a boy. Worked up to be a mate. Then I met the guv'nor and I left the sea to follow him.

SCHOMBERG

Why?

RICARDO

Why?
(*He stares at Schomberg.*)
Why should I tell you?

SCHOMBERG

You are by no means obliged to.

RICARDO

Because he spotted me, that's why. Like that!
(*Clicks his fingers.*)
He knew everything about me the moment he looked at me. And he . . . touched me inside somewhere.
(*He looks at Schomberg.*)
Waste of time telling you this, really, isn't it? It's outside your grasp. Isn't it?

SCHOMBERG

What did he spot . . . in you?

RICARDO

Who I am. What I am.
                    (*Pause.*)
Sometimes I have a girl – you know – and I give her a
nice kiss and I say to myself: 'If you only knew who's
kissing you, my dear, you'd scream the place down.'
Hah! Not that I'd want to do her any harm. I just feel
the power in myself.

SCHOMBERG

I see.

RICARDO

Do you? Well, you and me, for instance, we're sitting
here having a friendly chat, and that's all right. You're
not in my way. But you don't mean a thing to me.
You're no more to me than that fly over there. I could
squash you or leave you alone. I don't care what I do.
Or I might get Pedro to break your neck. He'd catch
you round the waist and jerk your head backwards –
snap! I saw him do it to a big buck nigger once who was
waving a razor about in front of the guv'nor. He does it
well. You hear a low crack, that's all – and then the man
drops down like a limp rag.
          (*He smiles at Schomberg.*)
Mind you, I wouldn't ask him to do it unless you
irritated me in some way. I'm a reasonable man.

SCHOMBERG

I know you to be a reasonable man. And I'm sure Mr
Jones is a reasonable man.

RICARDO

Mr Jones! He's no more Mr Jones than you are. You're
pig ignorant. He's a gentleman. I spotted it at once. And

he spotted me. Like that! And so I followed him. And
I've followed him ever since.
>   (*He bends down, touches his ankle.*)
Look. What am I doing?

SCHOMBERG

You're scratching your ankle.

RICARDO

No, I'm not.

Ricardo straightens, with a knife in his hand.

SCHOMBERG

Gott in Himmel!

RICARDO

Comes in handy. Suppose some little difference of
opinion crops up during game. You drop a card. You
bend down to get it and you come up ready to strike. Or
you stay under the table. You wouldn't believe the
damage you can do under a table with a thing like this.

SCHOMBERG

I would.

Ricardo slips the knife back into a sheath attached to his shin.

RICARDO

You know where I got this knife? From a savage in
Nicaragua. You know his brother.

SCHOMBERG

I ... ?

RICARDO

Pedro. He was Pedro's brother. We'd run into a bit of
trouble, you see, the guv'nor and me. So we were hiding
up a creek in Nicaragua. We were carrying a cash box
with 320 sovereigns in it and 500 Mexican dollars. The
Mexican dollars weren't much good in Nicaragua but

we were thinking of popping up to Mexico for a game of cards, you see. Do you follow me?

SCHOMBERG

Oh yes. Yes.

RICARDO

Well, we came across this pair of alligator-hunters, up this creek. So we shared their hut with them. It was all right. Fresh fish, good game, everything lovely. No trouble. And these certain people who were looking for us, you see, they gave it up, as a bad job. But, unfortunately, these savages smelt the cash box, you see. I saw them smell it. And then I spied them sharpening their knives behind some bushes. So I said to myself: 'Hullo. They mean business.' Antonio was his name. The brother. The trouble was we only had one revolver between us – the guv'nor's six-shooter. Only five chambers loaded. No more cartridges. Well, it was time for dinner. Broiled fish and roast yams.

EXT. NICARAGUAN CREEK. EVENING.

A fire. Jones, Ricardo, Pedro, and Antonio eating. Jones and Ricardo silent. Pedro and Antonio occasionally grunt to each other. They cut their fish with large knives. They do not look up.

RICARDO

How's the fish, guv'nor?

JONES

Terribly good.

Jones finishes his fish.

Pedro and Antonio are silent.

Jones wipes his fingers on a silk handkerchief. He sighs, puts his hand behind his back, as if to get up, draws a revolver and shoots Antonio in the chest.

Antonio pitches forward on to the fire.

Pedro jumps up, runs away. Ricardo springs on to his back, gets his hands round his neck, strangles him. They fall.

Ricardo continues squeezing. Pedro is still.

Jones walks over and looks at him.

He isn't dead.

RICARDO

Anyone else would have been dead. He's an ox.

Jones remains looking down on Pedro, gun in hand, while Ricardo goes towards Antonio's body.

Ricardo pulls the body away from the fire, picks up Antonio's knife, drags Antonio's body to a stream and kicks it in. The body sizzles.

EXT. THE CREEK. LATER.

Pedro tied to a tree.

The rope goes round his throat and trunk, a reef-knot under his ear.

Ricardo asleep.

Jones sitting, smoking, by the fire, a blanket round his legs.

EXT. THE CREEK. MORNING.

Pedro tied to the tree. Eyes rolling, tongue hanging out.

Along the beach Jones and Ricardo setting up a mast on a small boat.

Ricardo looks back at Pedro croaking.

RICARDO

I think he wants to say something, sir.

JONES

Oh, he's probably thirsty.

VICTORY

RICARDO

Shall I give him some water?

JONES

Well, if he's thirsty, he'll probably appreciate it.

Ricardo collects a jug of water. He takes it to Pedro.

Pedro drinks. After drinking, he stares at Ricardo.

Jones approaches.

RICARDO

He's asking to be finished off. As a favour.

JONES

Oh no, no. We'll take him with us. He could be useful.

RICARDO

But will he be manageable?

JONES

Oh, I think so. Cut him loose.

Ricardo takes the knife from Antonio's corpse. He approaches Pedro. Pedro twitches, sweats. Ricardo goes behind him. Pedro wriggles. Suddenly becomes still. Ricardo cuts him loose.

Pedro, freed, feels his limbs. He looks up at Jones. He crawls towards Jones, puts his arm around Jones's legs, embraces his legs. Jones withdraws his legs, gently.

Right, Let's be off.

INT. HOTEL BILLIARD ROOM.

Schomberg leans across the table to Ricardo.

SCHOMBERG

Look here. Do you mean to say that all this really happened?

RICARDO

No. I was making it up as I went along, just to help you
through the hottest part of the day. Bring me a glass of
sirop. I'm parched.

*Schomberg goes to the bar, takes a bottle of Sirop de Groseille
from a shelf, pours pink liquid into a tumbler, splashes soda-water
into it.*

This is a dead-and-alive hole. Playing cards here is like
playing cards in a nunnery. Bloodless. Dried-up nuns.

Schomberg brings the tumbler to him. He drinks.

SCHOMBERG

I don't expect you're making a fortune out of them,
either?

RICARDO

Peanuts.

SCHOMBERG

Then why do you stick here? Men like you – you need
excitement – you need a challenge worthy of your
mettle.

RICARDO

Yes, you're right. Challenge is the word. He needs a
challenge. He gets these lazy moods sometimes. He's in
one now. But give him a real challenge – and he'll tense
up tight as a drum and go straight to the heart of the
matter.

SCHOMBERG
(*intensely*)

Listen to me.
(*Ricardo looks at him.*)
Listen. I could put you on a track. On the track of a
man.

RICARDO

Who? The man in the moon?

SCHOMBERG

No, no. Listen to me. I'm serious. This man lives on an
island, alone. He's rich. He's a thief. He has plunder.
He has plunder stowed away on this island.

RICARDO

How much plunder?

SCHOMBERG

A lot.

RICARDO

How do you know?

SCHOMBERG

I know.

RICARDO

What kind of plunder?

SCHOMBERG

Minted gold.

RICARDO
(*muttering*)

Minted gold, eh?

Pause.

SCHOMBERG

And cash. I have cast-iron evidence of this.

RICARDO

Who is he?

SCHOMBERG

He's a Swede. A baron. A Swedish baron.

RICARDO

A baron, eh? These foreign titles are usually fake. I'm a student of all that kind of thing, you see. Still . . . it might interest the guv'nor. A fake baron. He likes a duel, the guv'nor, especially if it's with a hypocrite. He doesn't favour hypocrites.

SCHOMBERG

I'll give you everything. Directions, provisions, a boat.

Ricardo stares vaguely over Schomberg's shoulder.

RICARDO

Oh yes?

SCHOMBERG

A fishing boat. A child could handle it. And at this season the Java Sea is a pond. You wouldn't even get a wet face.

RICARDO

Well . . . it might be of interest.

Schomberg turns sharply and looks behind him.

JONES LEANING AGAINST THE DOOR, LOOKING AT HIM.

EXT. SAMBURAN VERANDA. NIGHT.

Lanterns. Heyst reading. Lena cutting pages of a book with a kitchen knife.

In background in the room the cylinder gramophone playing. Rosalia Chalier singing.

She looks up at him.

LENA

I've done it. The book is ready to be read.

HEYST

Ah Good.

He continues to read.

LENA

What are you reading?

HEYST

Poems.

LENA

Read one to me.

(*Pause.*)

Will you?

HEYST

They're French.

LENA

You mean in the French language?

HEYST

Yes.

LENA

Oh. I wouldn't understand, would I?

HEYST

No.

Pause.

LENA

Unless you told me what it meant?

He slowly looks up.

HEYST

Why not read something yourself, in English?

Pause.

LENA

I'm sleepy.

She stands, goes to him, kisses him lightly on the cheek, goes into the house.

He remains reading for a moment, then closes the book, turns out the lantern.

INT. BEDROOM. NIGHT.

Lena lying in the bed.

Heyst comes in, looks down at her.

HEYST

Are you asleep?

LENA

No. I'm not sleepy.

She reaches up, pulls him down. He sits on the bed. Her arms around his neck, she whispers.

Say something to me in French.

HEYST

Tu es très belle.

She looks into his eyes.

LENA

What does that mean?

He bends towards her. She flinches. He takes her face in his hands and kisses her gently.

INT. BEDROOM. NIGHT.

Later. Moonlight.

Under mosquito net Heyst lying on the bed. Lena sitting by him, bathing his naked chest and stomach with a sponge.

He lies still, looking up at her.

INT. JAVA SEA. DAY.

A boat far out to sea, becalmed. Heat. Three figures gradually discerned reclining in the boat. The mast slowly sways.

INT. MAIN ROOM. AFTERNOON.

Heyst standing in the open doorway, looking into a glass, trimming his beard.

Lena comes into the room. She takes the scissors, begins to trim his beard.

> **HEYST**
> There is no need –

> **LENA**
> Why not?

She trims his beard in silence and then gives him the mirror.

> There. Am I a good barber?

Heyst laughs, uncertainly, takes the scissors, puts them in a drawer.

Lena sits.

> You should try to love me.

> **HEYST**
> Try? But it seems to me –
> > *(Pause.)*
> What do you mean?

> **LENA**
> You should try to love me as people do love each other when it is to be for ever.
> > *(Pause.)*
> That is what I mean.

Heyst goes to her, looks down at her.

HEYST
Nothing can break in on us here.

He bends, lifts her out of the chair. She throws her arms around his neck, clasping him. He holds her, swings her round. She kisses him, then looks swiftly over his shoulder, gasps.

CHANG IN THE ROOM.

THE ROOM.

Lena disengages herself and slips swiftly into the bedroom.

Heyst stares at Chang.

Chang does not move.

HEYST
What do you want?

CHANG
Boat out there.

HEYST
Boat? Where?

CHANG
On reef. In trouble. White men.

Heyst stares at him.

HEYST
White men?

In background Lena appears at the bedroom door and watches them through the curtain.

Heyst leaves the room, followed by Chang.

EXT. CLEARING.

Low sun, ruddy glare, long shadows from trees.

Heyst running towards the jetty. He looks out to the reef.

EXT. THE REEF.

*The boat ricocheting against the rocks on the ocean side of the reef.
The water on the shore side of the reef is calm. Two figures
glimpsed lying in the boat. Another figure crouched, stumbling.*

HEYST AND CHANG IN CANOE.

They row the canoe to the reef.

*Heyst climbs onto the reef, holding rope which is attached to the
canoe. He attempts to control the rocking boat, slipping on the
rocks. He finally manages to attach the rope to the boat.*

*Heyst jumps into the canoe and he and Chang, with great effort,
pull the boat round the reef into calm water.*

They tow the boat back towards the jetty.

EXT. THE JETTY.

*Heyst and Chang climb out of the canoe on to the jetty. They look
down at the boat.*

EXT. THE BOAT.

The boat rocking gently up and down by the jetty.

*Jones, Ricardo and Pedro lying twisted in the boat. Their faces
are blotched, blistered.*

Ricardo tries to sit up, fails.

*A cork helmet floats alongside the boat. A large, earthenware jug,
uncorked, rolls about.*

RICARDO
(*hoarsely*)

Hello.

He suddenly stands, swaying.

Water.

Heyst kicks a large brass tap projecting above the planks. It does not budge.

HEYST
(*to Chang*)

Crowbar!

Chang runs to the end of the jetty.

Ricardo sits abruptly, choking.

RICARDO

Water.

Chang runs back with crowbar.

Heyst levers the tap with a jerk. Water trickles out of the pipe and suddenly gushes.

Ricardo crawls to the pipe, squats under it, clutches the end of the pipe, gurgles as he drinks, water soaking him.

Pedro sits up, charges, flings Ricardo away, sits under the pipe and drinks.

Ricardo picks up an oar and slams Pedro's head with it.

Pedro hangs on to the pipe. Ricardo hits him again. Pedro lets go of the pipe. Ricardo kicks him in the ribs. Pedro crawls away.

Ricardo looks back at Jones, who is still lying, supine. He helps Jones up, guides him to the pipe.

Here you are, sir. Steady.

Jones drinks.

HEYST WATCHING.

RICARDO AND JONES.

Ricardo looks up at Heyst.

RICARDO
Forty hours. No water.

Jones comes away from the pipe, tunic soaked. He steadies himself on Ricardo's shoulder, looks up at Heyst and smiles a ghastly smile.

HEYST
(to Ricardo)
Isn't that man of yours bleeding to death?

RICARDO
Man? He's not a man. He's an alligator.
(He shouts.)
Aren't you? Olé! Pedro! Dungheap! You're an alligator!
Aren't you?

PEDRO
(weakly)
Señor?

RICARDO
(to Heyst)
What did I tell you?

Heyst signals to Chang to stop the water. Chang does so and stands still, crowbar in hand.

JONES
I'm afraid we aren't presenting ourselves in a very favourable light.

HEYST
Please come ashore.

JONES

Very kind.

Helped by Ricardo from below and by Heyst from above, Jones climbs on to the jetty.

Ricardo follows.

Ricardo bends down, scratches his leg, stays crouched for a moment, looking up at Heyst. He then slowly stands upright.

EXT. ISLAND.

Long shot. Twilight.

Pedro climbs out of the boat with bags.

Heyst, Jones and Ricardo stand together.

Chang and Pedro stand on the periphery of the group.

Silence.

THE GROUP.

JONES

We are indebted to you.

He sways. Ricardo helps him.

RICARDO

Lost our bearings. Heading for Batavia. Lost our bearings. Ran out of water. Sun beating down. Thought we were dead.

HEYST

I am not able to offer you a share of my own quarters but I can give you a temporary home. Come.

He moves away.

Jones remains still.

JONES

It is like a dream.

HEYST

Sir?

JONES

A jetty, a white man, houses – it's a dream.
        (Pause.)
A lovely dream.

Jones, swaying on Ricardo's shoulder, smiles at Heyst.

LONG SHOT.

The group walking towards a bungalow.

JONES
(VO)

There is a settlement of white people here, I take it?

HEYST
(VO)

No, no. Abandoned. Abandoned. Long ago. I am alone.

They walk up the steps of the bungalow.

Chang tries to unlock the door. He puts his shoulder to it. It explodes in the silence, reverberating in the night.

They go in.

EXT. HEYST'S BUNGALOW: VERANDA. NIGHT.

Lena sitting in shadow. A lantern on the steps lights only her feet and the hem of her dress.

She watches Heyst approach. Across the clearing a small fire is now burning outside Jones's bungalow. Candlelight in the windows. Heyst walks up the steps, stops.

LENA

It's me.

Pause.

HEYST

You can't be seen. Good.

LENA

Why?

(*Heyst does not answer.*)

Why good?

HEYST

I don't know.

LENA

Who are they?

HEYST

I don't know.

EXT. CLEARING. NIGHT.

The two bungalows.

Moonlight. Stillness.

INT. THE BEDROOM. NIGHT.

Lena wakes up. She is alone. She gets up, goes to curtain, looks through it into main room. Heyst opening drawers, looking into them.

She goes into the room.

INT. MAIN ROOM.

A lantern is on low.

LENA

What are you looking for?

He shuts the drawer.

> HEYST

Did you see Chang in this room at all – last evening?

> LENA

No.

> HEYST

At any time?

Pause.

> LENA

What's the matter?

> HEYST

I left you asleep. What woke you?

> LENA

A dream. You've lost something. What is it?

> HEYST

What dream?

> LENA

You weren't by me. You had gone. I put my arms out. I turned to you, but you weren't there.

> HEYST

That's not a dream.

> LENA

What have you lost? I have touched nothing.

He turns to her.

> HEYST

Lena . . .

> LENA

We are still strangers to each other. You don't know me very well.

HEYST

I asked if you had seen Chang in here, last evening.

LENA

What has he stolen? Money?

HEYST

No, not money. There is no money.

LENA

What, then?

HEYST

Something . . . of a certain value.

LENA

Well, ask him to give it back to you.

HEYST

Mmnn.

>(*Pause.*)

Go back to bed. I'll come. I'll just smoke a cheroot on
the veranda.

>(*He touches her arm.*)

I'll come.

EXT. VERANDA. NIGHT.

Heyst walks on to the veranda, sits, lights cheroot.

LONG SHOT.

View of Heyst's veranda. Glow of the cheroot.

Ricardo in foreground, watching.

The cheroot is thrown into the night.

EXT. SAMBURAN ISLAND. DAWN.

High shot.

Glistening. Birds.

INT. JONES'S AND RICARDO'S BEDROOM. EARLY MORNING.

Jones asleep. Ricardo dressed. He slips quietly out of the room.

EXT. JONES'S BUNGALOW.

Ricardo comes out.

Pedro on veranda, folding the boat's mast. He places two oars beside it.

Ricardo steps into the clearing.

INT. HEYST'S BUNGALOW. MAIN ROOM.

Heyst comes out of bedroom, closes the door. He walks across the room, looks out towards the other bungalow.

EXT. CLEARING.

Ricardo up a tree, looking down on the clearing.

Pedro on the veranda.

Heyst appears, walking across the clearing to Jones's bungalow, knocks on the door, goes in.

Ricardo's eyes follow Heyst. He then looks back at Heyst's bungalow.

Chang suddenly standing by the side of the house. He disappears behind it.

Ricardo begins to descend the tree.

INT. JONES'S BEDROOM.

Jones in bed. The door closing, Heyst inside the room. Jones sits up.

HEYST

Good morning.

JONES

Good morning . . . to you.

HEYST

I hope you slept well.

JONES

Very well. Oh, terribly well. Thank you. Still quite weak, of course.

HEYST

Naturally.

JONES

We owe a great deal to you, Mr Heyst.

Pause.

HEYST

How do you know my name?

JONES

You introduced yourself to us last night.

HEYST

I don't recall doing so.

JONES

Don't you? How strange. But I am right, aren't I? Your name is Heyst, is it not?

HEYST

And yours?

JONES

Oh, mine is Jones. And his is Pedro.

Heyst turns to find Pedro sitting in the corner of the room, by the door.

INT. HEYST'S BUNGALOW. MAIN ROOM. MORNING.

Ricardo standing still in the room.

Silence.

He looks about the room, at the bookshelves, the painting, etc.

His eyes go to the closed door. He goes towards it, slowly, and soundlessly opens it.

The curtain.

A faint rustle from within. He carefully moves the curtain and looks in.

Lena, her back to him, combing her hair. Bare shoulders and arms.

INT. JONES'S BEDROOM.

> HEYST
> Where were you headed for – in your boat?

> JONES
> Madura.

Pause.

> HEYST
> Did you know I was living on this island?

> JONES
> You? I didn't know you existed, old boy.

Pause.

> HEYST
> Nevertheless, I believe there is something you want of me.

> JONES
> Oh?

HEYST

Yes. May I ask what it is?

JONES

Well ... Mr Heyst ... now that we have met ... I mean now that I know you exist ... there may be something I might want of you. But it's not urgent. I think I'll tell you what it is ... the day after tomorrow – after I have given the matter a little more thought.

HEYST

What matter?

JONES

Oh, the matter ... the matter ... You and I have much more in common than you think, you know.

HEYST

I do not see that.

JONES

Well, we *are* both gentlemen, aren't we?

INT. HEYST'S BUNGALOW. BEDROOM.

Lena turns sharply.

Ricardo springs, puts his hand to her mouth. He holds her tightly with his other arm.

INT. MAIN ROOM.

Chang. He stands, listening.

Scuffling, grunts, thuds, chair falling.

Chang leaves the room.

INT. BEDROOM.

Lena knees Ricardo in the groin. He falls back, sits abruptly against the wall.

He clutches his throat, squeezes his legs together. He stares at her.

She staggers, sits on the bed, adjusts her sarong around her, sits still, stares down at him.

A chair with a dress on it has overturned. Ricardo's slipper has come off.

Ricardo looks at her with a half-smile.

RICARDO

I wasn't going to hurt you. You surprised me, that's all.
                    (*Pause.*)
I didn't expect you, you see.
                    (*Pause.*)
Who are you?
          (*He massages his neck, grins.*)
You're not tame, are you?
          (*She remains still. He gazes at her.*)
You're a tiger.
                    (*Pause.*)
Listen, you wouldn't say anything ... would you ... to anyone ... about this?
          (*She slowly shakes her head.*)
Good girl.

LENA

What do you want?

RICARDO

Yes, you're a real tiger. Listen to me. I think we can be friends. What do you think? Do you think so yourself?
                    (*Pause.*)
You're my kind. Aren't you?

LENA

Am I?

RICARDO

Yes. I feel it. Here!

He punches himself in the stomach.

LENA

What do you want?

RICARDO

Money.

LENA

Whose money?

RICARDO

His money.
(*Pause.*)
Where does he keep it? Do you know?

LENA

What?

RICARDO

Does he keep it in the house?

LENA

No.

RICARDO

Sure?

LENA

Sure.

RICARDO

Where, then? Do you know?

She looks at him and then nods, slowly.

He takes her hand, clasps it.

You're my kind. Aren't you?

LENA

Yes.

RICARDO

Tell me something. Is he a good shot?

LENA

Yes.

RICARDO

So's my guv'nor. Better than good. I'm not so hot. This
is what I use.

He lifts is trouser leg. Lena studies the knife strapped to his shin.

LENA

Aah.

Suddenly Heyst's voice is heard.

HEYST
(*VO*)

Chang!

CHANG
(*VO, fainter*)

Sir?

HEYST
(*VO*)

Coffee ready?

CHANG

Sir.

*Ricardo turns to the door, reaches down, stays crouched, knife in
hand, facing the door.*

HEYST
(*VO*)

Lena!

LENA

Yes, in a minute.

She touches Ricardo's shoulder. He whips round to her, knife at her breast.

She points to a window high in the wall, picks up a chair, places it under the window. He moves to it.

INT. MAIN ROOM.

Heyst looking out of the front window. Chang comes in with a tray of coffee.

Heyst turns and looks towards the bedroom.

INT. BEDROOM.

Ricardo gone. Shutters swinging at the window.

Lena sees his slipper. She picks it up, stands in the centre of the room, aims.

> HEYST
> (*VO*)

Lena! Breakfast!

> LENA

Yes.

She throws the slipper through the window.

EXT. BUNGALOW.

Ricardo under the window. The slipper flies through it. He catches it, puts it on. He whistles shortly.

INT. BEDROOM.

Lena standing. Ricardo's whistle. She goes into the main room.

INT. MAIN ROOM.

Heyst is sitting at the table. Lena comes in. He looks at her.

> HEYST

Your face is white. What is it?

> LENA

No, nothing. I just felt a little giddy. I didn't want –

She sways. He goes to her.

> HEYST

You're ill.

> LENA

I'll –

Her eyes close.

He picks her up, carries her into the bedroom.

INT. BEDROOM.

He lays her on the bed, stands, closes shutters at the window. He sits with her. She clutches his hand, smiles, closes her eyes.

EXT. THE CLEARING.

Ricardo running along the verge of the clearing, keeping out of sight in the bush.

He arrives eventually at the other bungalow. He stops, takes a deep breath, composes himself, goes in.

INT. JONES'S BUNGALOW. BEDROOM.

Jones sitting cross-legged against the wall.

Ricardo comes in.

> RICARDO

Ah! Sir!

> JONES

Where have you been?

RICARDO

Oh, nosing around. Just nosing around. I knew you had
company. I saw him come in.

JONES

You're out of breath. What's the matter?

RICARDO

Matter? Nothing. Thought I'd have a little run, that's
all. Exercise.

Jones stares at him.

JONES

Exercise?

RICARDO

So you had a talk with him?

JONES

You ought to have been here.

RICARDO

I will be next time. Just play him easy. We don't want
him to start prancing. Play him easy. For at least a
couple of days. I think I can find out a lot in a couple of
days.

JONES

Oh yes? How?

RICARDO

By watching.

JONES

Why not pray a little, too?

RICARDO
(*laughing*)

That's a good one.

Pause.

JONES

You can be certain of at least two days.

Pause.

RICARDO

You trust me, don't you?

JONES
(*slowly*)

Trust you? Oh yes. I trust you.

RICARDO

We'll pull it off. Take my word.

JONES

Mmnn. I have a peculiar feeling about this. It's not like
anything else ... we've done. It's a different thing. It's a
sort of test.

INT. HEYST'S BUNGALOW. BEDROOM.

Lena asleep. Heyst leaves her.

INT. MAIN ROOM.

Heyst closes door to bedroom, softly. Turns.

Chang.

Silence.

CHANG

I go now.

HEYST

Oh?

CHANG

I no like this. I go.

Pause.

HEYST

What don't you like?

CHANG

I know plenty.

HEYST

Oh do you?

(*Pause.*)

Are you frightened of the white men? Is that why you stole my revolver?

Chang opens the front of his shirt, slaps his bare chest.

CHANG

No revolver! Look!

HEYST

Well, where have you hidden it?

He moves slightly towards Chang. Chang jumps back.

If you give me back my revolver, no one will be frightened.

CHANG

No revolver.

They stare at each other. Chang points to the bedroom.

I no like that.

HEYST

What?

CHANG

Two.

HEYST

Two? Two what?

CHANG

You no like that fashion, Number One, if suppose you know.

384

HEYST

What are you talking about?

CHANG

I go now.

He goes.

INT. JONES'S BUNGALOW. BEDROOM.

Jones in same position.

Ricardo sitting.

RICARDO

Mind you, I'll tell you the truth, sir, it's hard ... to be patient. I find it hard. I want to rip him, you see. I want to rip him and have done with it.

JONES

But if you ripped him, old chap, you might never find your precious money.

RICARDO

My precious money? You're after the money as much as me, aren't you?

JONES

Oh, money isn't everything, you know.

A knock at the door.

Heyst comes in.

Ah, Mr Heyst. Here you are again. Come in.

Heyst closes the door.

The door opens behind Heyst. Pedro comes in. He closes the door and stands by it.

HEYST

I'm sorry to intrude.

JONES

Not at all, not at all.

HEYST

I have come to tell you that my servant has deserted – gone off.

JONES

Oh really? Why has he done that?

HEYST

I think he didn't like your looks.

JONES

Whose looks? Not Martin's surely? I have always thought Martin was rather good-looking.

HEYST

All your looks. The point is that he is armed. He has a revolver. He doesn't like your presence here. I thought I should warn you.

JONES

But where has he gone?

HEYST

There's a native tribe on the other side of the island.

JONES

Oh, is there really?
            (*Pause.*)
Rather a bore to lose a good servant. They're not easy to find. However, we have one
            (*to Ricardo*),
haven't we? Why don't we let Mr Heyst have our Pedro?

HEYST

No. I couldn't possibly deprive you –

RICARDO

No, that's a good idea. Pedro can look after all hands.

JONES

He's a surprisingly subtle cook, actually. Aren't you, Pedro?

RICARDO

Damned good idea.

HEYST

It's really not necessary –

RICARDO

We'll send him over at once, to start cooking your dinner. I'll tell you what, I'll come and join you for dinner, in your bungalow, if I may? The guv'nor's still feeling weak, so I suggest we send his dinner over here, tonight.

> (*He turns to Pedro.*)

Like to cook special dinner for the gentleman tonight, Pedro?

> (*Pedro stares at him.*)

He's thrilled.

> (*Ricardo turns back to Heyst.*)

Have you got the key to the store-room on you, Mr Heyst? I'll give it to our Pedro.

Silence in the room. The three men stare at Heyst.

Heyst slowly takes out the key, gives it to Ricardo, leaves the room.

Silence.

I've got a little plan, sir.

Jones says nothing.

I think I'll shave.

He goes to his bag, takes out looking-glass, etc. Goes on to the veranda.

Pedro! Hot water!

EXT. VERANDA.

Ricardo takes off his shirt, hangs the glass, etc.

Jones watching him through the open door.

Pedro brings a pan of hot water, puts it down.

Ricardo places the key carefully on the veranda rail. He begins to shave, humming.

Jones watches him through the open door.

INT. HEYST'S BUNGALOW. BEDROOM. EARLY AFTERNOON.

Lena, lying, eyes open. Heyst bending over her.

LENA

I'm better.

HEYST

Can you walk?

LENA

Of course.
(She sits up, swings her legs to the side of the bed.)
I'm better. What is it?

HEYST

We must find Chang.

LENA

Find him? What –

HEYST

Come.

EXT. HEYST'S BUNGALOW.

Pedro, in front of house, stooping over fire, with saucepans.

Heyst and Lena pass by him without looking at him.

Pedro stands, stares after her.

Heyst and Lena go into the bush.

EXT. JONES'S BUNGALOW. VERANDA.

Ricardo on the veranda. He gazes at the two figures going into the bush.

Pedro running towards him.

Ricardo glances quickly inside the open door of the room, sees Jones sitting by the wall, eyes closed.

Ricardo walks quickly towards Pedro, stops him.

> PEDRO
> (*pointing*)

Woman!

> RICARDO
> (*whispering*)

Woman? Of course there's a woman. We know that.
Now shut up! Go back! Cook dinner!

Pedro goes back to the fire.

Ricardo looks up towards the forest.

EXT. THE FOOTHILLS.

Two white figures disappearing.

EXT. THE FOREST.

Heyst and Lena approaching Chang's hut.

Heyst goes in.

INT. CHANG'S HUT.

Empty. Signs of hurried evacuation.

Heyst leaves.

EXT. THE FOREST.

Lena waiting. Heyst to her.

HEYST

Gone. Let us go on.

LENA

Where has he gone?

HEYST

To the tribe.

INT. STORE-ROOM. AFTERNOON.

Ricardo ripping sacks. Flour, rice, dried fish, erupting from the sacks. Ricardo feverishly searching. Nothing. He stands still, sticks his knife into another sack, viciously rips it.

EXT. HILL PATH.

Heyst and Lena climbing up precipitous path. At its top is a barricade of felled trees.

HEYST

A barrier against the march of civilization.

They climb towards it.

They feared what was unknown, incomprehensible. And so they built this barricade. It's understandable. I must say I wish we were on the other side of it.

Lena seizes his arm, freezes.

VICTORY

LENA
Look!

EXT. THE BARRICADE.

Through piles of freshly cut branches, spear blades protruding.

HEYST AND LENA.

They stand still.

HEYST
Stay.
> (*She holds on to him.*)

I won't approach near enough to be stabbed, I promise you.

He moves forward.

EXT. THE BARRICADE.

Lena's point of view:

Heyst approaches the spears. He stops. Calls out in native language for Chang.

EXT. THE BARRICADE.

Spears pointing.

Chang suddenly appears through foliage, revolver in hand.

The spears withdraw.

LENA WATCHING.

HEYST AND CHANG.

CHANG
Not come any close, Number One.

HEYST

What harm can we do you?

CHANG

Men come after. Bad for these people. I shoot if you come. Now – finish!

HEYST

All right. Finish for me. But let the girl come through. I implore you.

Chang laughs.

CHANG

She even more bad trouble.

HEYST

No, no. These men – they do not know she is on the island.

CHANG

They know.
                    (*He points the gun.*)
They know.

The spears come back.

Lena watches as the spears return.

Heyst turns slowly from the barricade, goes back to her.

HEYST

He says no.

LENA

To what?

HEYST

He won't let you through.

LENA

Me? You were going to send me . . . in there? You wanted me to leave you?

(*He is silent.*)

I would not have gone. I would not have left you.

She takes his hand.

He leads her to a view of the sea, looks down.

HEYST

I've thought of their boat. But they have taken
everything out of her. The oars and the mast. To put to
sea in an empty boat would be death.
(*She looks inland, starts.*)
What is it?

LENA

Something moving.

HEYST

No doubt we are being watched. What does it matter?

He sits, stares out to sea.

THE SUN BEGINNING TO SINK.

LENA AND HEYST.

LENA

Perhaps they are our punishment.

HEYST

Punishment?

LENA

The way we live ... together. It is unlawful, isn't it?

He looks at her, laughs.

HEYST

You mean they are messengers of God? What God
could that be?
(*Pause.*)

Are you conscious of sin? I am not.

LENA

You took me up from pity. I threw myself at you. I am guilty.

HEYST
(*with emphasis*)

No. No. You are not guilty.
(*Pause.*)
Could I find the courage in me to cut their throats? The problem is I have nothing but a pen-knife. But even if it were a carving knife, would I have the courage? I've always thought cutting throats a vulgar, stupid exercise.
(*Pause.*)
But to be totally without power – to protect you – that is a bitter –

LENA

To protect me? It is you they are after.

HEYST

But why?

A gust of wind.

LENA

Look!

EXT. THE HEADLAND.

'*Black on a purple sea. Great masses of cloud piled up and bathed in a mist of blood. A crimson crack like an open wound zigzagged between them, with a piece of dark red sun showing at the bottom.*'

HEYST
(*indifferently*)

A thunderstorm.

INT. JONES'S BUNGALOW. EVENING.

Jones standing. He wears a smoking jacket and a cravat.

He picks up a gun from a table and puts it in a drawer. He places a chair.

He stands, uncertain. He goes to the drawer, takes the gun out, puts it in the pocket of his jacket. The gun weighs down the pocket. He takes it out. He rips his jacket off. He puts on a long, blue silk dressing-gown. He puts the gun in the dressing-gown pocket.

He looks into a mirror and tears his cravat off. He stands, trembling.

INT. HEYST'S BUNGALOW. EVENING.

Pedro laying the table. He goes out.

Thunder.

After a moment, Heyst and Lena enter.

They stare at the table, laid for dinner.

Heyst lights candelabra, takes it to the window, sets it on a table.

> HEYST
> To let them know we're back. Let's finish the game.

> LENA
> There are three places laid.

> HEYST
> We have a guest. The shorter one of the two. He is like
> . . . a jaguar. He is coming to dinner.

Lena sits in a chair.

> Something is being worked out. Perhaps they don't
> know what it is, either.

He picks up a table knife.

These are useless. Absolute rubbish – no edge, no point, no weight. A fork would be better.

LENA

No. You need a knife.

A whistle from outside.

Heyst walks to the window. Night has fallen. A flash of lightning.

HEYST

I have a crowbar somewhere. Could I stand in ambush by this door? Smash the first head that appears, scatter ... blood and brains? And then do it again? And then do it again?

LENA

No. It is a knife you need.

Heyst looks up at the painting of his father. He murmurs.

HEYST

He is responsible. The night he died I asked him for guidance. He said, 'Look on. Make no sound.' That is what I have done all my life. Until ... you.

The door opens. Ricardo comes in.

Mr Ricardo, my dear.

RICARDO

At your service, ma'am.
>   (*He flings his hat into a chair.*)
At your service.
>   (*To Heyst.*)
Don't like the look of the weather.
>   (*To Lena.*)
Pedro told me there was a lady about, but I didn't know I should have the privilege of seeing you tonight, ma'am.

(*To Heyst.*)

Had a pleasant walk?

HEYST

Yes. And you?

RICARDO

Me? I haven't moved. Why do you ask?

HEYST

Oh, you might have wished to explore the island. But I remind you it would not be totally safe.

RICARDO

Oh, that Chink. He's not much.

HEYST

He has a revolver.

RICARDO

So have you.

HEYST

Yes. But I'm not afraid of you.

RICARDO

Of me?

HEYST

Of all of you.

RICARDO

Oh. Aren't you?

The doors burst open. Pedro comes in with a tray. He sets dishes of rice and fish on the table and goes.

Extraordinary strong brute, ma'am, that one. Not pretty though, I'd agree with that.

Heyst sits. Ricardo sits.

Ricardo picks up a biscuit and eats it.

397

(*To Heyst.*)

Oh . . . before you start your dinner . . . sir . . . would you mind spending ten minutes with the guv'nor? He'd like to have a word with you.

(*Heyst looks at him.*)

He's not too well, and we've got to think of getting away from here.

HEYST

Getting away?

RICARDO

The best of friends must part. And, as long as they part friends, there's no harm done.

(*Pause.*)

Can I take you to him now? He's really keen to have a chat – before he can make up his mind to go away.

Heyst looks at Lena.

LENA.

She nods, almost imperceptibly.

INT. MAIN ROOM.

They all sit quite still.

Heyst stands abruptly. Ricardo's hand goes to his ankle, stops, scratches his leg.

Heyst goes to the door, looks out into the clearing. Lightning.

Ricardo takes Lena's hand.

She looks at him.

Heyst turns. Ricardo drops Lena's hand.

Lena stands, goes into the bedroom. The curtain falls behind her.

HEYST

Your man is outside.

RICARDO

Yes?

HEYST

Get rid of him.

RICARDO

You want him out of the way?

HEYST

Yes. Get rid of him.

RICARDO

You mean you want him out of the way before you let
me take you to the guv'nor?

HEYST

That is right.

Ricardo puts his fingers to his mouth and emits a piercing whistle.

A moment.

Pedro bursts in, looks wildly about. Ricardo raises his hand.
Pedro becomes still.

RICARDO

Go to the boat. Now! Understand?
                    (*Pedro stares.*)
The boat! At the jetty. Go there! You know what a boat
is?

PEDRO

Si . . . boat.

RICARDO

Go to the boat. And stay there. Till I whistle.
                    (*He whistles shortly.*)
Till I whistle.

399

(*Pedro goes.*)

The deal is on the square. God's honour. He'll stay there ... till I whistle. Will you come along now, sir?

HEYST

In a minute.

Heyst goes into the bedroom.

INT. BEDROOM.

The bedroom is dark. Heyst enters. A flash of lightning; Lena momentarily disclosed. He shuts the door, whispers.

HEYST

Lena.

LENA

Yes.

HEYST

You have a black dress. Put it on. Now.

Sound of material sliding. He waits.

She appears out of the dark.

LENA

I have it on.

HEYST

You have a dark veil. Where is it?

LENA

I have it.

HEYST

Listen. I am going to see the other man. You understand why?

LENA

Yes.

HEYST

Our friend is escorting me. As soon as we leave, go out
of the back door into the forest. Stay on the verge.
Cover your face with the veil, keep the house in sight.
Wait in the forest until you see three candles out of four
blown out and then one relighted. When you see that –
come back.

(*She takes his hand, gently, and holds it.*)

If you do not see that – before daylight – *do not come
back*. You understand me?

LENA

Yes.

HEYST

In that case, go to Chang. Yes – to Chang. The worst he
can do to you is shoot you, but he won't. I really think
he won't, if I am not with you. You understand?

LENA

Yes.

She raises his hand to her lips and kisses it.

HEYST

Lena . . .

He kisses her, leaves the room.

Lena alone.

INT. MAIN ROOM.

The bedroom door opens. Heyst comes in.

Ricardo is standing by the desk. He turns to Heyst and smiles.

EXT. THE CLEARING. NIGHT.

Thunder. Heyst and Ricardo walk towards Jones's bungalow.

They go up the steps. Ricardo opens the door.

RICARDO

Here he is, guv'nor.

INT. JONES'S BUNGALOW. BEDROOM.

Heyst and Ricardo come in.

Jones is standing, dressed in the blue silk dressing-gown, 'a painted pole'. His hands are in deep pockets.

Two candles are burning.

Heyst slowly walks into the room.

Ricardo stands, suddenly hesitant. He catches Jones's eye.

RICARDO

I'll pop back. I'm on a track.

He leaves the room abruptly.

Jones, startled, looks after him.

Heyst and Jones stand still.

JONES

Awfully close, isn't it?

HEYST

I haven't come here to discuss the weather.

JONES

No, I suppose you haven't.
          (*Suddenly.*)
Don't put your hand in your pocket! Don't!

INT. HEYST'S BUNGALOW. MAIN ROOM.

Lena sitting in black dress, under candelabra.

Ricardo comes in.

*He looks at her, adoring. He moves towards her. She raises a
hand. He stops still.*

RICARDO

I wouldn't harm you. You're my girl. You can feel how
quietly my heart beats. Ten times today when you, *you*,
swam in my eye, I thought it would burst out of my ribs
or leap out of my throat. It has knocked itself dead tired,
waiting for this evening. Feel how quiet it is.
> (*Pause.*)

Speak to me.

LENA

What is your name?

RICARDO

Martin Ricardo. Martin Ricardo.

LENA

That's a very nice name.

RICARDO

Yes. It is. Thank you.

He draws closer to her.

Have you found out ... where the plunder is?

LENA

Ah. Who knows where it is?

RICARDO

And who cares? You're right. You're my treasure.
You're my riches.
> (*Pause.*)

Still, the money must be somewhere. We'll find it. No
trouble. Yes. But what you want is a man, don't you? A
master that will let you put the heel of your shoe on his
neck. Don't you? I live for myself – and you shall live for
yourself too. These 'gentlemen' make a convenience of

403

people like you and me. You see, we can both be free,
you and me together. You have found your man in me.
Is that your thought?

Pause.

LENA

Yes.

RICARDO

I'll rip him. I'll rip them both. Never in his life will he
go into that room of yours again – never any more!

INT. JONES'S BUNGALOW. BEDROOM.

HEYST

I am not armed.

JONES

A question of prudence. That's all.
                    (*Pause.*)
I've heard of you, Mr Heyst.

HEYST

From whom?

JONES

We were staying at Schomberg's Hotel.

HEYST

Schom –

He stops.

JONES

What's the matter?

HEYST

Nothing. Nausea.
                    (*Pause.*)
Who are you?

JONES

Me? I'm just paying you a visit.

HEYST

For what purpose?

JONES

For your money.

Jones brings a handkerchief from his left-hand pocket and wipes his face. He raises his right hand in his right-hand pocket.

Don't move.

HEYST

I've told you, I am not armed.

JONES

You are armed. You are damn well armed!

Pause.

HEYST

What money?

Jones studies him. He is shivering.

JONES

I don't trust you at all, you know. I really think I should shoot you. Now.

HEYST

Yes. Do it. Why not?

JONES

Breeding. I suppose. Ha! But . . . don't misread me. I'm an adequate bandit.

HEYST

You're cracking an empty nut. There is no money.

JONES

Schomberg said there was! Martin told me there was!

(*He takes the revolver out of his pocket and cocks it.*)
Where did he go? Where is he? Why isn't he here with
me?

>   (*Violently.*)

He should be by my side!

>   (*He stills.*)

Money . . . money . . . one needs to play cards . . . to get
the game going . . . that's all.

>   (*Pause.*)

My life – I'll confess it – has been a search for new
impressions. I must say you've turned out to be
something quite out of common. That's the truth.

HEYST

There is no money. Schomberg is mad. He persecuted
the girl. He was possessed . . . with an insane and odious
passion for her. What he has told you of money is to do
only with malice and spite. Don't you see that?

Pause.

JONES

Girl? What girl?

>   (*Pause.*)

Girl?

HEYST

Oh, Mr Jones, you can't expect me to believe that you
didn't know I was living with a girl on this island.

Jones stares at him.

INT. HEYST'S BUNGALOW. MAIN ROOM.

RICARDO

With this.

He takes the knife out of its sheath.

Lena takes the knife out of his hand, gently.

LENA

Mmnn, yes.

She balances the knife in her hand.

RICARDO

It's been a good friend to me.
                    (*She holds it up to the light.*)
Listen, when we are going together about the world,
you'll always call me husband, won't you?

LENA

Of course.

INT. JONES'S BUNGALOW. BEDROOM.

Jones stands swaying against the wall. Heyst watches him.

JONES

A girl? Well, well.
                    (*He laughs.*)
Yes, that's why he shaved. He shaved under my nose.
For the girl.

HEYST

No, he –

JONES

Yes! I smelt it then. I tell you what, old chap, he's let me
down. That's what it is. A gentleman is no match for the
common herd, or, at least, that is the view of the
common herd. Your . . . girl is of the common herd too,
isn't she, your creature? You could hardly have found
her in a drawing-room.
                    (*He giggles.*)
He shaved . . . right in front of me.
                    (*He points the gun.*)
Come.

HEYST

The girl is not there.

They go out.

INT. HEYST'S BUNGALOW. MAIN ROOM.

Lena holding the knife.

LENA
(*softly*)
I'll be anything you like. I'll do anything you like.

Ricardo kneels, takes her foot, kisses it.

EXT. THE CLEARING. NIGHT.

Rain.

Jones and Heyst approaching Heyst's bungalow. Jones's revolver is at Heyst's back.

Through the lighted door they see Ricardo kneeling. He moves from her foot to her leg up to her stomach. He remains, nuzzling her stomach. She sits, throned, still, white.

Jones and Heyst stop.

JONES
Ah. So the girl isn't there?

CLOSE-UP: HEYST LOOKING.

JONES WHISPERING IN HEYST'S EAR.

JONES
Look on. Make no sound. Mud souls, obscene. Mud bodies. My . . . secretary. Look at it, kissing the belly of the nymph, and then up through her body to her lips.

INT. HEYST'S BUNGALOW. MAIN ROOM.

Ricardo's head moves up to Lena's breasts.

RICARDO

My love.

Lena, with the knife in her hand, looks down at him. She raises the knife.

A shot.

They fall apart.

Ricardo's head is grazed. He falls away, staggers to his feet.

Sound of running steps. Heyst comes in the door.

(*To Lena.*)

Stick him!

He rushes out of the door.

Heyst stands, looking down at Lena.

She is bending over, her hands over her face. She leans back, puts her hands to her breast. She looks up. Sees him.

LENA

Oh, my beloved.

Pause.

HEYST

Yes. He found you charming, the jaguar. Didn't he? And it amused you . . . to charm him. Didn't it? It amused you.

LENA

You mustn't make fun of me.

EXT. THE CLEARING.

Rain.

Ricardo, standing, holding his head.

Jones comes out of the shadows.

RICARDO

Guv'nor! I thought he'd done for you. He nearly had
me just now.

JONES

No, it wasn't him. It was me.

RICARDO

Eh?

JONES

It's me now, too.

He shoots him.

Ricardo falls.

INT. MAIN ROOM.

Heyst has turned away from her.

LENA

Don't make fun of me.

*She droops in the chair, sways, half off the chair. He goes to her,
holds her.*

The knife falls from her lap.

He tears her dress open.

A bruise of a bullet hole in her breast.

Her eyes open; looking down, she sees the knife on the floor.

Give me that. It's mine. I won it for you.

He gives her the knife.

What's the matter with me?

HEYST
(*very quietly*)

You have been shot.

LENA

Shot. Yes.

(*Pause.*)

Oh, my beloved. Take me in your arms, carry me out of this.

He lifts her in his arms, carries her to chaise-longue, gently lays her down.

She looks up at him.

Who else could have done this for you?

HEYST

No one.

Her eyes close.

EXT. THE CLEARING.

Jones sitting on the ground. Ricardo's body lies close by.

Jones observing Heyst through the lighted windows, blankly.

JONES'S POINT OF VIEW.

Heyst remains a moment, looking down at Lena. He then walks into the bedroom. He looks down at the bed, picks up an oil lamp, douses the bed with the oil, lights a match, sets fire to the bed.

He goes back into the main room, picks up another lamp, douses the room, sets fire to it.

EXT. SAMBURAN BAY. DAVIDSON'S BOAT. NIGHT.

Davidson staring towards the island.

VICTORY

EXT. THE ISLAND.

The house in flames.

EXT. JONES SITTING, MOTIONLESS.

EXT. THE JETTY. NIGHT.

Davidson arriving in a small boat with two sailors. They jump out of the boat, begin to run towards the house.

Out of the dark, Pedro lurches towards them, jumps at Davidson, seizes him. The two sailors pull him off, struggle with him.

Davidson runs towards the house.

Pedro and sailors rolling on the ground in the background.

EXT. THE HOUSE. DAVIDSON'S POINT OF VIEW.

The house ablaze. Heyst sitting with Lena in his arms.

Davidson rushes up the steps, is beaten back by the flames. He turns, sees Jones.

> **DAVIDSON**
> Help me, for God's sake!

Jones puts his hand behind him, picks up his revolver, points it at Davidson. Davidson freezes. Jones drops the revolver, stares blankly at him.

THE HOUSE.

The figures of Heyst and Lena no longer visible.

EXT. THE ISLAND.

Long shot.

The house, burning.

412

VICTORY

Davidson silhouetted at the window.

Jones still sitting, in the light of the flames, unmoving.

Camera holds on the scene.

Turtle Diary

Turtle Diary was produced in 1985. The cast was as follows:

NEAERA DUNCAN Glenda Jackson
WILLIAM SNOW Ben Kingsley
JOHNSON Richard Johnson
GEORGE FAIRBAIRN Michael Gambon
MRS INCHCLIFF Rosemary Leach
MISS NEAP Eleanor Bron
HARRIET SIMS Harriet Walter
SANDOR Jeroen Krabbe
PUBLISHER Nigel Hawthorne
MR MEAGER Michael Aldridge
LORRY DRIVER Gary Olsen
MAN IN BOOKSHOP Harold Pinter

Director John Irvin
Producer Richard Johnson
Production Designer Leo Austin
Photography Peter Hannan
Costume Designer Elizabeth Waller
Editor Peter Tanner
Composer Geoffrey Burgon

GIANT TURTLES SWIMMING IN THE SEA.

They are swimming towards a tropical beach. Brilliant sunlight. Camera pulls back to reveal that the film is on a video display in an aquarium.

Camera pans to turtles in a tank. Soaring, dipping and curving. They loop away and then swing towards the glass.

Camera pans to find William, looking at turtles. Black silhouettes of people holding children up to the glass.

Echoing footsteps, cries of children, running.

THE TURTLES.

WILLIAM.

He turns, walks away through the people. He passes Neaera. The camera stays with her. She is watching the turtles.

INT. AQUARIUM.

William passing green windows.

Glimpses of crab, lobster, tropical fish, toads, newts, etc.

Door of aquarium slams, echoes.

INT. BLOOMSBURY BOOKSHOP. DAY.

Harriet 23 on short stepladder reaching for a book. William at table handing wrapped book to a man.

> **WILLIAM**
> Thank you very much, sir.

Harriet descends ladder. William turns. Her bottom bumps into him.

> HARRIET
> (*giggling*)

Sorry.

> WILLIAM

Sorry for what?

A Woman approaches Mr Meager (elderly).

> WOMAN

There's a new book just come out. Could you . . . ?
Historical. Terribly well reviewed. Do you know what it
is?

> MR MEAGER

Er . . . let me see . . . I wonder . . .

He looks at William.

> WILLIAM

Might it be . . . *Servant to the King* by Jean Bright?

> WOMAN

That's it. How clever.

> WILLIAM

Yes, that's it. Going like a bomb with the menopausal
set.

> WOMAN

What did you say?

> WILLIAM

Going like a bomb, it's the best she's written yet.

Woman looks at him dubiously. Mr Meager coughs.

INT. PUBLISHER'S OFFICE. DAY.

Publisher kissing Neaera's cheek at reception area. They walk through open-plan office.

> PUBLISHER
>
> Lovely to see you. How are you?

> NEAERA
>
> Oh, fine.

> PUBLISHER
>
> You look wonderful.

> NEAERA
>
> Oh . . .

She laughs.

> PUBLISHER
>
> Come and have a drink.

He opens the door to his office. They go in.

> What will you have?

On the wall is a poster for Gillian Vole's Jumble Sale. *He points to it.*

> The success of the sales conference!

> NEAERA
>
> Really?

> PUBLISHER
>
> Sherry? Gin? Vodka?

Enter Second Publisher.

> SECOND PUBLISHER
>
> Neaera! Hello!

> NEAERA
>
> Hello.

SECOND PUBLISHER

See the poster?

NEAERA

Yes.

SECOND PUBLISHER

The success of the sales conference.

PUBLISHER

Sherry? Gin? Vodka?

SECOND PUBLISHER

Gin.

PUBLISHER

Not you.

NEAERA

Vodka. Why not?

PUBLISHER

Why not indeed!

> (*To Second Publisher.*)

What about you?

> (*To Neaera.*)

I think it's going to do even better than *Gillian Vole's Christmas*.

He gives her vodka.

Cheers. I'll have . . . let's see . . . what will I have?

SECOND PUBLISHER

Gin.

PUBLISHER

I hate gin.

SECOND PUBLISHER

No, I'd like one.

PUBLISHER

Yes, I know that. But what about me?

SECOND PUBLISHER
(*to Neaera*)

What's next?

NEAERA

Oh ... God ... I don't know.

PUBLISHER
(*to Neaera*)

I'll join you in a vodka. Why not?

NEAERA

Why not indeed?

PUBLISHER

What little animal have you got up your sleeve now?

NEAERA

What about a water beetle?

PUBLISHER

A water beetle! How lovely.
(*He pours.*)

What is it?

SECOND PUBLISHER

Shall I help myself?

NEAERA

Cheers.

PUBLISHER

Cheers.

Second Publisher pours a drink.

NEAERA

Well, it's just a beetle which lives in the water.

SECOND PUBLISHER
(*muttering*)

Promising.

NEAERA

Actually . . .

PUBLISHER

Mmnn?

NEAERA

Actually . . . I think I might have come to the end.

SECOND PUBLISHER

What do you mean?

NEAERA

I can't draw. I can't write.

PUBLISHER

Don't be silly.

SECOND PUBLISHER

A temporary condition.

PUBLISHER

Have another vodka.

EXT. PARSON'S GREEN. THE COMMON. EVENING.

An Underground train, above ground, passing the Common on its way to Putney Bridge.

The lights of the train. It slows down. Signals go from red to green.

The train moves.

EXT. STREET. EVENING.

Lamplight. Woman walking with greyhound. Man, dragging one leg, walking behind.

EXT. WILLIAM'S HOUSE. EVENING.

Lighted window on the ground floor. Mrs Inchcliff glimpsed through furniture. She is bending over a sideboard using an electric sander.

Camera pans to upper window. William looking out.

INT. WILLIAM'S HOUSE. WILLIAM'S ROOM. EVENING.

William staring out of the window.

WILLIAM'S POINT OF VIEW.

Couple with greyhound in the distance. Another train passes, going fast.

Shouts. Youths run into the children's playground. They jump on to the swings, swing violently.

INT. WILLIAM'S HOUSE. BATHROOM. NIGHT.

Bath-water running out. Hair in bath. Scum.

Sandor's bare legs leaving bathroom. He goes on to the landing.

INT. WILLIAM'S HOUSE. LANDING. MORNING.

In a corner of the landing a cooker, fridge and sink.

Sandor is heavy-set, moustached. He goes to the cooker, shovels food from a saucepan on to a plate. Some of the food spills on to the cooker. He turns off the gas, goes to his room, slams the door.

William comes out of his room, goes to the cooker, sees mess, grimaces, looks viciously towards Sandor's door. He takes rag, wipes cooker.

EXT. STREET. DAY.

Neaera wheeling a pushchair. On the pushchair a small tank and aquarium gear. She walks towards a large house in a square.

INT. NEAERA'S HOUSE.

The house consists of self-contained flats.

She pulls the pushchair up the stairs, arrives at her landing. A flat door opens. Johnson comes out. He wears a three-piece dark suit, carries a briefcase and overnight bag.

JOHNSON
Hello. What's that? Setting up an aquarium?

NEAERA
Yes.

JOHNSON
Really? How funny. I've had one for years.

NEAERA
Have you?

JOHNSON
Yes, I've been keeping fish for years. Black Mollies. Nothing flash. What are you going to put in yours?

NEAERA
I thought . . . a water beetle.

JOHNSON
Fascinating. Should make a fascinating pet. Any time you'd like some snails, let me know. I've got tons of them.
(*She stares at him.*)
They keep the tank clean, you see.

NEAERA
Oh. Well, thank you.

JOHNSON
I'd give you a hand setting that thing up, but I'm on my way to Heathrow.

NEAERA

Going somewhere nice?

JOHNSON

Oh, Amsterdam, Vienna. That sort of thing. Good luck
with the beetle.

EXT. THE COMMON. NIGHT.

*Miss Neap walking towards the house. She holds a theatre
programme in her hand. She sees a light in the front window.
Stops.*

INT WILLIAM'S HOUSE. MRS INCHCLIFF'S WORKROOM.
NIGHT.

*The room is crammed with furniture and objects, pieces of wood.
A workbench. Mrs Inchcliff sitting at it under a green-shaded
light, planing a piece of wood. She wears jeans, shirt and sandals.
William sits by her with a cup of tea.*

MRS INCHCLIFF

Have you ever done any of this?

WILLIAM

Oh ... once. Yes. A bit of it. When I had a house. I
used to make things for my girls.

MRS INCHCLIFF

What things?

WILLIAM

Oh ... you know ... this and that.

INT. FRONT DOOR.

*Miss Neap closing the door. She goes towards the room, hears
voices, stops.*

INT. WORKROOM.

MRS INCHCLIFF

Did you make things for your wife, too?

WILLIAM
(*laughing*)

My wife? No.

MRS INCHCLIFF
(*calling*)

Hello!

William turns to see Miss Neap hovering in the shadows of the hall. She comes forward into the doorway.

WILLIAM

Hello, Miss Neap.

MISS NEAP

Oh, hello.

MRS INCHCLIFF

Cup of tea?

MISS NEAP

Oh, no. No, thank you. I have to go to Leeds to see my mother in the morning.

WILLIAM

Do you come from Leeds?

MISS NEAP

Me? Oh yes. I do.

MRS INCHCLIFF

How is your mother?

MISS NEAP

Oh ... she's quite old now.

WILLIAM

Been to the theatre?

MISS NEAP

Oh ... yes.

WILLIAM

Good?

MISS NEAP

Mmnn.

WILLIAM

What was it?

MISS NEAP

Umm ... well, it was a farce.

WILLIAM

Ah.

MRS INCHCLIFF
(*to William*)

You should go up to the theatre some time. See a bit of life. Young man like you.

William laughs shortly.

MISS NEAP

Well ...

She smiles briefly, stands uncertainly.

EXT. THE SQUARE. NIGHT. 3 A.M.

Long shot. A figure sitting on a bench, alone. Orange sky. London hum.

EXT. THE SQUARE. NIGHT. 3 A.M.

Close shot. Neaera on the bench.

THE TURTLES.

They swoop in the tank, their flippers click against the glass as they turn.

VOICE

The Green Sea Turtle, *Chelonia Mydas,* is the source of turtle soup.

INT. AQUARIUM.

A boy listening to a recorded guide. In background, William listening.

VOICE

The Green Turtle swims 1,400 miles to breed and lay eggs on Ascension Island in the South Atlantic, halfway to Africa. Ascension Island is only five miles long – nobody knows how they find it.

INT. AQUARIUM.

William walks away towards the exit.

EXT. AQUARIUM. DAY.

William comes out. He bumps into Neaera, who is walking towards the entrance.

WILLIAM

Sorry.

They look at each other.

NEAERA

Sorry.

She goes in.

INT. AQUARIUM.

Neaera stands by the turtle tank. At the far end of the aquarium George (head keeper) standing among a group of children. They are asking questions. Words indecipherable. Echoes.

She moves towards the group, stops, hovers. The children run towards the exit. George walks away. Tentatively, she approaches him.

NEAERA

Excuse me.

GEORGE

Morning.

NEAERA

These turtles . . . how long have they been here?

GEORGE

The big ones? The big ones have been here about thirty years.

She looks at them, and then at him.

NEAERA

That's a very long time.

GEORGE

It is.

NEAERA

Are they happy?

He laughs.

GEORGE

Happy? No, I wouldn't think they're all that happy. Born for the ocean, you see.

NEAERA

Yes.

(*They stand.*)

Thank you.

INT. NEAERA'S FLAT. DAY.

The water beetle. It is lying on damp moss.

Voices of children from the street.

Neaera prods the beetle with a pencil into a little net, lifts the aquarium cover, lets the beetle into the water. The beetle swims down to a plastic 'shipwreck'. Neaera watches it, and then looks about her room.

The room is bright. A work table. A drawing board, etc. A number of illustrations on the wall, of children's books. Volumes of the books on shelves.

She picks up a china figure of a 1900 bathing beauty sitting on a turtle. She turns the figure to face the tank.

INT. BOOKSHOP. OFFICE. DAY.

William with coffee.

Mr Meager comes in, pours coffee.

MR MEAGER

Had bad news yesterday.

WILLIAM

What?

MR MEAGER

Penrose died.

WILLIAM

Penrose?

MR MEAGER

Yes, just like that.

WILLIAM

What ... you mean old ...?

MR MEAGER

Old Penrose. Yes. He wasn't all that old, either.

Through the office window, William sees Neaera enter the shop. He stands.

WILLIAM

Dear dear.

He goes into the shop.

INT. BOOKSHOP.

Neaera picks up a large book on turtles from a table and opens it. William joins Harriet.

HARRIET

What are you doing this weekend?

WILLIAM

Me? Oh ... nothing much. What about you?

HARRIET

I'm going to the country. Friends. Lovely house. In the Chilterns.

WILLIAM

Ah.

HARRIET

Do you like the country?

He looks at her blankly.

WILLIAM

What?

HARRIET

Do you like the country?

WILLIAM

The country. Yes. I used to, yes.

HARRIET

Used to? Well, what do you like now?

A customer approaches. She moves away. He looks across to Neaera, who is still reading the book. She closes it, goes to him.

NEAERA

I'd like this, please.

WILLIAM

Certainly.

He looks at the book. A large turtle on the cover. He wraps the book. Neaera puts cash on the table.

NEAERA

Have you anything else on sea turtles, apart from this?

WILLIAM

No. I don't think so, nothing else. We've got Carr, of course. Have you read Carr?

She looks directly at him, recognizes him.

NEAERA

Yes, I have.

WILLIAM

Oh, you have? Good book, isn't it?

NEAERA

Wonderful.

WILLIAM

Yes. Well, this one's pretty interesting too. It's –

A Man approaches, book in hand.

MAN

Have you got the sequel to this?

WILLIAM

Sequel? Is there one?

MAN

Somebody told me there was one.

NEAERA

Thank you.

Neaera leaves the shop. William glances at her and then looks at the book.

WILLIAM

No, this is the sequel to the one before, you see.

MAN

The one before?

EXT. ZOO. DAY.

William walking through the Zoo.

INT. AQUARIUM.

George cleaning tank windows. The suds run down the glass.

Suddenly reflected through the suds: William. He is standing still, looking at George. George turns.

GEORGE

Afternoon.

WILLIAM

Good afternoon. I just wondered ... these turtles ...

GEORGE

Yes?

WILLIAM

Any chance of looking at them ... from the other side?

GEORGE

Why do you want to do that?

433

WILLIAM

Oh ... curiosity.

GEORGE

I'll just finish this job. All right?

WILLIAM

Yes. Yes, of course.

George cleans the window. William stands.

TURTLES THROUGH THE SUDS.

INT. HEAD KEEPER'S ROOM.

George leads William through the room, on to planks across the back of the tank. They look down at the turtles.

GEORGE

That's not the colour they'd be in natural light. The colour fades here.

WILLIAM

Not too big a space for them, is it?

GEORGE

Not too big, no.

WILLIAM

Do you ever move them out?

GEORGE

When we clean the tank, yes. We put them in the filters.

WILLIAM

Is that difficult?

GEORGE

Bit awkward getting them through the hole, you have to mind their jaws. But it's not too difficult.

WILLIAM

Ah.

(Pause.)

Tell me, suppose some turtle freak decided to steal these turtles. What would he need for the job?

George begins to roll a cigarette.

GEORGE

What would he want to do with them – after he'd stolen them?

WILLIAM

Put them back in the sea.

GEORGE

Ah. Well, he'd need a trolley to get them out of here, and crates to put them in, and a van to take them down to the ocean.

WILLIAM

Wouldn't they dry out – on the trip?

GEORGE

Funny. You're the second person this week who's asked me about the turtles. No, drying out's no problem. Put them on wet sacks, you see. Throw a bucket at them every now and again. They'd be all right.

WILLIAM

A bucket?

GEORGE

Yes. To wet them down.

WILLIAM

But what about the Channel? Wouldn't it be too cold for them?

GEORGE

Cold water makes them a little sluggish but I think

they'd backtrack up the North Atlantic current till they
hit the Canary current or the Gulf Stream. They'd be in
home waters in three months.

WILLIAM

Mmnn. Who was the other person?

GEORGE

Eh?

WILLIAM

Who was the other person – who asked you about the
turtles?

GEORGE

A lady.

WILLIAM

Ah. Oh yes. Well, I might give you a ring some time.

GEORGE

Any time.
(*William takes out notebook.*)
George Fairbairn. Head Keeper. 722 2180.

WILLIAM

Thanks.

INT. WILLIAM'S ROOM. NIGHT.

*William in bed, smoking. Shouts of youths passing the house.
Mock groans and screams.*

EXT. THE COMMON. NIGHT.

A tube train in the distance, coming closer.

EXT. PLAYGROUND. NIGHT.

A swing sent up violently, tangled.

WILLIAM IN BED, EYES OPEN.

INT. LANDING. NIGHT.

Sandor shovelling food on to a plate. Cooker spattered. Slam of door.

THE WATER BEETLE. NIGHT.

The beetle swimming in the tank. Neaera's legs moving past the tank. The bathing beauty and the turtle. Neaera stands by the window, looking out. Her back.

EXT. FESTIVAL HALL. DAY.

People sitting on benches, reading the Sunday newspapers. Neaera comes into shot. She looks up at Hungerford Bridge. A train is passing.

EXT. TRAIN ON HUNGERFORD BRIDGE.

The sky is framed in each window as the carriages pass. Rectangles of blue. The train passes. Blue sky.

NEAERA'S FACE.

EXT. THE SQUARE. DAY.

Neaera approaches her house.

A car draws up. A chauffeur gets out, opens the back door.

Johnson gets out, with a briefcase. Chauffeur gives him a suitcase.

Johnson sees Neaera. The car drives away. He waits for her.

She crosses the road.

JOHNSON
Hello. How's the beetle?

NEAERA

Quite well, I think.

JOHNSON

Must pop in and see it some time. Trouble is, I'm
always rushing about. No rest for the wicked.

NEAERA

Where've you been this time?

JOHNSON

Oh, Bahrain, Abu Dhabi . . . you know, that kind of
thing.

INT. NEAERA'S HOUSE. STAIRS.

Neaera and Johnson ascending.

NEAERA

What do you do, exactly?

He laughs, puts fingers to lips.

JOHNSON

Top secret. God, I hate travelling. Well, love to your
beetle.
   (*He opens the door to his flat, turns.*)
Oh, what is it, by the way, male or female?

NEAERA

Female. There were no males available.

INT. WILLIAM'S HOUSE. BATHROOM.

Scum in bath. Hairs. William, gritting teeth, cleans the bath.

NEAERA'S TANK.

Neaera is kneeling by the tank. The beetle swims.

*Through the water in the tank, through the window, glimpses of
rooftop and sky.*

EXT. REGENT'S PARK. DAY.

Brilliant sun. People with ice-creams and soft drinks, rowing boats on the lake. A band playing. Children.

The Zoo in the distance.

William walking towards the Zoo. His face set.

INT. AQUARIUM. HEAD KEEPER'S ROOM. DAY.

> GEORGE
> What do you think of this?

He hands William a black baby turtle, nine inches long. William holds it. It waggles its flippers.

> WILLIAM
> Friendly.

> GEORGE
> They are.

George takes it, puts it in a small tank.

> WILLIAM
> Tell me . . .

> GEORGE
> Yes?

> WILLIAM
> What if this turtle freak . . . were to seriously propose a turtle theft . . . to the Head Keeper?

> GEORGE
> You mean me?

> WILLIAM
> You. Yes.

> GEORGE
> And you're the freak?

WILLIAM

I am. Yes.

GEORGE

I'd be with you all the way. Have a beer.

He goes to the fridge. Brings out two beers.

I've been telling them for years that we should let the big ones go, put them into the Channel. But they don't want to know. They're not interested in turtles here.

WILLIAM

I see. But how ... how do you think we would go about it?

GEORGE

Easy. Put them into the filters for about a week. Nobody would know they'd gone.

WILLIAM

You'd ... help me then?

GEORGE

Like a shot.

WILLIAM

But wouldn't they bring charges against you?

GEORGE

No, no. They wouldn't bring charges. I'm Head Keeper. I've been here for twenty-seven years. Anyway, don't forget the RSPCA. If I said keeping giant turtles here for thirty years was cruel, I don't think the Zoological Society would take it too far. Anyway, I'd do it. What about you?

(*William stares at him.*)

Do you want to do it?

Pause.

WILLIAM
Yes.

GEORGE
Well, let's do it. I'll let you know a couple of days in advance when we're going to clean the tank.

EXT. AQUARIUM. DAY.

George and William emerge into sunlight. They stand a moment.

EXT. ZOO.

Neaera approaching. She sees William and George talking. She stops.

EXT. AQUARIUM.

GEORGE
I'll give you a tip. Take them down to Cornwall.

WILLIAM
Why?

GEORGE
Well, it gives them a head start. They've got a long way to go.

EXT. ZOO.

William walks towards the exit. He sees Neaera.

Neaera walks towards William.

NEAERA'S FACE.

WILLIAM'S FACE.

INT. AQUARIUM.

It seems to be empty. Neaera walks towards George's office door. It is ajar. She looks in. He is writing at a table. He looks up.

NEAERA

Good morning.

GEORGE

Morning.

NEAERA

I wondered ...

GEORGE

Yes?

NEAERA

That man ... who was here just now ... I saw him going out ...

GEORGE

That's right. Tall chap.

NEAERA

I keep seeing him here.

GEORGE

Yes, he comes here quite a lot.

NEAERA

May I ask why?

GEORGE

He's interested in the turtles.

NEAERA

In what way?

GEORGE

He doesn't think they should be here.

442

NEAERA

Where does he think they should be?

GEORGE

In the sea.

INT. AQUARIUM.

Neaera standing alone. She suddenly discerns two figures by a tank, a man and a Girl. The man is murmuring. The Girl whispers.

GIRL

No. It's too late. It's too late.

NEAERA'S FACE, STRICKEN.

WILLIAM SITTING IN HIS ROOM, STILL. NIGHT.

NEAERA'S FACE.

INT. BOOKSHOP. DAY.

Neaera comes in. She sees William. He nods. She goes to the Natural History shelves. Opens books without seeing them. He approaches, stands with her, sorts books. She looks at him.

NEAERA

I wonder if you've time ... for a word?

WILLIAM

Of course. What about a drink? In about five minutes?

NEAERA

Oh, yes. Thank you.

INT. PUB. DAY.

Neaera at table. A plate of sandwiches on the table. William bringing drinks from the bar. He sits.

WILLIAM

My name's Snow, by the way. William Snow.

NEAERA

Mine's Duncan, Neaera Duncan.

WILLIAM

Neaera Duncan?

NEAERA

Yes.

WILLIAM

Gillian Vole, Delia Swallow – all the little animals?

NEAERA

Yes.

WILLIAM

Well, well. How funny. I used to read your books to my girls.

NEAERA

Really?

WILLIAM

When they were little.

She laughs shortly.

NEAERA

Well ... yes.

They drink.

WILLIAM

We've got them in the shop. Still popular. Got a new one coming out?

NEAERA

No.

(*Silence.*)

These turtles.

WILLIAM

Turtles?

NEAERA

You've been speaking to the Head Keeper.
> (*He drinks.*)

I have too. A little.
> (*Pause.*)

If you have any ... plan ... I'd like to come in with you.

WILLIAM

Plan? What kind of plan?

NEAERA

For releasing them.

WILLIAM

I don't follow you.

NEAERA

Putting them into the sea.

He laughs.

WILLIAM

What makes you think I have a plan to do that?
> (*Pause.*)

A dream, perhaps. But that's not a plan.

NEAERA

Well ... a dream.
> (*They stare at each other.*)

What would you need – to make it real?

WILLIAM

You'd need the co-operation of the Head Keeper.
You'd need crates – for the turtles. You'd need a van,
and you'd need a very cool head. I haven't got any of
those things. Well, that's not entirely true. I might have

445

the co-operation of the Head Keeper.
> (*She looks up.*)

You've done this kind of thing before, have you?

NEAERA

No. I haven't.

WILLIAM

You haven't touched your sandwich.
> (*He drinks.*)

You like turtles, do you?

NEAERA

They're in prison.

WILLIAM

They're not alone in that.
> (*Pause.*)

You could always write to *The Times* about it.

NEAERA

Nobody's interested in turtles. Except the Head Keeper.
And me.
> (*She looks at him.*)

And you.

He drinks, smiles.

INT. WILLIAM'S HOUSE. BATHROOM.

A piece of paper taped to a wall: PLEASE CLEAN BATH AFTER
USE'.

Miss Neap reading this. She leaves the bathroom.

She crosses the landing, knocks on William's door. He opens it.

WILLIAM

Yes?

MISS NEAP

Did you put up that notice?

WILLIAM

Notice?

MISS NEAP

In the bathroom.

WILLIAM

Oh. Yes. Yes, I did.

MISS NEAP

I always clean the bath.

WILLIAM

Oh ... I know ...

MISS NEAP

Always.

WILLIAM

It wasn't meant for you, it was meant for him.

MISS NEAP

I've never been so upset.

WILLIAM

It wasn't meant for you. It was meant for *him*.

MISS NEAP

Who?

WILLIAM

Him!

MISS NEAP

Well, why didn't you say so, on the wall?

WILLIAM

Yes ... sorry ... I should have done that.

She walks away.

447

EXT. THE COMMON. NIGHT.

William sitting. Orange sky. London hum.

INT. WILLIAM'S HOUSE. HALL. DAY.

*William flipping through Yellow Pages. He finds Van Hire.
Dozens of entries. Looks over them.*

Suddenly a sound from above. He turns, looks up the stairs.

SANDOR LOOKING DOWN AT HIM.

Sandor turns away. Footsteps on landing, door slams.

WILLIAM SHUTS THE DIRECTORY.

EXT. STREET. EVENING.

Woman with greyhound, followed by man dragging leg.

EXT. HOUSE. EVENING.

William at his window, looking down.

EXT. STATIONARY TUBE TRAIN. DAY.

*The train stands in a station above ground. A pigeon on the
platform.*

INT. TUBE TRAIN.

*The carriage almost empty. William sitting. The train hums. The
pigeon walks in. Doors close. The train moves.*

A MAN

Bloody pigeon. Christ!

William watches the pigeon.

*The train stops. Dark station. Doors open. Pigeon walks out.
Doors close. Train moves.*

William's face against blurred, moving background.

NEAERA SWIMMING IN THE OCEAN.

A white shadow coming up from below. A shark, growing closer.

NEAERA
(*VO*)

This isn't mine, this isn't mine!

INT. NEAERA'S FLAT. NIGHT.

She is asleep in a chair. She sits up, abruptly, murmurs.

NEAERA

Not mine.

She looks at a clock. The time: 3.45. Silence.

BEETLE IN TANK.

Plants shrouded in green webs of algae. White, ghostly strands of old meat. Plastic shipwreck.

INT. NEAERA'S FLAT. NIGHT.

Neaera opens the telephone directory. She flips to the letter S. She finds a list of seven W. Snows. She looks at the telephone, does not move.

EXT. THE SQUARE. NIGHT.

Neaera is sitting on a bench. A Policeman approaches her.

POLICEMAN

Morning.

NEAERA

Is it?

POLICEMAN

Well, it will be soon. Getting some air?

NEAERA

Yes. It's very close.

POLICEMAN

Feeling all right?

NEAERA

Yes. Thank you.

POLICEMAN

Do you live near here?

NEAERA
(*gesturing*)

In that house.

POLICEMAN

Ah. Well, good morning.

NEAERA'S POINT OF VIEW.

The Policeman walking away. His steps echo.

INT. NEAERA'S FLAT. DAWN.

Neaera opening the windows. She looks at the telephone directory, still open at the list of Snows. She looks at her clock: 5.00. She sits down, lights a cigarette.

EXT. MUSEUM STREET. DAY.

A bus stops at bus stop. Neaera gets off. She walks towards the bookshop.

The bookshop is closed, dark. She walks up and down the street, looking in other shops.

Harriet drives up in a Citroën Deux-Chevaux. She goes to the shop, unlocks the door, goes in, locks the door. Neaera goes to the window, looks in. Harriet turns the lights on. She picks up the post, notices Neaera, takes post to the inner office.

Neaera stands.

Harriet returns with brown-paper bags, puts money into the till.

She sees Neaera again, looks at her watch, goes to the door, unlocks it.

NEAERA
Good morning.

HARRIET
Good morning.

Neaera goes in.

INT. BOOKSHOP. DAY.

HARRIET
Can I help you?

NEAERA
Will Mr Snow be in today?

HARRIET
It's his day off.

NEAERA
Could you give me his phone number? It's urgent.

HARRIET
I'm sorry. I'm afraid I can't do that.

NEAERA
I think he may be ill.

HARRIET
Ill?

NEAERA

Would you ring him yourself – just to make sure he's all right?

HARRIET

He looked perfectly all right yesterday.

NEAERA

It's urgent.

HARRIET

But if you're a friend of his, you'd have his number.
            (*Neaera stares at her blankly.*)
All right, I'll ring him. Who shall I say it is?

NEAERA

Neaera Duncan.

HARRIET

What, the one who does the *Gillian Vole* books?

NEAERA

Yes.

HARRIET
(*smiling.*)

We stock them here, you know. Hold on a minute.

Harriet goes into the office. Neaera watches her dialling through the window.

Harriet puts the receiver down, scribbling on a piece of paper. She comes out.

No answer.

NEAERA

No answer?

HARRIET

Do you want his address?

452

She gives Neaera the piece of paper.

NEAERA

Oh. Thank you.

HARRIET

He's probably asleep.

NEAERA

It isn't personal ... you know. I mean ... it's nothing
personal at all, really.

HARRIET

Well, there's his address anyway.

NEAERA

Thank you.

She leaves the shop.

EXT. MUSEUM STREET.

A taxi. Neaera hails it, gets into it.

INT. TAXI. MOVING.

DRIVER

Do you know the street?

NEAERA

No. Don't you?

DRIVER

I'm a suburban driver. I don't know London. I'm a
Jehovah's Witness. We think God's going to step in and
put things right in a couple of years. There won't be any
taxis then.

NEAERA

What will there be?

DRIVER

The Lord will take care of the righteous. We've been interested in the year 1986 for some time.

NEAERA

What will you do if nothing happens in 1986?

DRIVER

A lot of people ask that question. I'll tell you –

They pass very loud road works. The road works drown his voice.

NEAERA

What?

DRIVER

The Lord will provide.

NEAERA

I think it's somewhere off Fulham Broadway.

He turns and looks at her.

EXT. WILLIAM'S HOUSE. DAY.

The taxi draws up. Neaera gets out. She goes up the steps, rings the bell.

Mrs Inchcliff opens the door.

MRS INCHCLIFF

Yes?

NEAERA

Is Mr Snow here?

MRS INCHCLIFF

Yes. Right up to the top.

Neaera goes in.

INT. WILLIAM'S HOUSE.

Neaera goes up the stairs. At the top landing she stands, lost.

Sandor is at the cooker, stirring a saucepan. He stares at her.

                    NEAERA
    Mr Snow?

He points to a door.

                    SANDOR
    That one.

She knocks on the door. William opens it.

                    WILLIAM
    Good Lord! Hello. What a surprise.
                    (*She stares at him.*)
    Come in.

INT. WILLIAM'S ROOM.

He closes the door.

                    WILLIAM
    What's the trouble? You look done in. Have some
    coffee. Sit down.

He pours coffee. Gives it to her. She sips.

    What is it? You don't look well.

                    NEAERA
    I'm sorry, I've never done anything like this before, you
    must think I'm mad, they gave me your address at the
    shop, I said it was urgent, she was very nice –

                    WILLIAM
    Urgent? What?

NEAERA

Don't be angry. I know I don't know you, we don't
know each other – but I –

WILLIAM

Drink your coffee.

NEAERA

It was a dream. Nonsense, of course, anyway I couldn't
sleep, I mean I wasn't in bed, just dropped off, in a
chair, I couldn't sleep, you see, I must have dropped off,
it was the middle of the night, there was this shark
coming up out of the depths, in the sea, green water, a
white glimmer, a shark, it woke me up, coming towards
me, I woke up –

WILLIAM

A shark?

NEAERA

Yes.

He gives her a cigarette and lights it.

WILLIAM

Drink your coffee.

She inhales the cigarette.

NEAERA

I have my own cigarettes, in my bag.

WILLIAM

You had this dream . . . of a shark?

NEAERA

Yes.

WILLIAM

And what does that mean?

NEAERA

Death.

Pause.

WILLIAM

Does it?

NEAERA

Yes.

WILLIAM

Well ... how awful. How awful for you.

NEAERA

No. It wasn't mine.

WILLIAM

What?

NEAERA

It wasn't mine.

WILLIAM

What do you mean?

NEAERA

It was yours.

WILLIAM

My what?

NEAERA

Your death.

Pause.

WILLIAM

Oh, thanks.

(*Pause.*)

How do you know?

457

NEAERA

I knew.

WILLIAM

But this shark ... was coming up through the water
towards *you*. You said that. So where do I come into it?

NEAERA

No. It was coming up through the water towards you.

He laughs.

WILLIAM

Jesus Christ.
> (*Silence.*)

So you came here because you thought I was dead? You
thought I'd done myself in? Well, here I am, as you see.
In the pink.
> (*He sits.*)

As you see.

She smokes.

NEAERA

You see, they do say that when you dream of yourself
you're actually dreaming about someone else.

WILLIAM

Yes. Nice and convenient, that. As a theory. I must
remember that.

NEAERA

Anyway, I think we should forget all about these turtles.

WILLIAM

You've taken the words out of my mouth.

NEAERA

It's ridiculous.

WILLIAM
Dangerous too. You know that big male? He could take
your hand off with one bite. Probably will, too.
Irritation. I mean, they haven't actually *said* they want to
swim back to Ascension Island, have they? Probably
quite comfortable where they are. After all, they've been
there for thirty years. You get used to things.

NEAERA
Yes. That's right.

INT. BOOKSHOP. MORNING.

Harriet in the office, making tea. William reading a paper.

HARRIET
Did Miss Duncan ever reach you?

WILLIAM
Oh, yes. She did.

HARRIET
Was it all right, giving her your address?

WILLIAM
Yes, fine. Silly of me not to have given it to her before.

HARRIET
I didn't know she was a friend of yours.

WILLIAM
Haven't known her long.

HARRIET
Funny, meeting authors.

She pours water into the pot.

WILLIAM
That's a pretty dress.

HARRIET

Oh. Thank you.

INT. PUB. EVENING.

William and Harriet at a table (the same table as William and Neaera).

HARRIET

I thought you'd never ask.

WILLIAM

Ask what?

HARRIET

Me. Out.

WILLIAM

Oh. Yes. Did I?

HARRIET

Yes. You did.

WILLIAM

I thought you asked me.

HARRIET

Well, perhaps I did.

They drink.

Do you like working in the bookshop?

WILLIAM

I love it. Love it. I love all the shapes and sizes.

HARRIET

What, of the books?

WILLIAM

No. The customers.

HARRIET

Oh, do you?

WILLIAM

Don't you?

HARRIET

If you don't like it, why do you stay?

WILLIAM

Ah. Well, I did have ambitions once. I was going to discover the Amazon.

HARRIET

Hasn't it been discovered?

WILLIAM

Yes.

(*Pause.*)

You're nice anyway.

INT. RESTAURANT. EVENING.

William and Harriet at table, sitting with food and two bottles of wine, one empty, one half empty.

HARRIET

Have you ever been married?

WILLIAM

I must have been. I had two daughters. They were little once. They used to sit on my lap.

HARRIET

Were you a good father?

WILLIAM

They thought so. But they were only children at the time. Yes, I was married. I was 'in business'. Out in the big world. A long time ago. Didn't like any of it. So I

461

thought I'd find a nice little corner, in a nice little bookshop, and keep out of trouble. See?

HARRIET

No.

WILLIAM

What about you? Are you going to go far?

HARRIET

Why not? Don't you think I'm intelligent?

WILLIAM

Very.

HARRIET

And capable?

WILLIAM

Very. I think you'll go far.

He pours wine.

HARRIET

What about women?

WILLIAM

What about them?

HARRIET

What *about* them?

WILLIAM

Oh, *women*. No, no.

HARRIET

What do you mean, no, no?

WILLIAM

I've been on a sabbatical for years.

HARRIET

Why?

462

(*He drinks.*)
Don't you miss it sometimes?

WILLIAM
It? Oh ... *it*. Yes, I suppose I do miss it, sometimes.

HARRIET
Might as well get some fun out of life.

WILLIAM
Is that your motto?

HARRIET
It obviously isn't yours.

WILLIAM
Oh, I don't know. Here we are. Painting the town red.

HARRIET
I saw *Les Enfants du Paradis* the other day. Do you
remember what Arletty says?

WILLIAM
What?

HARRIET
C'est si simple, l'amour.

WILLIAM
Funny lot, the French.

EXT. WILLIAM'S HOUSE. NIGHT.

Harriet's car draws up.

INT. CAR. NIGHT.

HARRIET
Don't you want to come to my place?

WILLIAM
No. You'll love my place.

463

INT. WILLIAM'S HOUSE.

William and Harriet creeping up the stairs. They peer round the top landing. Sandor making coffee. He stares.

> **HARRIET**
> (*cheerfully*)

Hello.

They go into the room.

INT. WILLIAM'S ROOM. NIGHT.

The door closes. Lamplight through the window. He kisses her. She whispers.

> **HARRIET**

Remember Arletty.

INT. WILLIAM'S ROOM. MORNING.

Church bells.

Harriet and William naked in bed. She is asleep. He looks down at her. A knock on the door. Mrs Inchcliff's voice.

> **MRS INCHCLIFF**
> (*VO*)

Telephone.

Harriet wakes up.

> **WILLIAM**

Telephone.

He gets up, puts on a dressing-gown, goes out.

INT. HALL.

William comes downstairs, picks up the telephone. Mrs Inchcliff glimpsed in her workroom in background.

WILLIAM

Hello?

GEORGE
(*VO*)

This is George Fairbairn.

WILLIAM

Oh, hello.

GEORGE
(*VO*)

The big day is coming up, Thursday week.

WILLIAM

Ah, I see.

GEORGE
(*VO*)

Are you still on?

WILLIAM

Yes. Yes.

GEORGE
(*VO*)

You'll need crates. Do you want the measurements?

WILLIAM

Oh. Right. Right. Just a minute.
(*He picks up pad and pencil.*)
Yes. Right.

GEORGE
(*VO*)

Four feet long, twenty-eight inches wide, one foot deep.

WILLIAM

Right.

GEORGE
(*VO*)

If you can drop the crates off, I'll have them boxed and
ready for pick-up.

WILLIAM

OK. Right.

GEORGE
(*VO*)

Drop them off about seven, Thursday week.

WILLIAM

Right.

GEORGE
(*VO*)

See you then.

WILLIAM

Oh, listen. I'll ring to confirm.

GEORGE
(*VO*)

Confirm?

Miss Neap comes down the stairs and goes to the hall table.

WILLIAM

Yes.

GEORGE
(*VO*)

I thought you had confirmed.

WILLIAM

Just ... give me a few days.

GEORGE
(*VO*)

Do you want to scrub round it?

WILLIAM

Just give me a couple of days.

GEORGE
(*VO*)

All right. Ring me in a couple of days then.

Phone down.

WILLIAM

Morning, Miss Neap.

MISS NEAP

Good morning.

She picks up the Sunday Express *from the hall table. He goes up the stairs.*

INT. WILLIAM'S ROOM.

William enters. Gets into bed.

HARRIET

Who was it?

WILLIAM

No one.

She touches his face.

INT. HALL.

Miss Neap with the Sunday Express *in her hand, looking at herself in the hall mirror.*

INT. BOOKSHOP. DAY.

A large American Woman and a small American man enter the shop. The Woman approaches Mr Meager. In background, in a corner of the shop, William and Harriet are whispering.

WOMAN

I want to look at some guide books. You have guide books?

MR MEAGER

Certainly. Which part of England?

WOMAN

William Shakespeare country.

MR MEAGER

Miss Sims, would you help this lady? Guide book to the Cotswolds.

HARRIET

Oh, yes.

WOMAN
(*to husband*)

You go and buy some antiques or something. Come back in ten minutes.

HUSBAND

Sure thing.

He goes towards the door.

Neaera comes in.

He lets her pass.

HARRIET
(*to woman*)

Over here.

She leads Woman to a table.

William sees Neaera. She goes to the Poetry section.

Harriet glances at her.

WOMAN
(*to Harriet*)
You know a place called Hog's Bottom?

HARRIET
No, I ...

WOMAN
Isn't it close by Stratford-upon-Avon?

HARRIET
It could be, easily.

William has moved across to Neaera. She looks at him. They speak quietly.

NEAERA
Have you thought any more – about the matter?

WILLIAM
I thought we agreed –

NEAERA
We didn't agree anything.

WOMAN
(*to Harriet*)
OK, give me two of those and one of those. Where the hell's my husband?

NEAERA
Have you spoken to the man?

WILLIAM
Well ... yes. He phoned.

NEAERA
With what news?

WILLIAM
Thursday week ... is the day.

Harriet gives the Woman her books, takes cash.

HARRIET

Thank you, madam.

Husband enters shop.

WOMAN

Where have you been?
                    (*She gives him package.*)
Take this.

They go out.

Neaera goes towards the door.

HARRIET

Hello.

NEAERA

Oh, hello.

She goes out.

William stands by Harriet.

WILLIAM

I've got to have a drink with her.

HARRIET

Why?

William does not reply, sorts a pile of books.

INT. PUB. DAY.

William and Neaera at the table.

Silence.

WILLIAM

So you . . . you want to do it.

470

NEAERA

Yes.

Pause.

WILLIAM

How do you know I'm competent?

NEAERA

I don't.

WILLIAM

And what about you?

NEAERA

I don't know.

Pause.

WILLIAM

I think it's crazy. We could end up in prison. Or worse.

NEAERA

Well, don't do it.

WILLIAM

No. All right. We'll do it.

They sit.

INT. HARRIET'S CAR, MOVING. NIGHT.

HARRIET

Oh, I got those tickets.

WILLIAM

What tickets?

HARRIET

For the Queen Elizabeth Hall.

WILLIAM

Oh, yes. Yes.

HARRIET

There are eight altogether.

WILLIAM

Eight what?

HARRIET

Recitals! Have you forgotten?

WILLIAM

No, no. Great.

She drives.

Eight, eh?

INT. RESTAURANT. BOOTHS. NIGHT.

Neaera in a booth, alone. The booth shakes as people sit in the next booth.

Neaera has finished her meal. She sits with wine, coffee and a book.

William's and Harriet's voices from the next booth.

WILLIAM
(*VO*)

What are you going to have?

HARRIET
(*VO*)

I don't know.

WILLIAM
(*VO*)

I'm having Steak au poivre.

HARRIET
(*VO*)

Where's that? I can't see it.

WILLIAM
(*VO*)

There. Down there.

HARRIET
(*VO*)

Oh yes. Oh I ... no, I'll have scampi.

WILLIAM
(*VO*)

Scampi. Provençal?

Neaera finishes her wine and stands.

HARRIET
(*VO*)

No ... yes. Provençal. That's rice, isn't it?

WILLIAM
(*VO*)

More or less.

HARRIET
(*VO. Laughs*)

More or less?

Neaera moves past the booth, looks at the couple with a prepared smile. They look up. They are not William and Harriet.

INT. HARRIET'S FLAT. NIGHT.

Harriet lying in William's arms. They are naked. She kisses him.

HARRIET

We've been invited to a party.

WILLIAM

We?

HARRIET

Yes.

473

WILLIAM

Who by?

HARRIET

Nick and Ros. They want to meet you.

WILLIAM

When?

HARRIET

Saturday.

WILLIAM

No. I can't. I'm sorry. I've got some odd jobs to do. I've
told myself I'm going to do them on Saturday, you see.
I've set Saturday aside.

HARRIET

Odd jobs?

WILLIAM

Yes.

Pause.

HARRIET

What does that woman want?

WILLIAM

What woman?

HARRIET

Miss Duncan.

WILLIAM

Nothing. She doesn't want anything.

HARRIET

Nothing?

WILLIAM

Nothing.

TURTLE DIARY

INT. TELEPHONE BOX. EARLY EVENING.

William talking.

> **WILLIAM**
> Wait a minute. Just a second. I'm making a note:
> £15.99p a day, 7p a mile, £80 deposit?

> **VOICE**
> That's right.

> **WILLIAM**
> Right. That's OK.

> **VOICE**
> Right.

> **WILLIAM**
> Thursday the fourteenth.

> **VOICE**
> Thursday the fourteenth. Got it.

> **WILLIAM**
> Thank you.

> **VOICE**
> Right. OK, Mr Quinn.

William puts the telephone down, picks it up, dials another number.

He suddenly sees Miss Neap walking along the pavement. He turns away. He puts a coin in. George's voice.

> **GEORGE**
> (*VO*)
> Hello.

> **WILLIAM**
> Mr Fairbairn?

GEORGE
(*VO*)

Yes.

WILLIAM

It's William Snow.

GEORGE
(*VO*)

Oh, hello.

William looks over his shoulder, sees Miss Neap stroking a cat on the pavement. He turns back to the telephone.

WILLIAM

Thursday's fine.

GEORGE
(*VO*)

Oh is it? Good.

WILLIAM

I'll be there.

GEORGE
(*VO*)

Good.

WILLIAM

That lady will be with me.

GEORGE
(*VO*)

Lady?

WILLIAM

Yes. You know her.

GEORGE
(*VO*)

Oh, her? Yes. Right. Good. Safety in numbers.

476

WILLIAM

I hope you're right.

GEORGE
(*VO*)

It'll go like clockwork. How about the crates?

WILLIAM

They'll be there.

GEORGE
(*VO*)

I hope so. Otherwise they'll be sitting on your lap.

WILLIAM

Bye.

GEORGE
(*VO*)

Bye.

INT. BOOKSHOP. EVENING.

The shop is closed. Mr Meager and William. Harriet in background.

MR MEAGER

Yes, he's made a remarkable recovery, as a matter of fact.

WILLIAM

Oh good.

MR MEAGER

I was quite taken aback, when they told me he was still alive. I thought he was a doomed man myself. Oh well, good night.

WILLIAM *and* HARRIET

Good night.

477

Mr Meager goes out.

William and Harriet turn out the lights in silence.

WILLIAM

Right, then.

HARRIET

Well, have a good time ... with your odd jobs.

He goes to the door.

EXT. BOOKSHOP. EVENING.

Harriet locks up. They stand.

HARRIET

Want a lift?

WILLIAM

No. It's all right. I'll walk up to the station.
            (*Pause.*)
Are you going to the party?

HARRIET

I don't know.

Pause.

WILLIAM

Well ... till Monday.

HARRIET

Yes.

He kisses her lightly, turns away. She gets into her car.

INT. CAR.

Harriet driving. The car passes William, walking. She does not turn.

INT. TUBE TRAIN. DAY.

William sitting with planks of wood. The train stops. The doors open. William, with some difficulty, carries the planks through the door.

INT. WILLIAM'S HOUSE. HALL. DAY.

Planks of wood leaning against the wall. William, carrying planks, opens the front door, leans planks against the wall.

INT. WILLIAM'S HOUSE. WORKROOM. EVENING.

William sawing wood with a hand saw. He is surrounded by wood. On a chest lie rope and ring bolts.

Mrs Inchcliff comes in.

> MRS INCHCLIFF
> What are you making?

> WILLIAM
> Turtle crates. I'm going to steal three sea turtles from the Zoo and put them into the sea.

> MRS INCHCLIFF
> Sounds a good thing to do. Nice to have a man doing something in here again. Charlie was never out of here. Do you want to try his Black and Decker?

She goes to a cupboard and brings it out.

> Here.

William looks at it.

> WILLIAM
> Frighten the life out of me, these things.

> MRS INCHCLIFF
> Try it.

He does.

> MRS INCHCLIFF

What do you think?

> WILLIAM

It works.

INT. MISS NEAP'S ROOM. NIGHT.

Miss Neap sitting alone. Hammering from below.

MRS INCHCLIFF'S KITCHEN. NIGHT.

Mrs Inchcliff is making tea and sandwiches. Hammering above. She puts the plates on a tray. The hammering stops. She looks up.

INT. WORKROOM. NIGHT.

The three crates are finished. Open boxes, no lids. Mrs Inchcliff comes in with tray. She surveys crates.

> WILLIAM

What do you think?

> MRS INCHCLIFF

Beautiful.

> WILLIAM

With tools you can do anything.

> MRS INCHCLIFF

With tools and a man.

Miss Neap comes downstairs. She looks round the door, sees crates.

> MISS NEAP

What lovely things. What are you going to put into them?

WILLIAM

Turtles. I'm going to put some sea turtles into them and take them down to the sea.

MISS NEAP

Ah, the sea. Yes. It always seems so far away. Even though the Thames goes into it.

The front door closes. Sandor appears, looks round the door. He carries newspapers under his arm and a packed briefcase.

SANDOR

Good evening.

He sees the crates, goes to them, examines them, looks at William.

SANDOR

You did this?

WILLIAM

That's right.

SANDOR

Quite good.

WILLIAM

Thanks.

SANDOR

Quite good.

INT. WILLIAM'S ROOM. EVENING.

William looking out of the window.

The lights of the tube train.

The woman with the greyhound walking slowly along the pavement.

No man.

He turns from the window.

481

INT. NEAERA'S HOUSE. DAY.

Neaera ringing the bell of Johnson's flat. He opens the door. He is wearing a sweater.

JOHNSON

Oh, hello. How are you?

NEAERA

You're here. Oh good. I wasn't sure.

JOHNSON

Yes, I'm here this week.

NEAERA

Well, could you possibly feed my beetle? I have to be away Thursday and Friday –

JOHNSON

Of course.

NEAERA

Thank you so much. There's a sort of lamb chop – well, the remains –

JOHNSON

Yes. Quite.

NEAERA

Here's the key.

JOHNSON

First rate. It will be an honour.

She gives him the key. A sudden male cough from inside Johnson's flat. She looks at Johnson. He smiles.

Would you like to show me where the remains ... are?

NEAERA

Remains?

JOHNSON

Of the lamp chop.

NEAERA

Oh yes. Of course.

He follows her to her door. They go into her flat.

INT. NEAERA'S FLAT. SITTING-ROOM.

On the table a large map spread out. Neaera goes into the kitchen.

Johnson follows.

NEAERA

There.

JOHNSON

Ah. Right. It will be done.

NEAERA

Thank you.

They go back into the sitting-room.

JOHNSON

I do think you're a wonderful mother to your beetle.

She laughs.

Johnson notices a large book on turtles open on the table. He looks at it, then at the map.

Going somewhere nice?

NEAERA

Cornwall.

JOHNSON

Cornwall? Really? I was born there.

NEAERA

Really?

JOHNSON

Yes, I was born in Cornwall.

He smiles.

INT. BOOKSHOP. DAY.

William and Mr Meager. Harriet in background.

WILLIAM
(*to Mr Meager*)
Listen, I wonder if you'd mind if I took Friday off.
Personal matter. Illness.

MR MEAGER

Serious?

WILLIAM

Well ... you know ...

MR MEAGER

Family?

WILLIAM

First cousin.

MR MEAGER

Heart?

WILLIAM

No. Feet.

MR MEAGER

Feet?

WILLIAM

Gout.

MR MEAGER

Ah. Can be nasty.

WILLIAM

I don't trust doctors.

MR MEAGER

Quite right. Yes, yes. That'll be all right.

He moves away.

Harriet joins William, whispers.

HARRIET

What is it?

WILLIAM

Nothing.

HARRIET

Where are you going?

WILLIAM

It's private.

HARRIET

Look, you're not compelled to tell me anything at all,
you're quite entitled to take a day off without having to –

WILLIAM

Look –

HARRIET

– without having to explain yourself to me, you're a
perfectly free man, I just asked, that's all, I realize I
shouldn't have asked –

WILLIAM

Harriet –

HARRIET

I'm quite grown up you know –

485

WILLIAM

I know, but –

HARRIET

I still like you, whether you – whatever you –

WILLIAM

Everything isn't sex. There are other things that are
private.

A customer enters the shop. Harriet goes towards him.

HARRIET
(*brightly*)

Yes, sir. Can I help you?

EXT. ZOO. DAY.

Camera moves across the Zoo. A telephone is ringing.

INT. ZOO: RECEPTION.

The telephone is ringing. A Man picks it up.

MAN

Zoo here.

WILLIAM
(*VO*)

Hello, is that the Zoo?

MAN

Zoo here.

*The following sequence is intercut between William in a coin box
and the receptionist. Man in Zoo's reception.*

WILLIAM

I think you should be warned. I'm going to steal some
of your animals.

MAN

Oh yes? What kind of animals.

WILLIAM

Big ones.

MAN

When are you going to do it?

WILLIAM

Soon.

MAN

How are you going to do it?

WILLIAM

I'm not going to tell you.

MAN

I see. Well, thanks for letting us know.

WILLIAM

Not at all.

EXT. NEAERA'S HOUSE. EARLY EVENING.

Neaera stands with two suitcases.

William draws up in a large van. He gets out.

WILLIAM

Hello. We'll put your cases in the back. What have you
got in there?

NEAERA

Blankets, pillows.

WILLIAM

Oh.

*He opens the back of the van. Three crates. Rope, etc. Blankets
and pillows.*

INT. VAN.

Neaera sitting in passenger seat. William climbs in.

>   NEAERA
> The crates are beautiful.

>   WILLIAM
> Oh good. Listen, I'm very nervous about this van. I've
> never sat so high up for a start. But the most important
> thing is – I – you see – it's the width. It's so wide. I'm
> not used to it. Will you tell me if I'm too close to parked
> cars, or the kerb – as we go?

>   NEAERA
> Yes.

>   WILLIAM
> Thank you.

EXT. LONDON STREET.

Van being driven slowly down the street. Rain.

INT. VAN.

>   WILLIAM
> Where the hell are the bloody wipers?

He tries various switches, finds wipers.

>   NEAERA
> Too close!

>   WILLIAM
> Blast!

He veers away.

EXT. ZOO. WORKS GATE. EVENING.

George standing with a trolley. Van draws up. William gets out, goes to the back door. George goes to Neaera's window. She winds the window down.

GEORGE

Good evening.

NEAERA
(smiling)

Good evening.

George to back door. They take out the crates and put them on the trolley.

WILLIAM

Are they all right?

GEORGE

Perfection.

WILLIAM

See you at eight.

GEORGE

I'll be here. So will they.

INT. KEBAB HOUSE. EVENING.

William and Neaera at a table. Greek music, a candle, retsina.

WILLIAM

Cheers.

NEAERA

Cheers.

WILLIAM

Here's to our friends.

NEAERA

Yes.

They drink.

Why did you choose Polperro?

WILLIAM
Oh, I don't know. Pretty name. Plenty of sea.

NEAERA
Yes.

WILLIAM
Do you agree?

NEAERA
Sounds fine.

WILLIAM
Do you keep animals?

NEAERA
I have a water beetle.

WILLIAM
Does she want to go to Polperro? She could ride on the back of the turtles.

NEAERA
She's a freshwater beetle. You know what her motto is?

WILLIAM
What?

NEAERA
East, West, Home's Best.

WILLIAM
But it's not our motto, is it?

NEAERA
No.

WILLIAM
Perhaps we can ride on the back of the turtles.

NEAERA

Bum a ride on the turtles?

WILLIAM

Is that what we're doing?

NEAERA

I don't know. I haven't really . . . thought.

WILLIAM

No. I haven't *thought*, either. Makes a change, doesn't it?

NEAERA
(*grinning*)

Yes, it does.

EXT. ZOO. WORKS GATE. EVENING.

George trundling a crate covered with tarpaulin on a trolley. He places it beside another trolley covered with tarpaulin.

Another Keeper passes.

KEEPER

Hello, George. What you got in there?

GEORGE

Turtles.

KEEPER

Oh yes? What are you doing with them?

GEORGE

Giving them a holiday. They need it.

KEEPER

Well, I don't know if they bloody need it, but I bloody need it. See you.

He goes.

INT. RESTAURANT.

Waiter with food.

WAITER
Two Doner Kebabs.

He sets them down, goes.

NEAERA
Looks delicious.

WILLIAM
We're going to need it. We have a long way to go.

NEAERA
How long?

WILLIAM
Two hundred and fifty miles.

NEAERA
I've packed a flask of coffee.

WILLIAM
Have you? So have I.

She laughs.

NEAERA
Have you?

EXT. ZOO. WORKS GATE. EVENING.

George waiting with three trolleys covered with tarpaulin. The van draws up. William gets out, opens the back door. They take the tarpaulins off, put the crates in the back of the van, followed by one trolley.

Neaera joins them. They all look at the turtles. They lie on their backs, with their flippers pressed against their sides, their mouths open. They sigh.

NEAERA

So there they are.

WILLIAM

There they are.

GEORGE

Got the champagne?

WILLIAM

Champagne?

GEORGE

For the launching.

WILLIAM

I'll get some on the way.

GEORGE

I took the liberty of laying on a bottle. Give you both a little send-off.

INT. HEAD KEEPER'S OFFICE.

George opening champagne.

GEORGE

It's not every day I send my turtles out into the world, you know. Something of an occasion.

He pours into stemmed glasses.

Here's to the launching.

NEAERA

Here's to you.

WILLIAM

Here's to us.

They all drink.

EXT. ZOO. WORKS GATE. NIGHT.

William and Neaera in the van. George saluting. The van moves. George suddenly shouts after them. The van stops abruptly. George runs to the van. William lowers his window.

> GEORGE
>
> Don't forget to give them a bucket of water every three hours. To wet them down.

> WILLIAM
>
> Bucket? I haven't got a bucket.

> GEORGE
>
> Any garage. Easy.

> WILLIAM
>
> Every what?

> NEAERA
>
> Three hours.

> GEORGE
>
> Good luck.

William turns ignition. The van moves away. Neaera waves.

> WILLIAM
> (*muttering*)
> A bucket every three hours!

EXT. BAKER STREET. NIGHT.

Van moving. Rain.

EXT. BAYSWATER ROAD. NIGHT.

Van moving.

EXT. OFF-LICENCE. HAMMERSMITH. NIGHT.

The van is parked outside a brightly lit off-licence. William can be seen at the counter.

INT. VAN.

Neaera sitting.

Sound of a police siren. A police car draws up, parks in front of the van. A policeman gets out, goes into the off-licence.

OFF-LICENCE.

Neaera's point of view.

Through the off-licence window, William at the counter, a woman wrapping a bottle of champagne. The policeman stands next to William. William looks at him, looks away. He gives the woman money. Man behind the counter gives the policeman cigarettes. Woman gives William the champagne. Policeman gives the man money, takes cigarettes. Policeman and William approach the door together. Policeman lets William go first. William emerges, comes to the van. Policeman stands, unwrapping cigarettes. William gets into the van.

WILLIAM

Christ!

He drives away.

EXT. CHISWICK HIGH ROAD. NIGHT.

Van driving.

INT. VAN.

Neaera looking at map by torchlight.

NEAERA

We stay on the M4 until after Swindon. Then we go through Chippenham, Trowbridge, Frome, Shepton Mallet, Glastonbury, Taunton, Exeter, Plymouth, across the Tamar, go through Looe, and there's Polperro.

She looks out suddenly.

Too close!

WILLIAM
Christ!

He veers away.

EXT. CHISWICK ROUNDABOUT.

The van goes round the roundabout, missing the M4.

INT. VAN. NIGHT.

NEAERA
No. That's the North Circular. You missed it.

WILLIAM
Damn!

EXT. ROUNDABOUT.

The van goes round again.

EXT. M4.

The van driving.

INT. VAN.

WILLIAM
Where's this from?
                    (*Passionately.*)
'Ship and boat diverged; the cold damp night breeze
blew between; a screaming gull flew overhead; the two
hulls wildly rolled; we gave three hearty cheers and
blindly plunged like fate into the lone Atlantic.'

NEAERA
Moby Dick.

WILLIAM

Right!

The van drives on.

NEAERA

Blindly plunged like fate into the lone M4.

Pause.

WILLIAM

Yes, that's it.

THE TURTLES SIGHING.

EXT. M4.

The van driving.

EXT. DARK TOWN.

The van driving through a narrow street.

INT. VAN.

NEAERA

Too close!

WILLIAM

It's so bloody wide! I'm not used to driving a thing like this. I'm not used to driving at all. I haven't had a car for years.

NEAERA

You had a car once, did you?

WILLIAM

Once.

Pause.

NEAERA

I'm sorry I can't drive.

WILLIAM

That's all right.

Pause.

NEAERA

I think you're driving very well.

They drive on.

EXT. LAYBY. LATE AT NIGHT.

The van parked. A large articulated lorry.

INT. VAN.

William and Neaera drinking coffee, eating sandwiches.

WILLIAM

Lovely sandwiches.

NEAERA

Oh, good.

WILLIAM

It didn't occur to me that you'd make sandwiches. I thought we'd have to find some in some lousy café.

NEAERA

Ah, well ...

WILLIAM

Is this home-made bread?

NEAERA

You mean did I bake it myself?

WILLIAM

Yes.

NEAERA

No. I didn't.

WILLIAM

Ah.

NEAERA

But it is good bread.

WILLIAM

Bloody good. Good cheese too.

NEAERA

Cheese gives you strength.

WILLIAM

Does it?

A sudden knock on the van door. They jump. A face at the window. William winds the window down.

MAN

Got a light, mate?

WILLIAM

Light? Yes. Just a moment.

He gets out of the van and closes the door. He gives the Man a light.

MAN

Thanks. Nice night.

THE LIGHTED VAN. MAN'S POINT OF VIEW.

Neaera sitting. In background the crates clearly discernible.

WILLIAM

It is.

MAN

Going far?

499

WILLIAM

Somerset.

MAN

Do it often?

WILLIAM

What?

MAN

This trip.

WILLIAM

No. No, not very often.

MAN

What have you got in the back there? Coffins?

William laughs.

WILLIAM

Coffins? No, no. Not coffins.

MAN

Well, they look like coffins.

WILLIAM

Do they?

MAN

You'd be surprised the kind of people you get on the road sometimes. Particularly at night.

WILLIAM

Really?

MAN

Oh yes. Well, ta-ta.

WILLIAM

Good night.

The Man goes towards the lorry. William gets back into the van.

TURTLE DIARY

INT. VAN.

WILLIAM
Let's go.

They drive away.

MAN IN LORRY.

He smokes, watching the van drive away.

INT. VAN. DRIVING.

WILLIAM
What's the time?

NEAERA
One o'clock.

WILLIAM
We've got to find a garage. We've got to find a bucket.
No point in throwing three dead turtles into the sea.

She looks back.

NEAERA
They're breathing.

EXT. COUNTRY ROAD. NIGHT.

Van approaches a dark garage.

INT. VAN.

NEAERA
Closed.

EXT. COUNTRY ROAD. NIGHT.

Van approaches a dark garage.

INT. VAN.

> WILLIAM
>
> Oh my God.

EXT. COUNTRY ROAD. NIGHT.

Van approaching a lit garage.

INT. VAN.

> WILLIAM
>
> Open.

EXT. GARAGE. NIGHT.

William putting cap on petrol tank. He goes towards the pay booth.

INT. PAY BOOTH.

Man behind the counter. William pays.

> WILLIAM
>
> Do you have a bucket, by any chance?

> MAN
>
> A bucket?

> WILLIAM
>
> Yes.

> MAN
>
> A bucket.

He crosses the room. Picks up a bucket.

> What about this?

> WILLIAM
>
> Thank you. Can I fill it with water?

> MAN

Just outside. Bring the bucket back though, won't you?

> WILLIAM

Of course.

> MAN

It's not mine, you see. It belongs to the guv'nor's wife.

> WILLIAM

Does it?

> MAN

Yes. She'd be lost without her bucket.

EXT. GARAGE.

William filling bucket. He goes to the back of the van, empties the bucket. He fills the bucket again. Empties it again.

MAN IN BOOTH. WATCHING.

William brings the bucket back into the booth.

> WILLIAM

Thank you very much.

> MAN

Like it?

> WILLIAM

What?

> MAN

The bucket.

> WILLIAM

Yes. Lovely.

> MAN

It is a lovely bucket, yes.

WILLIAM

Good night.

He walks to the door.

INT. VAN. NIGHT.

William looks back at the turtles.

WILLIAM

Do you think they've any idea?

NEAERA

No. But when they find themselves in the ocean they'll just do what turtles do in the ocean. That's what I think.

WILLIAM

Swim.

NEAERA

Yes.

WILLIAM

You think so? You sure they won't drown – out of shock?

(*She looks at him.*)

Well, we'll soon find out.

NEAERA

How soon?

WILLIAM

About fifty miles.

THE MOON. BROKEN CLOUDS.

THE ROAD. CATS' EYES ON THE ROAD.

WILLIAM DRIVING. NEAERA ASLEEP.

EXT. THE TAMAR BRIDGE.

The van crosses it.

INT. VAN.

> WILLIAM
> (*softly*)

Christ.

> NEAERA

What?

> WILLIAM

We've forgotten something.

> NEAERA

What?

> WILLIAM

The tide. It might be out.

EXT. POLPERRO.

The van comes downhill into Polperro.

INT. VAN.

> WILLIAM

We're here. What's the time?

> NEAERA

Two-thirty.

THE VAN STOPS.

INT. VAN. NIGHT.

They look at Polperro in the moonlight.

Silence.

EXT. POLPERRO.

They get out of the van, quietly, and walk towards the harbour.

INNER HARBOUR.

The tide is in. Boats bobbing. William and Neaera come round the corner. They speak together.

WILLIAM and NEAERA

It's in!

The wind hits them in the face. They run up an incline to the outer harbour.

In the outer harbour, waves crashing, spray flying, sea breaking halfway up steps, wind, moon in quick clouds.

THE VAN.

They run to the van, open the doors, take out the trolley. She steadies the trolley. He tips the first crate on to it. He hauls the trolley towards the harbour. She follows with rope.

EXT. HARBOUR. BREAKWATER. NIGHT.

They ease the crate off the trolley and lower it with the rope through the ring bolts.

THE TURTLE'S FACE.

WILLIAM UPENDS THE CRATE AND TILTS IT.

THE TURTLE HITS THE WATER AND DIVES.

WILLIAM AND NEAERA HUG AND KISS EACH OTHER.

SECOND TURTLE ON THE TROLLEY.

TURTLE DIARY

TROLLEY WHEELED TOWARDS HARBOUR.

CRATE UPENDED.

TURTLE DIVES.

THIRD TURTLE ON THE TROLLEY.

CRATE UPENDED.

TURTLE DIVES.

CRATES THROWN INTO THE SEA.

THE SEA.

Turtles swimming. In background, William and Neaera on the breakwater. They run down to the beach and into the surf.

THE BEACH.

WILLIAM
The champagne!

He runs back to the van. She stands, looking out to sea.

He runs up the incline towards her, with bottle and two cups. The cork pops. The champagne flows.

NEAERA
Here's wishing them luck!

WILLIAM
To the turtles!

They drink, and, giggling, drink again.

THE WAVES SILVER UNDER THE MOON.

THE BEACH.

William waves.

WILLIAM

Bye bye!

They finish the bottle, he hurls it into the sea.

They hug each other.

EXT. CAR PARK. NIGHT.

The van drives in quietly. Shafts of headlights illumine other vans and caravans. Silence. The van stops. The lights go off.

An owl. Distant sound of the sea.

INT. BACK OF VAN.

They arrange the blankets and pillows.

They lie down, on their backs.

Silence.

WILLIAM

Well, we did it.

NEAERA

Yes.
> (*Pause.*)

You were wonderful.

WILLIAM

Oh . . . I don't know.
> (*Pause.*)

You were pretty good yourself.

NEAERA

Thank you.
> (*Pause*)

Good night.

WILLIAM

Good night.

EXT. CAR PARK. AFTERNOON.

The car park is packed. Dozens of people, children. Refreshments and souvenir stands at the entrance. Bright sun.

INT. VAN.

Neaera wakes up. She turns over, sees William still asleep. She looks out of the window, surveys the car-park scene. She gets up, quietly leaves the van.

EXT. CAR PARK.

Neaera threading her way through people.

INT. VAN.

William wakes up. He turns, sees Neaera's pillow. He sits up, looks out of the window. He opens the doors and gets out.

EXT. CAR PARK.

William stands, frowning in the sun. He sees Neaera, who is leaning against the car-park wall. He goes to her.

WILLIAM

How are you feeling?

NEAERA

All right.

EXT. HARBOUR.

William and Neaera walk along the harbour. The tide is out. Boats sitting in the mud. Broken glass and rubbish.

509

Fishermen on the quayside. Boxes of fish. William looks into the boxes, casually.

> WILLIAM
> (*to a fisherman.*)
> What time was the high tide? Could you tell me?

> FISHERMAN
> Seven o'clock in the morning.

> WILLIAM
> Thank you.

They walk away and up to the breakwater.

In the mud, spars of broken crates stuck.

William turns to her.

> They got away.

EXT. POLPERRO.

The van leaving Polperro.

EXT. THE TAMAR BRIDGE. DAY.

The van crossing the Tamar Bridge.

EXT. VAN MOVING. NIGHT.

INT. VAN. NIGHT.

William and Neaera silent.

IN ROADSIDE CAFÉ. NIGHT.

William and Neaera at table, with tea.

A bottle of ketchup.

The café is empty.

INT. VAN. NIGHT.

William bent over the wheel.

EXT. WILLIAM'S POINT OF VIEW.

Flashing light, shadows, red tail-lights.

INT. VAN.

> WILLIAM
> My eyes are going.

> NEAERA
> Why don't you stop?

> WILLIAM
> Let's get there.

EXT. HAMMERSMITH FLY-OVER.

Van moving.

EXT. NEAERA'S HOUSE. NIGHT.

The van drives up.

INT. VAN.

William switches off the engine. They sit.

> NEAERA
> Are you all right?

> WILLIAM
> A bit tired. What's the time?

> NEAERA
> Midnight.
> (*Pause.*)
> Have you kept track of the expenses?

WILLIAM

I'll add it all up after I take the van back tomorrow. She did twenty miles to the gallon, you know.

NEAERA

Did she? Good. Well, good night.

WILLIAM

Good night.

They look at each other, briefly. She gets out. He jumps out.

Your blankets – your pillows.

NEAERA

Oh yes.

EXT. VAN.

They open the back door, put blankets and pillows into the case.

WILLIAM

Is that it?

NEAERA

Yes. Thanks.

WILLIAM

No. Thank you.

NEAERA

Good night.

He watches her go up the steps and into the house.

INT. NEAERA'S FLAT.

She enters. Puts the light on in the hall. The sitting-room door is closed. She goes to it, opens it.

INT. SITTING-ROOM.

Glow from the tank. A man's legs. A figure stands. She puts the light on. Johnson.

JOHNSON

Sorry to startle you. I dropped in a cleaning squad. I was just checking their work rate.

NEAERA

Cleaning squad?

JOHNSON

My snails.

NEAERA

Ah.

She looks in the tank.

RED SNAILS IN TANK.

INT. NEAERA'S FLAT. ROOM. NIGHT.

JOHNSON

Sorry to startle you. Your beetle's in damn good form, I must say. Very jolly.

NEAERA

Thank you ... for looking after her.

JOHNSON

Well, I'll say good night.

He goes to the door, turns.

Good trip?

NEAERA

Yes.

JOHNSON

Good. Good.

He goes.

She looks after him.

INT. WILLIAM'S ROOM. MORNING.

William gets out of bed. He puts on a dressing-gown and leaves the room.

INT. BATHROOM.

Hair and scum in the bath.

William staring down. He grits his teeth.

INT. LANDING.

William goes to the cooker.

The cooker is grimed with food. He stares at it.

He goes across the landing to Sandor's door, knocks.

Sandor opens the door. He wears a dressing-gown and slippers.

SANDOR

Yes?

WILLIAM

Too much!

SANDOR

What?

WILLIAM

Too much!

SANDOR

What are you saying?

WILLIAM

You clean that cooker.

SANDOR

Who clean cooker? Who say?

WILLIAM

You clean cooker. And bath! I say.

William pokes him in the chest.

SANDOR

Mind. Go slow. I caution you. Piss off. All best.

WILLIAM

No. Not all best. All bleeding worst.

He grabs the lapel of Sandor's dressing-gown.

Clean the cooker!

Sandor turns William round, thrusting his arm behind his back. William flings his arm back and hits Sandor in the face. They both fall to the floor.

Sandor gets William in a scissors grip. He tightens his legs round William's ribs. They lie on the landing.

WILLIAM'S FACE.

It is pressed against the carpet. Sound of Sandor's breathing above him. Sound of a train approaching. William's nose sniffing the carpet.

EXT. THE COMMON. DAY.

The train moving. Signals green. Red signals flash.

INT. LANDING.

Sudden upheaval.

Sandor rolling down the stairs.

William crouched on the landing.

SANDOR.

He stares up at William.

WILLIAM.

He stares down at Sandor.

Mrs Inchcliff runs up the stairs.

> MRS INCHCLIFF
> What's happening? Why is everyone lying on the floor?

Silence.

> SANDOR
> We have collision. Down we tumble.

Mrs Inchcliff looks up at William. He looks down.

INT. AQUARIUM. DAY.

Empty turtle tank.

Neaera looking at it. She goes to the office door, knocks, enters. George is there.

INT. OFFICE.

> GEORGE
> Hello! Come in. Sit down. You're back. How did it go? What happened?

> NEAERA
> They went. They went into the sea . . . and they went off.

GEORGE

Wonderful.

NEAERA

Unless you've had any reports – I mean of turtles being picked up, off the Cornish coast.

GEORGE

No reports.

NEAERA

Well . . . we did it.

GEORGE

That's terrific.

NEAERA

Yes. We did it.

She suddenly cries.

He puts his arm around her.

GEORGE

They'll be very pleased, you know.

NEAERA
(*crying*)

Who?

He holds her.

GEORGE

The turtles. They'll be really happy.

INT. WILLIAM'S ROOM. MORNING.

William hobbling about the room. He limps, curses. He massages his ribs, shoulders, arm. Curses.

He suddenly stops, lifts his head, sniffs.

Sound from the cooker on landing.

William opens the door very quietly, peeps through the chink.

SANDOR AT COOKER.

Sandor shovels food from pan on to plate, goes to his room, shuts door.

William goes on to the landing and stares at the cooker. It is filthy.

William picks up cloth, holds it under tap, goes across landing, knocks at Sandor's door.

SANDOR

Who is it?

WILLIAM

Me.

Sandor opens the door. William holds up wet cloth.

Clean the cooker.

SANDOR

I clean your cooker right enough. I break your bones.

William shoves the cloth into his face and knees him in the crutch. Sandor doubles over. William forces his head down and knees him in the face.

SANDOR ON FLOOR, FACE BLOODY.

WILLIAM'S FACE, UNCERTAIN.

SANDOR'S FEET FLYING OUT.

WILLIAM HITTING WALL.

INT. WILLIAM'S ROOM.

William lying on his bed. Mrs Inchcliff sitting by him. He opens his eyes.

518

WILLIAM

Where am I?

MRS INCHCLIFF

On your bed.

Pause.

WILLIAM

Where's Sandor?

MRS INCHCLIFF

At the hospital. To get his nose done.

Pause.

WILLIAM

How did I get here?

MRS INCHCLIFF

We carried you.

WILLIAM

Who?

MRS INCHCLIFF

Sandor and me.

William looks at her.

A girl phoned.

WILLIAM

Oh? When?

MRS INCHCLIFF

About ten minutes ago. I said you were sleeping.

WILLIAM

Well, I was, wasn't I?

INT. GEORGE'S FLAT. MORNING.

The flat is on the top floor of a house in Hampstead. It is light, airy, silent.

George and Neaera are in bed. She is in his arms. He kisses her cheek, moves to get out of bed.

NEAERA

Where are you going?

GEORGE

Coffee?

NEAERA

No. Stay.
                    (*She kisses him.*)
Stay.
                         (*Pause.*)
All right, you can go now.

He moves.

No. Stay.
                    (*She snuggles into his chest.*)
I'll make the coffee.

GEORGE

You don't want to make coffee.

NEAERA

No. I don't.

GEORGE

Well, listen. Will you just let me know when you're ready to order breakfast?

NEAERA

Yes. I'll let you know.

They lie close.

I'm ready to order.

GEORGE

What do you want?

He takes her in his arms.

INT. WILLIAM'S ROOM. MORNING.

William sitting up in bed in pyjamas, with coffee and toast.

Footsteps. A knock at the door.

WILLIAM

Hello?

Harriet comes in.

HARRIET

I came to give you a lift. What's the matter?

WILLIAM

A slight chill. I think I'll stay where I am today.

HARRIET

Oh. Did you catch it on your day off?

WILLIAM

Possibly.

HARRIET

How was your day off?

WILLIAM

Oh, OK.

HARRIET

What did you do?

WILLIAM

I went to Cornwall.

HARRIET

Cornwall?

WILLIAM

Yes.

HARRIET

That's ... a very long way, isn't it?

WILLIAM

It bloody is.

HARRIET

With that woman?

WILLIAM

That's right. She did well.

HARRIET

Did she?

WILLIAM

Yes. We put these turtles into the sea, you see.

HARRIET

You what?

WILLIAM

Turtles. We stole three turtles from the Zoo and took them to Cornwall and put them into the sea. That's why I needed the day off, in order to do that.

HARRIET

I don't understand.

WILLIAM

Why not?

Pause.

HARRIET

I don't understand ... what you're talking about.

WILLIAM

It's simple. That's what we arranged to do and that's
what we did.

HARRIET

Turtles.

WILLIAM

Yes.

(*Pause.*)

Want a piece of toast?

HARRIET

Thank you.

She sits on the bed.

William gives her a piece of toast.

WILLIAM

Here you are. They're on their way to Ascension Island
now.

HARRIET

Who are?

WILLIAM

The turtles. Marmalade?

HARRIET

You're very chirpy this morning.

WILLIAM
(*grinning*)

Am I? Yes – I suppose I am.

*A sharp knock at the door. Mrs Inchcliff comes in without waiting
for a response.*

Harriet jumps up from the bed. William stares.

MRS INCHCLIFF

I think there's something wrong.

WILLIAM

Wrong?

MRS INCHCLIFF

Miss Neap. She won't answer the door.

William gets out of bed.

I haven't seen her all morning.

William goes to the door.

LANDING.

William and Mrs Inchcliff go down the stairs to the floor below.

THE FLOOR BELOW.

William and Mrs Inchcliff approach Miss Neap's door.

THE HALL.

The front door of the house opens. Sandor comes in, a large plaster over his nose. He stops, looks up the stairs.

MISS NEAP'S DOOR.

William knocks at Miss Neap's door. No reply. He tries the handle.

WILLIAM

It's open.

In background Harriet appears on the stairs.

He opens the door.

INT. MISS NEAP'S ROOM.

The room is dark, curtains drawn. William turns on the light. Miss Neap is sitting by a table in an armchair. One arm hangs over the side of the chair. Her head lolls. A large Snoopy dog is at her feet.

Mrs Inchcliff and William go to her. William feels Miss Neap's pulse. On her lap, a Book of Common Prayer *open at 'For the Burial of the Dead at Sea'.*

Behind her, on the table, an empty bottle of pills, a glass, a photograph of a girl of ten standing with her parents. An envelope propped up, addressed to Mrs Inchcliff.

THE LANDING AND STAIRS.

Harriet looking down into Miss Neap's room.

Sandor runs up the stairs, goes into the room. William turns from Miss Neap, murmurs something, looks up, sees Harriet, comes out of the room, goes up the stairs to Harriet, puts his arm around her, takes her up the stairs.

Mrs Inchcliff comes out of the room, goes swiftly down to the telephone, starts to dial.

Sandor remains, looking down at Miss Neap.

Over this, Mrs Inchcliff's voice.

                    MRS INCHCLIFF
                      (*reading*)
    'I have made all the arrangements for the cremation and
    have paid by cheque.'

INT. MRS INCHCLIFF'S KITCHEN.

Mrs Inchcliff, William and Sandor at kitchen table. A bottle of whisky. Mrs Inchcliff reading the letter aloud.

MRS INCHCLIFF

'I don't want a funeral service of any kind. I don't want anyone to be present. Please do not notify my mother until after the cremation. No flowers. Thank you. Flora Neap.'

Mrs Inchcliff puts the letter on the table. Sandor pours her a drink.

I never knew.

Pause.

WILLIAM

We never asked.
                        (*Pause.*)
She was just Miss Neap.

MRS INCHCLIFF

Do you think it's right – no service, no one there, no flowers?

WILLIAM

It's what she wanted.

SANDOR

Do it how she wanted.

Silence.

WILLIAM
(*to Sandor*)

How's your nose?

SANDOR

Nose no problem. But I am grotty a little. Minor temperature. I have slightly vertigo, I stand up, room goes round, floor is slanty. And you? How is your health?

WILLIAM
My floor's pretty slanty too.

Sandor raises his glass.

SANDOR
I drink to Miss Neap.

They all raise their glasses, drink.

INT. NEAERA'S FLAT. EARLY EVENING.

It has changed: brighter, crisper. Flowers. Bottles on the sideboard. Neaera different. Her hair, her dress, etc. Her doorbell rings. She walks quickly to it and opens it. Johnson.

JOHNSON
Hello.

NEAERA
Oh, hello.

JOHNSON
Wondered if you'd like to pop in and have a drink?

NEAERA
A drink?

JOHNSON
We've been neighbours for years. But we've never had a drink.

NEAERA
I'd love to. But I'm expecting someone in a minute.

JOHNSON
Ah. Another time, perhaps.

NEAERA
Mmnn.

                    JOHNSON
Snails behaving?

                    NEAERA
Busy cleaning up.

                    JOHNSON
Actually, they have tiny radio transmitters in them, so I
get to know everything that goes on in your flat.

                    NEAERA
Must make pretty dull listening.

                    JOHNSON
Well, I'll try again when I get back.

                    NEAERA
Where this time?

Johnson smiles.

                    JOHNSON
Oh ... usual kind of thing. Bye.

He goes.

She turns to look at the snails in the tank.

EXT. ZOO. DAY.

William walks towards the aquarium with a bottle of champagne.

INT. AQUARIUM.

*William walks through the aquarium. He notes two baby turtles
in the tank. He goes into the office.*

INT. OFFICE.

George and Neaera sitting with sandwiches.

GEORGE

Hello.

WILLIAM

Just passing by. Thought I'd drop this off.

NEAERA

Perfect. We're just having our lunch.

GEORGE

Couldn't be better.

George stands. Gets glasses.

NEAERA

Like a sandwich?

WILLIAM

No, no.

GEORGE
(*to William*)

Oh, I told them, by the way. I told them I'd set them
free. Left you two out of it. I said I was getting in a
couple of babies and I'd set them free too, when the
time comes.

WILLIAM

What did they say?

GEORGE

They made a few noises and then they shut up.

He opens the bottle and pours. They drink.

WILLIAM

Good. Well, I have to go.

NEAERA

Do you?

WILLIAM

Yes, back to work.

NEAERA

I'll come out with you.

GEORGE
(*to William*)
Come back and see how the babies are getting on.

WILLIAM

I will.

NEAERA
(*to George*)
Don't drink all the champagne.

INT. AQUARIUM.

Neaera and William walking through the aquarium.

WILLIAM

Listen. What about doing it again – in about twenty years' time?

NEAERA

You mean when the babies are grown up?

WILLIAM

Yes.

NEAERA

Why not?

WILLIAM

I'll ring you nearer the time.

NEAERA
(*smiling*)
Right.

TURTLE DIARY

They stop. Neaera puts out her hand. He takes it. They look at each other.

Well, cheerio then.

WILLIAM
Cheerio.

He opens the door. A shaft of brilliant sun. He goes out. She stands a moment. She turns, walks back towards the office.

EXT. ZOO.

Long shot. William walking towards the exit.

THE GIANT TURTLES, SWIMMING IN THE OCEAN.

Reunion

Reunion was produced in 1989. The cast included:

HENRY Jason Robards
HANS STRAUSS Christian Anholt
KONRADIN VON LOHENBURG Samuel West
GRÄFIN VON LOHENBURG Françoise Fabian
LISA, Henry's daughter Maureen Kerwin
HERR VON LOHENBURG, Konradin's father Jacques Brunet
MRS STRAUSS, Hans's mother Barbara Jefford
HERR STRAUSS, Hans's father Bert Parnaby

Director Jerry Schatzberg
Producer Vincent Malle
Production Designer Alexandre Trauner
Director of Photography Bruno de Keyzer
Costume Designer David Perry
Editor Martine Barraque
Music Philippe Sarde

EXT. A PRISON YARD. DAY.

Black and white film.

A line of men marching towards a door. They are naked to the waist, some holding their trousers up.

German guards accompany them.

They file through the door into a room. The camera stays at the open door.

INT. EXECUTION ROOM. DAY.

The room is bare. Two windows at the back. Winter sunshine slanting in. A rafter along the ceiling in front of the window.

Butcher's hooks hanging down.

A tall man in SS uniform stands straight-backed by the window.

The men file in and stand along the wall.

The door closes with a clang.

EXT. BAUER HOUSE: GARDEN. 1932. DAY.

Silent shot. A little girl on a swing under a tree, pushed by her father. In background two other children.

INT. SCHOOLROOM. 1932. DAY.

Silent shot. Konradin 16 entering the room and standing. The class looking at him. Hans (Henry when sixteen) looks up. Sounds of Central Park gradually grow on the soundtrack. Barking dogs.

REUNION

EXT. CENTRAL PARK, NEW YORK. 1987. SUMMER. DAY.

Henry 70 sitting on a park bench, looking into space. He is casually dressed.

A little girl, Alex 5, playing with a ball on the grass. The ball bounces away. She follows it. Two large dogs charge down the hill towards her. She sees them, cries out, falls. The dogs swerve away. She sits, crying.

Henry hears her cries. He stands, looks about him in panic, sees her, stumbles down the grass verge towards her.

He takes her in his arms.

> **HENRY**
> Alex, Alex, it's all right, I'm here, it's all right, I'm here.

INT. HENRY'S LAW OFFICE. DAY.

Activity up and down corridors, telephones ringing, etc.

Henry in his office on the phone. He wears a dark suit.

> **HENRY**
> *(into phone)*
> Tell him we can handle that. Sure. See I have the papers here by Wednesday ... I'm back Thursday ... Just have it on my desk for when I get back. We'll give 'em hell ... What? ... Germany ... Oh yeah? You fought there? Which side were you on?
> *(He laughs.)*
> Say no more. Sure, sure. I'll give them all your love. Bye.

He puts the phone down. His Secretary comes to the desk.

> **SECRETARY**
> Here's your ticket. And your travellers' cheques. And some cash.

HENRY

Uh-huh.

She puts them in a leather wallet.

SECRETARY

And here's the inventory.

He takes it. We glimpse a typed list in German.

HENRY

OK.

He puts it into the wallet. The Secretary smiles.

SECRETARY

And that's it.

HENRY

Good. Fine.

INT. NEW YORK RESTAURANT. DAY.

Lisa (in her thirties) at a table. Henry sitting. He kisses her on the cheek.

HENRY

How is she? Is she OK?

LISA

Sure she is.

HENRY

I got such a shock. You don't know how big they were –
the dogs. I blame myself.

LISA

Dad, she's perfectly all right. She's forgotten all about it.

HENRY

It's just that I was ... my mind was ... I wasn't paying
attention ...

LISA

Listen. Why are you taking this trip?

HENRY

Why?

LISA

You don't have to go. You don't want to go. Why are you going?

HENRY

I have to take care of this . . . thing.

LISA

You could do it from here. You know that. Your secretary could do it for you. I could do it for you. You don't have to go all the way over there yourself. Do you? What's the point?

HENRY

I want to do it myself. I have to go and do it myself.
          (*He takes her hand.*)
I'll be fine. Really. I'll be fine. I promise you.
                    (*He smiles.*)
I'm not a child.

WAITER

Are you going to have an aperitif before lunch, Mr Strauss?

HENRY

Sure. Give me a Bloody Mary.
                    (*To Lisa.*)
What about you?

LISA

I don't want anything.

REUNION

INT. PARK AVENUE APARTMENT. DAY.

The apartment is spacious, uncluttered.

Light slants through the wide windows. Traffic sounds, distant.

Stillness.

*Henry is standing by the window, looking out. A man in
chauffeur's uniform comes into the far end of the room, holding a
suitcase.*

> CHAUFFEUR
>
> Ready, sir?

> HENRY
>
> What's the time?

> CHAUFFEUR
>
> Four o'clock.

> HENRY
>
> OK.

He walks to the door.

SILENT FLASH.

Hans swinging on horizontal bar.

INT. KENNEDY AIRPORT. FIRST-CLASS CHECK-IN.

Coming up on to a computer:

Strauss, Henry
Lufthansa 324
New York–Stuttgart (return)
First class – Seat D3

SILENT FLASH.

*Father in officer's uniform with sword and Iron Cross standing
next to a Nazi.*

REUNION

INT. PLANE.

Henry sitting in first class.

ANNOUNCEMENT
(*in German*)
Captain Richter and his crew welcome you aboard this
Lufthansa flight to Stuttgart. Your flight time will be –

SILENT FLASH.

Marlene Dietrich crossing her legs in The Blue Angel.

INT. STUTTGART. HOTEL AM SCHLOSSGARTEN. RECEPTION.

RECEPTIONIST
Mr Strauss. Yes indeed. Thank you very much. Room
654. Have a nice stay, Mr Strauss.

Another Man escorts Henry to the elevator.

MAN
Is this your first time in Stuttgart?

HENRY
No.

INT. HOTEL BEDROOM. STUTTGART. NIGHT.

*Henry standing, looking about the room. He switches on the
television set. A discussion programme. Henry opens his suitcase.
He starts to unpack. On the screen the Presenter is talking to a
studio filled with young people (in German).*

PRESENTER
Now look at this.

Laurence Olivier in Henry V *comes up on the screen.*

OLIVIER
Then will he strip his sleeve and show his scars,

And say, 'These wounds I had on Crispin's day.'
Old men forget; yet all shall be forgot,
But he'll remember with advantages
What feats he did that day. Then shall our names,
Familiar in his mouth as household words,
Harry the king, Bedford and Exeter,
Warwick and Talbot, Salisbury and Gloucester,
Be in their flowing cups freshly remember'd.

The clip ends. the Presenter speaks.

PRESENTER

Now what was Laurence Olivier doing? Laurence Oliver
was acting a man who is himself acting – who is putting
on an act.

Henry goes into the bathroom.

INT. HOTEL BATHROOM. DAY.

Henry unpacking his shaving materials.

PRESENTER
(*VO*)

Henry the Fifth actually feels very uncertain indeed
about the battle ahead but is able to hide this
uncertainty by putting on a mask – by acting! Now here
is a quite different case. Or is it?

*Suddenly the voice of Judge Freisler screaming. Henry stops
unpacking and, suddenly riveted, stares into the mirror. He goes
into the other room.*

INT. HOTEL BEDROOM. DAY.

Judge Freisler on the television screen screaming. Black and white.

PRESENTER
(*VO*)

Now that man – is he an actor? Is he acting? Is he simply

playing the part of a cruel and sadistic judge? Or is he real? Is he the real thing?

Henry switches the television set off abruptly.

INT. HOTEL BAR. EARLY EVENING.

Henry comes into the bar. It is empty apart from a Japanese Businessman and the Bartender. They are talking.

> BARTENDER
>
> Yes, in Hanau. A very big company.

> BUSINESSMAN
>
> Oh yes. I know. But in Japan too. In Japan it is advancing very fast.

> HENRY
>
> A beer. Dutch. You have Dutch beer?

The Bartender shrugs.

> BARTENDER
>
> Yes.

He opens the bottle of beer.

> BUSINESSMAN
>
> You are American?

> HENRY
>
> Yes.

> BUSINESSMAN
>
> You are also developing superconductors in America.

> HENRY
>
> Superconductors?

> BUSINESSMAN
>
> Sure. They're going to revolutionize electronics. We were just talking about it. You don't know about them?

REUNION

HENRY

No.

BUSINESSMAN

They're going to change the world. Automobiles will
run on electric magnets. Pollution will be finished. It
will be a beautiful new, clean world. Listen – it's not
going to just change the world, it's going to save the
world. We're going to save the damn world and we're
going to make a lot of damn big money. Believe me.
You should get into it now. Take my advice. You can't
lose.

The Bartender leans across the bar to Henry, smiling.

BARTENDER

It will be good for Germany too.

EXT. HOTEL AM SCHLOSSGARTEN. NIGHT.

*Henry comes out of the hotel and walks into the park. A group of
winos on a park bench with bottles. He approaches the Opera
House and stops to look at it. It is brightly lit.*

EXT. SHOPPING ARCADE. NIGHT.

*Henry walking through the arcade. He passes a shop window
containing guns of all sizes. A tramp sits on a doorstep shouting.
He looks across the arcade at a McDonald's hamburger
restaurant. A group of punks eating.*

INT. HOTEL RECEPTION. MORNING.

Henry at the desk.

HENRY

What flights are there tonight for New York?

RECEPTIONIST

New York?

543

REUNION

HENRY

Yes.

RECEPTIONIST

Your room?

HENRY

654. Strauss.

She looks at the computer.

RECEPTIONIST

But you have reserved your room until Wednesday.

HENRY

I know. But I want to know what flights there are tonight.

RECEPTIONIST

The same as Wednesday. The same as every night.

HENRY

I see.

He turns and goes out of the hotel.

EXT. WIDE ROAD. STUTTGART. DAY.

Henry walks towards the corner, stops, looks about. At the corner is a tall office block. An elderly man approaches. Henry stops him.

HENRY

Excuse me. Do you speak any English?

The Man stares at him.

MAN

Little. A little.

HENRY

You are from Stuttgart?

MAN

Oh yes. Yes.

HENRY

Was there a school here? At this corner? The Karl
Alexander Gymnasium? Was it here?

MAN

Bombed.
                    (*He gestures.*)
Kaputt. Gone.

HENRY

Thank you.

The Man clicks his heels, bows.

MAN
(*in German*)
At your service.

INT. TRAVELLING TAXI. DAY.

Henry looking out. Radio playing.

EXT. MODERN STUTTGART.

Henry's point of view.

INT. WAREHOUSE OFFICE.

*A Man at a desk. Henry sitting at the desk. The Man is looking
at a file.*

MAN

Strauss. Yes.

He looks up for a moment at Henry and then picks up the phone.

(*In German.*)
Herr Strauss is here. Lot 415.

(*To Henry.*)

Follow me please.

They go out into the corridor.

Go down there, please. Take the elevator to the fifth
floor. Someone is waiting.

HENRY

Thank you.

He begins to walk down the corridor.

INT. WAREHOUSE. FIFTH FLOOR.

A Man removing sheets from furniture and tea chests.

MAN

You will ring that bell when you have finished, please.

HENRY

Yes. Thank you.

*Henry walks slowly through the furniture: heavy oak chairs,
tables, dressing tables, etc. He rummages in a tea chest,
unwrapping German newspaper. He looks at the date – 1934. He
bring out a long-stemmed wine glass, blue Meissen plates, a
Jewish candlestick.*

*From another tea chest he unwraps Cézanne and Van Gogh
prints and some books. Following this, coins, a tiger's claw, a
Roman fibula, an elephant's back tooth. A Corinthian coin. He
looks carefully at the coin and slips it into his pocket.*

*He goes to the next tea chest and unwraps an Iron Cross and an
officer's sword. He stares at them.*

INT. WAREHOUSE OFFICE.

Henry with Man.

MAN

OK?

HENRY

It's all in very good condition.

MAN

Yes, I think so.

HENRY

I want you to sell it and I want the money to go to
charity.

MAN

Yes, if you wish. What charity?

HENRY

Oh ...

MAN

There are hundreds of charities. You have a preference?

HENRY

The blind.

The Man writes, murmurs.

MAN

The blind.

INT. SCHOOLROOM. 1932.

Silent shot. Slow motion.

Konradin 16 entering the room and standing.

EXT. A LAKE. DAY.

*At the far side of the lake a procession with banners. A chorus of
voices singing in the distance.*

547

REUNION

INT. SCHOOLROOM. 1932.

*Boys at their desks, including Hans, are looking up, staring at
Konradin.*

*The Headmaster whispers in Herr Zimmerman's ear and goes
out.*

*Konradin stands still. He wears a light-grey suit, pale-blue shirt,
dark-blue tie.*

*Herr Zimmerman shows Konradin to a desk and walks
backwards to his own chair. Konradin sits.*

> HERR ZIMMERMAN
> Would you please give me your surname, Christian
> name and the date and place of your birth.

Konradin stands.

> KONRADIN
> Graf von Lohenburg. Konradin. Born 19th of January
> 1916. Burg Lohenburg. Württemberg.

He sits.

THE BOYS.

*The boys, scruffy, untidy, ink-stained, stare at Konradin, who sits
erect and composed, elegant.*

HANS WATCHING KONRADIN.

KONRADIN AT HIS DESK.

*Konradin taking pencils from his briefcase. His fingers: long,
clean.*

EXT. SCHOOLYARD. DAY.

Flag-raising ceremony. The school at attention. The ceremony ends. Two boys approach Konradin. One clicks his heels. Hans in the background.

VON HANKHOFEN
Lohenburg. Baron von Hankhofen. How do you do?

KONRADIN
How do you do?

VON HANKHOFEN
May I introduce you to Prince Hubertus Petershagen Wildenheim?

The Prince clicks his heels and bows.

THE PRINCE
How do you do?

KONRADIN
How do you do?

THE PRINCE
I believe you know my cousin – Count Dietrich Petershagen Wildenheim?

KONRADIN
Dietrich?

THE PRINCE
You stayed at his father's castle at Wimpfen-am-Neckar.

VON HANKHOFEN
Duke Eberhard Ludwig was shooting there.

KONRADIN
No, no, I'm afraid your cousin is confusing me with somebody else.

THE PRINCE
Somebody else?

549

KONRADIN

Somebody who looks like me perhaps?

He grins, turns and walks into school. The Prince and Baron look at each other. Hans studies them.

INT. SCHOOL CLOAKROOM. AFTERNOON.

Boys milling about. Hans packing his case. Through the window Konradin seen walking to the school gates. Hans looks after him.

INT. STRAUSS HOUSE. PARLOUR. DAY.

Hans drinking tea.

DR STRAUSS

One of the oldest families in Germany. They go back to the twelfth century. Look them up in the encyclopaedia. Very, very distinguished. Warriors. Great German warriors.

HANS

What were our ancestors – I mean in the twelfth century?

DR STRAUSS

Cattle dealers.

HANS

Distinguished.

DR STRAUSS
(*smiling*)
I don't imagine they were all that close to the Emperor.
(*They drink their tea.*)
What's he like, your friend?

HANS

He's not my friend. Anyway, he keeps himself to himself. Which suits me.

REUNION

INT. GYM.

The class running round the gym, with exhortations from the gym instructor, 'Muscle Max'.

MUSCLE MAX
Right! Stop! Stand easy. Now watch this.

He goes to the horizontal bar, stands to attention under it, stretches up his arms and then jumps. He raises his body slowly inch by inch, then turns to the right, to the left, etc. He then swings faster and faster and lands lightly on his toes.

Right! Were you watching?

THE CLASS
Yes, sir.

MUSCLE MAX
Who's going to be the first volunteer?

HANS
Me, sir.

MUSCLE MAX
You? All right, come on then.

Hans goes to the bar. He jumps up and grasps the rod. He raises his body from right to left and from left to right, hangs on his knees, swings upwards and rests for a second on the bar, then swings faster and faster, jumps over the bar and lands on his feet.

During all this Konradin's eyes have not left him.

As he lands there is surprised laughter from some of the boys, applause from others.

Good, Strauss. I didn't know you had it in you.

Hans's and Konradin's eyes meet.

REUNION

INT. SCHOOLROOM. MORNING.

Hans taking some Greek coins from his briefcase. He studies them through a magnifying glass. In background Konradin watching. Konradin strolls across to Hans's desk.

KONRADIN

Greek?

HANS

Yes.

KONRADIN

I collect too. May I look?

Hans gives him the magnifying glass. Konradin looks through it.

Yes, Pallas Athena. I have it. Who's this?

HANS

Alexander the Great.

The Master walks in, bangs on his desk with a ruler.

MASTER

Good morning. Everybody sit down.

Konradin goes to his desk.

EXT. SCHOOL GROUNDS. DAY.

Reutter, Müller and Frank approach Konradin. Hans is in the background, reading.

REUTTER

Lohenburg, I'm not sure that you know what we three are known as?

KONRADIN

No. what?

REUTTER

The Caviar of the class.

KONRADIN

Oh? Why?

MÜLLER
(*grinning*)

Because we're the most intelligent, well-read,
knowledgeable and artistic people in the class.

KONRADIN

Good lord. Are you really?

FRANK

Oh yes, there's no doubt about it. You can ask anyone.

KONRADIN

Oh? Who shall I ask?

FRANK

Us!

He laughs.

REUTTER

The thing is, we'd like to invite you to take part in a
play-reading we're giving on Thursday – to a rather
select audience.

KONRADIN

What's the play?

MÜLLER

Hamlet.

FRANK

We thought you might like to read the part of the Prince
yourself.

KONRADIN

But I'm not an actor, I'm afraid. And I've never
understood *Hamlet*. And anyway I'm very busy these
days. So sorry.

553

Konradin turns and walks away, glancing at Hans.

INT. SCHOOLROOM. DAY.

Hans standing addressing the class.

HANS

Hamlet is a classic example of schizophrenia, of split personality. On the one hand, he laments the deterioration of civilized values, the decline in standards, the breakdown of moral systems, the failure of the state – and on the other hand he treats people like rubbish, kills Polonius without a sign of remorse, is vicious to his mother, drives Ophelia crazy, coldly sends Rosencrantz and Guildenstern to their deaths. The great Sigmund Freud would describe this as a classic case of schizophrenia.

Bollacher mutters in a low voice.

BOLLACHER

Sigmund Freud! Sigmund Freud is a Jew!

Silence.

Hans turns slowly and looks at Bollacher.

MASTER

Thank you, Strauss. Very interesting.

INT. GYM. DAY.

Six boys swinging from rings throwing medicine balls at lines of pins.

Bollacher tying his shoelaces. Hans throws his ball at Bollacher. It hits him on the head. Bollacher turns angrily. Hans continues to swing.

REUNION

EXT. STUTTGART STREET. DAY.

Konradin walking. Hans walking a way behind him. Konradin slows. Hans slows. Hans accelerates, passes Konradin, nods perfunctorily, walks on.

Konradin calls after him.

KONRADIN

Hello!

Hans turns. Konradin catches him up.

Which way are you going?

HANS

Karalshohe.

KONRADIN

We're going the same way.

They walk.

Who's Freud?

HANS

Didn't you hear what Bollacher said? He's a Jew.

KONRADIN

No, apart from that.

HANS

You mean you haven't heard of him?

KONRADIN

Well, vaguely. What is he exactly?

HANS

Well . . . he's a doctor. Of the mind. He writes books about the mind.

KONRADIN

Oh.

They walk on.

Are they any good?

HANS

Terrific. I haven't read all of them, of course.

They walk on.

What do you think of the school?

KONRADIN

Well ... I don't know, really. I can't compare it with any other, you see.

HANS

Why not?

KONRADIN
(*laughing*)

I've never been to school before! Pathetic, isn't it? I've only ever had private tutors.

HANS

Really? Why?

KONRADIN

Well ... my father was Ambassador – first to Brazil – and then to Turkey. So ... I had these tutors.

HANS

Ah.

They walk on.

KONRADIN

What do *you* think of the school?

HANS

I can't wait to get to university and meet some girls.

They laugh and walk on.

REUNION

STUTTGART STREET.

High shot of the two boys walking up a hill, talking vigorously.

EXT. KONRADIN'S HOUSE. DAY.

The boys walking towards the house, talking.

> KONRADIN
> I think America might be good. Yale University. Have
> you heard of it?

> HANS
> Of course. But how's your English?

> KONRADIN
> Not bad.

They stop at a pair of great gates.

> I live here.
> > (*He extends his hand.*)
> See you tomorrow.

*They shake hands. Konradin opens the heavy gate and walks up
the oleander-bordered path towards an arch. Through the arch
can be seen the lower level of a double staircase. Hans watches
Konradin disappear. Hans turns away and begins to run up the
hill.*

EXT. BAUER HOUSE. GARDEN. DAY.

*The Bauer children playing on the swing. Hans passes on his way
to his own house. He waves at the children. They wave back.
Hans goes into his house.*

INT. STRAUSS HOUSE. DAY.

*Hans comes in the front door. He hears two voices from the
sitting-room. His Father and another man. He stops, listens.*

FATHER

But what kind of claim is that? It doesn't make any sense!

ZIONIST

It's our homeland! Palestine is our homeland.

FATHER

What, after two thousand years?

ZIONIST

Yes.

FATHER

But it's absolutely ridiculous! It's as if ... it's as if Italy claimed Germany because it was once occupied by the Romans!

ZIONIST

No it isn't.

FATHER

Anyway I was born in Stuttgart – not Jerusalem.

ZIONIST

And what about Hitler?

FATHER

A temporary illness – like measles. Once the economic situation improves Hitler will go out of fashion. He won't be necessary. Can't you see that? I know the German people. This is the land of Goethe, of Schiller, of Beethoven! They're not going to fall for that rubbish.

ZIONIST

And the Jews?

FATHER

Twelve thousand Jews died for Germany in the last war! Proudly! I was wounded twice! I have the honour to tell you I was awarded the Iron Cross first class by my country. Yes – I'm proud to be a Jew – but I'm also proud to be a German!

ZIONIST

You're a Jew? What kind of Jew?

FATHER

A German Jew! We go to synagogue on Yom Kippur and we sing 'Silent Night' at Christmas.

ZIONIST

You're mad.

The Zionist comes out into the hall fastening his briefcase. He sees Hans and points back into the room.

He's mad.

He leaves the house. Hans goes into the sitting-room.

INT. SITTING-ROOM. DAY.

FATHER

They're such dangerous fools, these people!

MOTHER

Hello, Hans.

HANS

I just walked up the hill with Lohenburg.

FATHER

So narrow-minded! It drives me mad!

MOTHER

Why do you get so excited?

FATHER

Excited! It's a serious matter, that's why! These people can't think. They're just panicking. They're distorting the truth. They have everything totally out of proportion. All they do is make things worse!

MOTHER

You have a dozen patients waiting for you. They've been sitting in your office for twenty minutes.

FATHER

Yes, yes.

(*To Hans.*)

How's school?

HANS

All right.

Father stands a moment and then speaks quietly.

FATHER

I would like to remind you of what happened on my fiftieth birthday.

(*He looks at them both.*)

Do you remember? I'll tell you. The Mayor of this town gave a reception for me at the town hall. You were both at my side. They played *Eine kleine Nachtmusik* in my honour. It was a splendid occasion. They wished to show their respect for me and they did so. Their respect for a German Jew. Remember that.

He leaves the room.

Mother turns to Hans.

MOTHER

What's he like? Is he nice?

HANS

Who?

MOTHER

Lohenburg.

HANS

Oh, he's all right. It's nothing to make a fuss about. We're not friends or anything.

REUNION

EXT. SCHOOL YARD. MORNING.

Boys milling. Hans stands alone. Konradin enters the yard, looks about, sees Hans, walks through the crowd towards him. They shake hands. Boys turn and stare.

The bell rings. Konradin and Hans go into the school together, ignoring the others.

Outside the school walls a Nazi truck goes by.

> VOICE
> (*through the loudspeaker*)
> Vote for the National Socialist Party! Vote for the
> National Socialist Party!

Hans and Konradin seen through coffee-shop window, talking earnestly.

Hans and Konradin standing in doorway, talking, laughing. Pouring rain.

Hans and Konradin running downhill. Bright sun.

INT. LIVING ROOM. DAY.

Schubert Lieder *playing on a gramophone.*

Heavy oak furniture. Blue Meissen plates and long-stemmed wine glasses, purple and blue, on a dresser.

The camera pans across the room into a conservatory.

INT. CONSERVATORY. DAY.

Mother sitting under a rubber tree sewing. The front door closes. She lifts her head.

> MOTHER
> (*calling*)

Hans?

REUNION

HANS
(*out of shot*)

Mother!

*The music continues. Hans and Konradin coming into the
conservatory.*

Mother, this is my friend Konradin von Lohenburg.

She smiles, gives Konradin her hand. He kisses it.

MOTHER
Good afternoon, Konradin. I'm very happy to meet you.

KONRADIN
That's very kind of you, Mrs Strauss.

MOTHER
I hear you've lived in Turkey, South America . . . is that
right?

KONRADIN
Oh yes. But I prefer Germany. I think the beauty of
Germany is unbeatable.

HANS
We want to start making some trips into the Black
Forest . . . seeing the country . . . on weekends . . . would
that be all right?

MOTHER
Staying the night, you mean?

HANS
Yes.

MOTHER
Where?

KONRADIN
Oh . . . inns . . .

MOTHER
Well, I don't see why not. As you say, we do live in a
very beautiful country. You should both ... see as much
of it as possible ...

INT. LANDING.

Hans leading Konradin to his room.

KONRADIN
What a charming woman, your mother.

They go into Hans's room.

INT. HANS'S BEDROOM.

*The window looks down into the valley, the vineyards spreading
across the hills.*

*Konradin looks at the prints on the walls (Van Gogh, Cézanne,
Japanese etchings) and then examines the books on the shelves
(Goethe, Schiller, Kleist, Hölderlin, Rilke, Tolstoy, Dostoevsky,
Lermontov, Pushkin, Turgenev, Gogol, Shakespeare, Byron,
Baudelaire, Balzac, Flaubert, Stendhal, Verlaine, Rimbaud).*

KONRADIN
This is quite a library.
(*He stares at the Russian titles.*)
The Russians aren't in the original, are they?

Hans laughs.

HANS
No! I haven't had time to learn Russian yet.

KONRADIN
Thank God for that. Should I read Dostoevsky?

HANS
You certainly should. He's tremendous. He's ... I don't
know ... gigantic.

He takes a book from the shelves and gives it to Konradin.

Here. *Crime and Punishment*. Start with that.

KONRADIN

Wonderful. Thanks.

Hans takes Konradin to a corner of the room to see his collection. Konradin examines the items with great interest. The collection consists of corals from the Red Sea, topazes, malachites, a Roman fibula, the iron point of a javelin, some Roman coins, a tiger's tooth.

Suddenly, Dr Strauss's voice is heard on the stairs.

FATHER
(out of shot)

Hans.

He comes in, sees Konradin, clicks his heels, stands stiffly and puts out his hand.

How do you do? I am Dr Strauss.

Konradin bows slightly. They shake hands.

I am greatly honoured, Herr Graf, to have the scion of such an illustrious family under my roof. I have never had the pleasure of meeting your father, but I knew many of his friends, particularly Baron von Klumpf, who commanded the Second Squadron of the first Uhlan regiment, Ritter von Trompeda of the Hussars and Putzi von Grimmelshausen, known as 'Bautz'. I am sure your father must have told you of Bautz, who was a bosom friend of the Crown Prince? One day, so Bautz told me, his Imperial Highness, whose headquarters were then at Charlesroi, called for him and said to him, 'Bautz, my dear friend, I want to ask you a great favour. You know Gretel, my chimpanzee, is still a virgin and badly needs a husband. I want to arrange a wedding to

564

which I will invite all my staff. Take your car and travel round Germany and find me a healthy, good-looking male.' Bautz clicked his heels, stood to attention and said, 'Jawohl, Imperial Highness.' Then he marched out, jumped into the Crown Prince's Daimler and travelled from zoo to zoo, all over the country. Finally a fortnight later he came back with an enormous chimp called George V. There was a fabulous wedding, everybody got drunk on champagne, George V and Gretel were sent off into their cage for their honeymoon and Bautz got the Ritterkreuz with oak leaves.

He roars with laughter.

Hans and Konradin are silent.

Father clicks his heels.

I do hope, Herr Graf, that in future you will look upon this house as your second home. Please commend me to your father.

He bows, leaves the room.

Silence.

Konradin continues to examine the collection. Hans stands by the window, his eyes closed, fists clenched. Konradin speaks quietly.

KONRADIN
This is a great collection. I like your room.

Hans turns abruptly, looks at Konradin keenly.

I really like it.

EXT. ROAD INTO BLACK FOREST. DAY.

Hans and Konradin cycling fast.

EXT. CASTLE OVERLOOKING GORGE. DAY.

Long shot. A white castle juts out from the hillside.

EXT. CASTLE TERRACE. DAY.

Hans and Konradin walk onto the terrace and look down into the gorge.

Hans whistles.

> **KONRADIN**
> It is true, isn't it? It is the most beautiful country in the world.

> **HANS**
> Yes. It's true.

They look down.

> Mind you, I haven't been anywhere else. Well – not really.

Konradin grins.

> **KONRADIN**
> Take my word for it.

EXT. A RIVER. DAY.

Hans and Konradin, swimming, racing across the river. They reach the bank together.

> **KONRADIN**
> A dead heat!

EXT. SMALL MOUNTAIN TOWN. CAFÉ IN THE SQUARE. DAY.

Hans and Konradin eating ice-cream.

A truck drives into the square carrying SA troopers. They get out and begin to paste Nazi posters on the walls. They are fat and ugly.

*They shout at each other. One trooper becomes entangled in a
poster. Hans and Konradin laugh into their ice-cream.*

INT. SCHOOLROOM. DAY.

*The class writing an essay, heads bent over their desks. The
Master leaning back in his chair. Silence.*

*Gradually, from the street sounds of martial music through a
loudspeaker, shouting, marching feet. Hans looks up and out of
the window.*

The Master watches him.

> MASTER
> Strauss! You're dreaming. What are you dreaming?

> HANS
> I wasn't dreaming, sir.

> MASTER
> Stop dreaming. Get on with your work. Concentrate.

Hans slowly looks down at his paper.

CINEMA SCREEN. BLACK AND WHITE.

Marlene Dietrich in The Blue Angel. *She is in her underwear.
She crosses her legs.*

EXT. BLACK FOREST ROAD. DAY.

Hans and Konradin cycling along the empty road.

*In a field they see a boy running after a girl. They fall into the
grass. Hans and Konradin cycle on.*

EXT. BLACK FOREST. A RUINED CASTLE. DAY.

*A great dead tree rises up through the ruin. A church steeple can
be seen in the distance through a gap in the wall.*

REUNION

The boys walk towards the ruin and sit down.

They take packets of sandwiches from their knapsacks.

HANS

Have one of these.

KONRADIN
(*taking a sandwich*)

Thanks.

They munch.

You know ... I don't know what we're going to do about this question of sexual desire. It's a terrible problem.

HANS

Yes. The trouble is, I just don't know any girls. How about you?

KONRADIN

Not really. Only cousins.

They sit, munching.

Delicious sandwich. What is it?

HANS

Chicken.

KONRADIN

Wonderful flavour. Honestly. I've never tasted chicken like it.

HANS

Of course, sexual desire is just an appetite like anything else. And sexual intercourse is the appetite satisfied.

KONRADIN

You mean it's like eating this sandwich?

HANS

Exactly!

They laugh.

Church bells suddenly begin to ring. They look up at the church spire.

Do you feel anything . . . ? When you hear those bells?

KONRADIN

Yes. I feel something.

HANS

What? What do you feel?

KONRADIN

Oh . . . you know . . . something . . .
                    (*Pause.*)
What about you? Do you feel anything?

HANS

Aah . . . Yes . . . I think I do.

INT. INN. BEDROOM. NIGHT.

The boys lying in their beds. Moonlight.

KONRADIN

Tell me . . .

HANS

What?

KONRADIN

You remember this afternoon – when we were standing in the chapel – you said you felt something.

HANS

Yes.

REUNION

> KONRADIN

What was it? What did you feel?

Hans thinks.

> HANS

God knows.

They burst into laughter, gradually subside.

> KONRADIN

I've never had a friend before, you know. I mean, I have
parents, relations – I know other people – but you're my
first friend.

EXT. KONRADIN'S HOUSE. DAY.

*Konradin and Hans walking towards the house, knapsacks on
their backs. They stop at the gates.*

> KONRADIN

Great trip.

> HANS

It certainly was.

> KONRADIN
> (*casually*)

Like to come in and see my room?

> HANS

Oh. Yes.

*They go through the gate and walk down the drive towards the
arch. Hans looks around and sees stables to his left. They pass
under the arch. Hans looks up at the villa, which is set high above
the ground and at the double staircases that lead up to the terrace.
They begin to climb up towards the villa. They arrive at the main
door. Konradin knocks lightly. The door opens. A servant lets
them in, bows.*

REUNION

Konradin leads Hans up the wide staircase. Oak-panelled walls, pictures of bear hunts, fighting stags, portraits of ancestors, etc.

One door open. A lady's bedroom. A four-poster bed. White curtains moving in the breeze. On a dressing-table Hans glimpses bottles of scent, tortoiseshell brushes inlaid with silver, photographs in silver frames. His glance focuses on one photograph which has a striking resemblance to Adolf Hitler.

KONRADIN

Up another flight I'm afraid.

They go on.

INT. KONRADIN'S ROOM.

View from the window of a large garden with a fountain and a small Doric temple.

KONRADIN

Here's my collection.

He takes out of cotton-wool Greek coins, a pegasus from Corinth, a minotaur from Knossos, a goddess from Gella, a glass bowl from Syria, a jade Roman vase, a Greek bronze figure of Hercules. A Corinthian coin. Hans examines the objects carefully, looks at Konradin and smiles.

HANS

Fantastic.

Konradin picks up the Corinthian coin.

KONRADIN

Why don't you have this?

HANS

Have it?

KONRADIN

Yes. Keep it. As a present.

Hans takes the coin and looks at it.

HANS
Thanks.

EXT. SMALL GERMAN TOWN. RAILWAY STATION PLATFORM.
DAY.

*A train arriving. A great bell is clanging on the face of the engine.
Gertrude 18 standing on the platform. The train stops. Konradin
and Hans get out. They approach Gertrude.*

KONRADIN
Gertrude, may I introduce Hans Strauss.
(*To Hans.*)
The Gräfin von Zeilarn, my cousin.

Hans bows and kisses her hand.

EXT. RAILWAY STATION FORECOURT. DAY.

*Nazi posters on the walls. Swastikas. The Hammer and Sickle. A
pony and trap stands. Gertrude and the boys get into it. The
driver flicks his whip and trots off.*

EXT. NARROW COUNTRY ROAD. DAY.

*The pony and trap. Suddenly round a corner a group of Hitler
Youth appears, marching. The driver slows the trap. The group
marches past.*

GERTRUDE
Aren't they handsome!

KONRADIN
Would you say so?

GERTRUDE
Well, I've just said so.

The trap drives on.

KONRADIN

I think they're pretty boneheaded.

GERTRUDE

Do you?

HANS

It's quite possible to be boneheaded and handsome at
the same time, isn't it?

GERTRUDE

What do you mean by boneheaded?

KONRADIN

Unintelligent.

GERTRUDE

Not like you, you mean?

KONRADIN

Quite. Not like us.

GERTRUDE

Well, why don't you both join the Hitler Youth
yourselves – so that it can benefit from your
intelligence?

Konradin laughs, winks at Hans.

EXT. ZEILARN ESTATE. DAY.

*Gertrude, Konradin and Hans on the grass. The remains of the
picnic. A servant stands by a table.*

GERTRUDE
(*to Konradin*)
Where are you going for the summer?

KONRADIN

I think Sicily. And you?

GERTRUDE
(*shrugging*)

Oh ... Baden Baden.
            (*She turns to Hans.*)
Where do you go?

HANS

We're going to Switzerland.

GERTRUDE

Really? I'd be careful if I were you. I hear lots of rich
Jews go to Switzerland to stuff themselves with Swiss
cheese.

Silence.

KONRADIN

Hans is Jewish.

HANS

But I'm not rich.

GERTRUDE

You're Jewish?

HANS

Yes.

GERTRUDE

But you don't look it!

HANS

Don't I?

Gertrude giggles, puts a hand to her mouth.

GERTRUDE

Oh dear ... I see why you haven't joined the Hitler
Youth!

KONRADIN

Are you falling in love with the Nazis, Gertrude?

GERTRUDE

Well, it's all pretty exciting, don't you think? I mean,
don't you feel the new spirit in Germany? You feel it
everywhere. Anyway, I think they have the good of
Germany at heart. I really do. So does Daddy. And
Mummy.

*In the distance, by an orchard, two riders on horseback appear.
Gertrude looks up.*

Oh look, there they are. I must go.

She stands. The boys stand.

(To Hans.)

Glad to meet you. But are you absolutely sure you're
Jewish? You really don't look it.

*She smiles, waves, walks away across the lawn towards the
orchard.*

Konradin and Hans walk towards the gate.

HANS
(to Konradin)

Don't I look Jewish?

KONRADIN

No, I don't think you do.

HANS

But what does a Jew look like?

*Laughter from the orchard. They turn and look. Gertrude with
her parents. Gertrude waves. The parents do not.*

PONY AND TRAP TRAVELLING.

Konradin and Hans sitting, looking at the countryside.

EXT. STREET. DUSK.

Hans and Konradin approaching Hans's house.

They see smoke rising from the house next door (the Bauer house). They stop and look at each other.

> HANS
>
> What's that?

They run towards the house, stop and stare. The Bauer house is a burnt-out ruin.

They run towards the Strauss house.

INT. STRAUSS HOUSE. HALL. DAY.

Hans and Konradin come through the front door into the hall. They hear sobbing. They stop. The sobbing continues. Mother comes out of the sitting-room and goes to them. Her face is drained.

> MOTHER
>
> A tragedy. A tragedy.

> HANS
>
> What?

> MOTHER
>
> The children ... the children ... they died.

> HANS
>
> Died?

A further burst of sobbing from the sitting-room.

> But ... how ... did someone ... do it?

> MOTHER
>
> No. No one did it. It was an accident. No one did it.
>> (*She cries, softly.*)
> No one did it.

REUNION

EXT. BAUER HOUSE, SMOKING. DAY.

Hans and Konradin walking slowly through the garden towards the house.

The charred ropes of the swing dangle from the burnt tree.

They walk slowly through the wreckage (blackened walls, burnt furniture, burnt toys). They stand in silence.

> HANS
>
> I knew these children.

Pause.

> KONRADIN
>
> It's terrible.

> HANS
>
> God doesn't exist. How can he exist?

> KONRADIN
>
> These ... things ... these catastrophes ... have happened ... throughout history.

> HANS
>
> So what? How can this God allow three innocent children to be burnt to death? Tell me.

> KONRADIN
>
> He can't control every accident of fate.

> HANS
>
> You mean he doesn't care?

> KONRADIN
>
> I didn't say that.

> HANS
>
> He either doesn't exist – or he exists and is all-powerful, in which case he is monstrous, or he exists and has no power, in which case he is pointless.

KONRADIN

That's too neat.

HANS

Well, what *is* the answer? How can you excuse the
burning to death of three children, for God's sake?

KONRADIN

I'm not excusing it! How can you accuse me of excusing
it?

HANS

Can't you hear their screams?

KONRADIN

God didn't kill them.

HANS

But he let them die!

They stand.

KONRADIN

But there is good ... in the world ...

HANS

I know. But somehow ...

KONRADIN

What?

HANS

There's no one in charge. There's no one in control. Is
there?

Pause.

KONRADIN

There must be.

REUNION

EXT. A BRIDGE. DAY.

Hans is leaning over the bridge, looking down at the river. Girls in boats float by, laughing.

Konradin joins him.

> KONRADIN

Hans.

> HANS

Hello.

They shake hands.

> KONRADIN

How are you?

> HANS

All right.

They walk towards a large open-air café.

Hundreds of people. An orchestra playing 'An der Weser'. Young Nazis at tables. The Nazi salute given in greeting.

> KONRADIN

I had a word with my pastor about our talk – about God. I told him what you said. I asked his opinion.

> HANS

What was it?

> KONRADIN

He said that what you said was blasphemy.

> HANS

Do you think it's blasphemy?

> KONRADIN

No.

They pass a news kiosk. The Vendor offers Konradin a copy of the Völkischer Beobachter.

REUNION

VENDOR

Take it. It's free.

They look at the headlines: 'SHALL GERMANY BE FREE OR A
COLONY OF FRANCE?', 'HITLER OR DESTRUCTION'.

KONRADIN

This paper is banned by the government.

He shoves it into a wastebin.

*They walk along the terrace. Some Nazis look up at them as they
pass.*

They sit at a table.

HANS

What do you think of them – the Nazis?

KONRADIN

Not much.
            (*Konradin waves to a waiter.*)
I mean, they have no real ideas, do they? They just like
dressing up and marching about. Bullies. Just primitive,
really.

HANS

What about Hitler?

KONRADIN

Oh, he just rants and raves, doesn't he?

*Suddenly at the far end of the terrace a table overturns. SA men
jump up, shouting. A man runs along the terrace. They chase
him. The man rushes by the boys' table. The boys stand. An SA
man collides with Hans. Hans stands his ground. The SA man
pushes him. Konradin hits the SA man on the jaw. Chaos.*

EXT. A LAKE. DAY.

*Konradin and Hans sitting at the side of the lake with tankards of
beer. Their clothes are dishevelled.*

REUNION

VENDOR

Take it. It's free.

They look at the headlines: 'SHALL GERMANY BE FREE OR A COLONY OF FRANCE?', 'HITLER OR DESTRUCTION'.

KONRADIN

This paper is banned by the government.

He shoves it into a wastebin.

They walk along the terrace. Some Nazis look up at them as they pass.

They sit at a table.

HANS

What do you think of them – the Nazis?

KONRADIN

Not much.
(*Konradin waves to a waiter.*)
I mean, they have no real ideas, do they? They just like dressing up and marching about. Bullies. Just primitive, really.

HANS

What about Hitler?

KONRADIN

Oh, he just rants and raves, doesn't he?

Suddenly at the far end of the terrace a table overturns. SA men jump up, shouting. A man runs along the terrace. They chase him. The man rushes by the boys' table. The boys stand. An SA man collides with Hans. Hans stands his ground. The SA man pushes him. Konradin hits the SA man on the jaw. Chaos.

EXT. A LAKE. DAY.

Konradin and Hans sitting at the side of the lake with tankards of beer. Their clothes are dishevelled.

REUNION

At the other side of the lake, they can discern a procession with banners. Voices sing in the distance.

> HANS
>
> I'm frightened.

INT. STRAUSS HOUSE. SITTING-ROOM. EVENING.

Hans, wearing a dinner-jacket, standing, listening to the radio.

> RADIO ANNOUNCER
>
> In the Reichstag elections Hitler has won a resounding victory. The National Socialist Party has received 13,750,000 votes. Their seats in Parliament have increased by 123 – from 107 to 230.

Hans turns the radio off. Mother comes into the room.

> MOTHER
>
> You look so handsome.
> > (*She adjusts his tie.*)
> Are you looking forward to it?

> HANS
>
> I am. I'm really grateful.

> MOTHER
>
> Where's your ticket?

He takes ticket from pocket.

> HANS
>
> Here.
> > (*He kisses her.*)
> Thank you.

EXT. STUTTGART OPERA HOUSE. NIGHT.

Cars and carriages arriving, etc. Posters announcing Fidelio. *Trucks full of cheering Nazis driving by. Hans walking towards the entrance.*

REUNION

INT. STUTTGART OPERA HOUSE. AUDITORIUM.

The orchestra tuning up. Hans walks to a seat on the aisle midway down the stalls. He sits. People milling into the auditorium.

Suddenly room is made at the door by the front row of the stalls. The audience seems to focus on the door. The Lohenburgs make their entrance. Konradin comes in first. He is followed by his mother, the Countess. She is dressed in black with a tiara of diamonds, diamond necklace and diamond ear-rings. The Count has grey hair and a grey moustache. A diamond-studded star shines on his jacket. They stand, receiving bows graciously. At last they move to their seats. Konradin greets various people.

The family sits down. The lights go down.

HANS SITTING IN THE DARK.

The opera in action.

THE INTERMISSION.

Hans slipping quickly out of the auditorium. Applause behind him.

Hans walks up into the foyer. A great room with marble columns, crystal candelabra, gold-framed mirrors, cyclamen-red carpets, honey-coloured wallpaper. Hans leans against one of the columns at the far end of the room. The audience comes in from the auditorium, filling up the foyer.

The Lohenburg family appears at the other end of the room and begins to walk slowly up its length, nodding to acquaintances. The crowd gives way for them. It is a regal procession.

Hans waits. They draw nearer. Hans stares at the beautiful Countess and then at Konradin. Konradin sees him. He gives no sign of recognition. His eyes flick away. They pass by.

INT. STRAUSS HOUSE. HANS'S BEDROOM. MORNING.

Hans wakes up suddenly with a gasp. He is sweating. His Father leans over him.

> FATHER
> What is it? What is it? Are you all right?

> HANS
> Yes, yes. Nothing. I had a nightmare.

> FATHER
> What nightmare?

> HANS
> Just a dream. A bad dream.

Father puts his hand on Hans's brow.

> FATHER
> Hmmnn. Perhaps you should stay at home today.

> HANS
> No, I'm all right. What's the time?

> FATHER
> Half-past seven. How was the opera?

> HANS
> I must get ready.

He jumps out of bed.

EXT. SCHOOL. MORNING.

Konradin standing. He sees Hans approach. Hans walks straight past him and into the school.

INT. SCHOOLROOM. MORNING.

Bollacher standing reciting Latin verbs. Konradin is looking at Hans. Hans avoids his gaze.

REUNION

INT. SCHOOL CORRIDOR. MORNING.

Bell ringing. Boys milling about. Hans walking down the corridor. Konradin calls after him. Hans goes on. Konradin runs down the corridor and catches him up.

KONRADIN
What's going on? Why aren't you speaking to me?

Hans does not speak.

I don't understand.

HANS
You don't understand?

KONRADIN
No.

He stands, breathing hard. Hans looks at him. They speak in hushed whispers as boys pass up and down the corridor around them.

HANS
Why did you cut me?

Konradin looks at him.

KONRADIN
Cut you?

HANS
Yes. Why?
(*Pause.*)
Are you ashamed of me?

KONRADIN
No. Not in any way.

HANS
I don't like being humiliated. I refuse to be humiliated.

REUNION

KONRADIN

It is not my aim ... to humiliate you. You're my only
friend. You know that. You're the only friend I have.

HANS

Then why did you cut me?

KONRADIN

I didn't ... cut you.

HANS

Oh don't be so damn stupid!

Konradin turns away.

Why have you never introduced me to your parents?
You ignored me last night because of them. I know that.
I want to know why!

*Boys look at them curiously. They are outside the doors of the
gym. Konradin looks through the window. The gym is empty.*

KONRADIN

All right. Come in here.

INT. GYM. MORNING.

*The boys walk into the gym. Konradin closes the door. They walk
across the gym to the horizontal bars.*

KONRADIN

I'll tell you why. But you won't like it.
(*He pauses.*)
You're a Jew. My mother hate Jews.

They stare at each other.

I didn't *dare* introduce you. She would have insulted you
– somehow. My mother comes from a highly ...
distinguished family. For hundreds of years Jews didn't
exist for her people – they were scum of the earth,

585

untouchables. She detests them, she's afraid of them, she has never spoken to a Jew in her life! If she was dying and nobody but your father could save her she wouldn't let him touch her. And she hates you even more because you are my friend. She thinks you've corrupted me, she thinks you're the Devil, a Bolshevik Jewish Devil!

(*He laughs, stops.*)

I've fought for every hour I've spent with you. I fight her
... all the time about you!

HANS

And your father?

KONRADIN

My father? Oh, my father has a sense of humour. He calls you 'Little Moses'. He calls me a child.

HANS

I see.

KONRADIN

Anyway, he thinks the Jewish problem is bound to be resolved, sooner or later. He thinks it'll resolve itself.

HANS

How?

KONRADIN

I don't know.

HANS

But what is the Jewish problem, exactly?

They stare at each other.

KONRADIN

Oh, don't look at me like that! Am I to blame for all this? Am I responsible for my parents? Am I to blame for the world? Why don't you grow up and face the facts? Face reality.

(*Pause.*)

Look. I should have told you all this before but I'm a coward. I couldn't bear to hurt you. Try to understand.

HANS
(*slowly*)
Yes. You're right. We have to face reality.

They walk across the gym to the door and go out.

EXT. STUTTGART STREET. EARLY EVENING.

Hans and Konradin carrying heavy briefcases walking up the hill towards Konradin's house. They are silent. They arrive at the gates and stop.

HANS
It'll be very hot in Sicily, won't it?

KONRADIN
Yes, very hot. But we're quite near the sea. So I shall probably swim every day. What do you think it'll be like in Switzerland?

HANS
Not so hot.

They stand.

KONRADIN
Let's stay friends. I don't think we should allow – all this – to spoil our friendship. Do you?

HANS
No.

KONRADIN
So we will go on being friends. Won't we?

HANS
Yes. Yes, of course. Naturally.

Konradin extends his hand.

KONRADIN

Have a good holiday.

They shake hands.

HANS

See you in September.

Konradin opens the gates. Hans continues to walk up the hill.

MONTAGE: SUMMER IN GERMANY 1932.

A group of little girls giving the Nazi salute, beaming.

Newsreel in cinema: A parade of Hitler Youth through crowded streets.

A band playing martial music.

Hitler's arrival in Berlin. Vast crowds greeting him.

Couples dancing on an open-air terrace. The song 'I Want a Man, a Real Man'.

Newsreel in cinema: Communist demonstrations against Fascism.

Fires breaking out.

A pretty little girl in white, with flowers, giving Nazi salute.

Newsreel in cinema: gunfire in the streets.

A Berlin fashion parade.

Newsreel in cinema: Nazi march through working-class district.

Workers running from the police.

Panic in the streets.

Vast torchlight processions.

REUNION

INT. SCHOOLROOM. DAY.

September. The new term. Herr Pompetski walks into the room. He wears a swastika in his buttonhole. He takes his place at the desk. The class is silent.

Hans and Konradin are at their usual places. They look older.

POMPETSKI
I am your new history master.
> (*He looks round the class.*)

Gentlemen, there is history and history. History which is in your books now and history which is about to be made. You know all about the first but you know nothing about the second because certain dark powers have an interest in keeping it hidden from you. We'll refer to them as 'dark powers' for the moment anyway – powers which are at work everywhere, I am afraid – in Russia, in America and in our own beloved country. They are an evil destructive force, intent upon undermining our morals and poisoning our national heritage. I propose to devote some time in examining this critical period in our history, which I personally trust will prove to be a turning of the tide.

The camera closes in on Hans's face.

Pompetski's speech goes on, becoming distant and finally inaudible.

You have all heard how the Dark Ages followed the fall of Rome. Do you believe it can have been pure chance that soon after the German emperors' descent on Italy the Renaissance began? Or isn't it more than probable that it was German blood which fertilized the fields of Italy, barren since the fall of Rome? Can it be a coincidence that a great civilization was born so soon after the arrival of the Aryans?

EXT. SCHOOLYARD. DAY.

Flag-raising ceremony. The Nazi flag. The majority of masters and boys giving the Nazi salute. Hans stands at attention. The ceremony ends. The boys mill about. Hans and Konradin come face to face.

HANS
Hello.

KONRADIN
Hello, Hans. How are you?

They shake hands warily.

How was Switzerland?

HANS
Quite good. Good cheese.

They both smile, thinly. The bell rings.

INT. SCHOOL ENTRANCE HALL. DAY.

Hans comes in. Bollacher, Erhardt and some others turn and look at him.

Erhardt holds his nose. The others grin. Bollacher calls.

BOLLACHER
Strauss! Wait a minute!

Hans stops, turns.

Konradin comes into the hall and stops, watching.

Bollacher walks up to Hans. He holds a sticker. He lifts it up to Hans's face.

Read this.

HANS
Take it away. Take it away from my face.

REUNION

BOLLACHER

Read it. Read it aloud!

They stare at each other.

All right. I will.

> *(He reads.)*
'The Jews have ruined Germany. German people –
awake!'

Konradin takes a step towards Bollacher.

KONRADIN

Bollacher –

Bollacher turns, looks sharply at Konradin. Konradin stops.

*Bollacher moves closer to Hans. He sticks the sticker on to Hans's
jacket.*

BOLLACHER

Why don't you go back to Palestine where you came
from? Jew boy.

*Hans hits him. They fight. Konradin watches. Bollacher falls,
hits his head. Pompetski comes down the main stairs.*

POMPETSKI

What's this?

BOLLACHER

Sir! He attacked me!

POMPETSKI
> *(to Hans)*

Did you attack him?

HANS

Yes.

POMPETSKI

Why?

HANS

He insulted me.

POMPETSKI

Oh, really? What did he say?

HANS

He told me to go back to Palestine.

POMPETSKI

But that's not an insult, Strauss. It's sound, friendly
advice.

(*To Bollacher.*)

Be patient. Now all of you get back to your classrooms.
We will have order in this country and I shall have order
in this school.

EXT. STREET. DAY.

Hans walking up the hill by himself.

EXT. STRAUSS HOUSE. DAY.

Hans approaching his house. He stops.

*A Nazi is standing outside the house with a large poster:
'Germans! Avoid all Jews. Whoever has anything to do with a
Jew is defiled.'*

*Father comes out of the house dressed in officer's uniform with
decorations including Iron Cross first class. He holds an officer's
sword. He stands to attention beside the Nazi. Mother can be seen
through a curtain at the window.*

*A crowd gathers. It begins to mutter. Low jeers directed at the
Nazi. A Nazi truck arrives. Jeers and catcalls from the truck.
The Nazi rolls up the poster and climbs into the truck. The truck
drives away. The crowd drifts away.*

Hans walks slowly to the house. He stops in front of his Father.

Father looks at him, takes him by the arm and leads him into the house.

INT. STRAUSS HOUSE. SITTING-ROOM. DAY.

Father, Mother, Hans.

FATHER
(*to Hans*)

Sit down.

He does.

We have something to say to you which we know will be a shock to you, but it must be said and it must be done.
(*Pause.*)
Your mother and I have decided to send you to America, for the time being anyway, until the storm has blown over. You will stay with your uncle in New York. He'll look after you and arrange for you to go to university. You can't go to a university here. You know that. You're not a fool.
(*Pause.*)
We are staying here. We intend to join you . . . later. Please accept this. Please don't speak.
(*Pause.*)
I have booked you on the *Bremen* which sails on October 5th.

INT. SCHOOLROOM. DAY.

Hans clearing his desk, putting papers and books into a briefcase. Other boys lounging about.

Bollacher and Erhardt stand by the window singing softly.

BOLLACHER and ERHARDT
Little yid – we bid you farewell
May you join Moses and Isaac in hell

Little yid – never come back,
or we'll break your filthy, lousy neck.

Hans leaves the room.

EXT. STREET. EVENING.

Hans walking up the hill. Konradin steps out of a doorway.

Hans stops. Konradin comes towards him.

KONRADIN

When are you going?

HANS

Tomorrow.

Pause.

KONRADIN

I'm sorry it's come to this. But it probably makes sense
– just for the time being. The country will be in a state
of flux for a while, I should think. But the fact is we
want a new Germany and we're going to get it.

Hans looks at him, expressionless.

Listen . . . I want to tell you . . . I believe in Hitler. I met
him in Munich recently. He really impressed me. He's
. . . totally sincere, you see. He has such . . . he has true
passion. I think that he can save our country. He's our
only hope.

Hans stands staring at him.

Look. I'm sure that in a couple of years you'll be able to
come back. Germany needs people like you. I'm sure
that the Führer will be willing to choose between the
good Jewish elements and the . . . undesirable Jewish
elements.

(*Pause.*)

594

I've learnt so much from you, you know. You've taught
me to think. You have. Truly.
                    (*He extends his hand.*)
Good luck.

*Hans does not take his hand. They stand still. Hans turns away
and runs up the hill. Konradin opens the gates and goes in.*

EXT. NEW YORK PIER. WINTER. DAY.

*Hans walking on to the pier. He is greeted by his uncle. His uncle
embraces him. He then takes him by the arm and walks along the
pier with him, talking quietly.*

INT. STRAUSS HOUSE. NIGHT.

Father closing all windows.

He goes into the kitchen, turns on the gas.

He goes up to the bedroom.

INT. STRAUSS HOUSE. BEDROOM. NIGHT.

Father gets into bed, holds his sleeping wife.

INT. STRAUSS HOUSE. KITCHEN. NIGHT.

The hissing gas.

INT. COURTROOM. DAY.

*Black and white. Judge Freisler screaming at Alex (Henry's
granddaughter), who stands in the dock wide-eyed. Cut to Lisa
(Henry's daughter) lying on the floor between two pairs of
jackboots, her hand stretched out, sobbing.*

INT. HOTEL BEDROOM. PRESENT. NIGHT.

Henry wakes up sweating.

INT. HOTEL. DAY.

Henry at reception desk.

> **HENRY**
> I would like to stay for a few more days. Is that all right?

> **RECEPTIONIST**
> How many days would that be?

> **HENRY**
> Oh . . . three of four. Perhaps five.

> **RECEPTIONIST**
> Yes, that will be fine.

> **HENRY**
> Will you cancel my flight?

> **RECEPTIONIST**
> Of course.

EXT. KONRADIN'S HOUSE. DAY.

Taxi drives in through the gate, under the arch and up the winding road to the villa.

Henry gets out and goes into the house.

INT. KONRADIN'S HOUSE. DAY.

Henry stands for a moment in the hall and looks about. The architecture has not altered but the hall is completely bare. A coat rack along the wall.

Four Girls descend the stairs. They look at him.

> **HENRY**
> Excuse me . . . does anyone speak English?

> **GIRL**
> Yes.

REUNION

HENRY

What is this house now?

GIRL

This house?

HENRY

Yes. What ... happens here?

GIRL

This is a special house for income taxes. Special income taxes department of Stuttgart.

HENRY

Oh.

GIRL

Can I help you?

HENRY

I would like information about a family who lived here. Called Lohenburg. Before the war.

GIRL

Taxes information?

HENRY

No, no. Just ... what happened to them?

GIRL

I do not know them.

HENRY

Is there anyone ...?

GIRL
(shrugs and points up the stairs)
Up there, perhaps.

HENRY

Thank you.

597

The Girls go out.

*Henry walks up the stairs and comes face to face with the doors of
mother's bedroom. The doors have not been changed. Henry opens
the door and looks in.*

INT. ROOM. DAY.

The room is bare. A long oval table. Chairs.

*A large television screen. Henry stands still, looking at the room.
Suddenly an inner door opens. A Man appears, stops abruptly.*

> MAN
> (*in German*)

Can I help you?

> HENRY

I'm sorry, I ... Before the war a family called
Lohenburg lived here. I wonder if you have –

The Man interrupts him politely, shrugging.

> MAN
> (*in German*)

I'm so sorry, I speak no English.
> (*He mutters.*)

Lohenburg? Yes ... yes.
> (*He smiles and speaks in English.*)

Our Director ... of this place ... is here ... what is it?
... not today ...?

> HENRY

Tomorrow?

> MAN

Yes. yes. Tomorrow. He knows ... this house, the
history ...

> HENRY

Tomorrow. I'll be back.

MAN

Lohenburg ... ja ...

Henry looks at him expectantly. The Man goes to the door, opens it wide, bows.

Tomorrow ... yes?

Henry steps on to the landing. The Man closes the door.

EXT. COUNTRY ROAD. DAY.

A taxi approaches the gates of a large estate. It goes through the gates and drives up to the house. Henry gets out of the taxi. He climbs the steps to the front door, rings the bell and waits. A Servant opens the door.

SERVANT

Guten Morgen.

HENRY

Good morning. Can you tell me – if the von Zeilarn family is still in residence here?

SERVANT
(*in German*)

This is the home of the Gräfin von Zeilarn und Lizen, yes.

HENRY

Is the Gräfin – by any chance – here?

Pause.

SERVANT

She is at home, yes.

HENRY

Will you give her my card?

He gives the Servant the card. The Servant withdraws.

Henry turns and looks out at the grounds.

The Servant returns.

> **SERVANT**
> This way please.

INT. ZEILARN HOUSE. DAY.

The Servant leads Henry into the drawing-room.

The Gräfin is a tall woman in her early seventies. She stands erect.

> **HENRY**
> Thank you so much for seeing me.

> **GRÄFIN**
> *(looking at card)*
> I don't recall our meeting.

> **HENRY**
> It was many years ago.

> **GRÄFIN**
> But you are American.

> **HENRY**
> Yes.

> **GRÄFIN**
> Did we meet in America?

> **HENRY**
> No, no. Here. In this house.

She frowns.

> **GRÄFIN**
> In this house? Please sit down.

They sit.

HENRY

I was brought to see you by Konradin von Lohenburg.

GRÄFIN

By whom?

HENRY

Konradin von Lohenburg.

She stares at him.

Your cousin.

GRÄFIN

When was this?

HENRY

In 1932.

The Gräfin glances out of the window.

GRÄFIN

Wonderful days.
  (*She looks back at him.*)
I remember no such meeting.

HENRY

I am not in the least surprised. I was a young boy of no
... consequence. It is a very long time ago.

GRÄFIN

But what were you doing in Germany ... in 1932?

HENRY

I lived here, with my family, in Stuttgart.

GRÄFIN

You said you were an American.

HENRY

I have become an American. I left Germany in 1932.

GRÄFIN

Why?

HENRY

I am Jewish.

Silence. The Gräfin is expressionless.

This is my first visit to Germany . . . for fifty-five years.

GRÄFIN

And what can I do for you?

Pause.

HENRY

I was a close friend of Konradin von Lohenburg.

GRÄFIN

Were you?

HENRY

I don't know what happened to him. I would like to know what happened to him. Did he survive the war? Do you know . . . Madame? Can you tell me?

She stands.

GRÄFIN

It is not a subject I am willing to discuss. I trust you will find your visit to Germany of interest. Please excuse me.

She inclines her head and leaves the room.

He remains standing.

INT. STUTTGART STATE ART GALLERY. DAY.

An exhibition of the photographs of John Copelans. Henry walking through the gallery, looking at them.

Over this a general rumble of passing people: murmurs and

snatches of conversation in many languages. Bursts of laughter from schoolchildren.

Henry walks through the crowd and into the lobby. His eye drifts over the posters and postcard counter. He suddenly stiffens. He walks to a poster and bends down to examine it. It is an announcement of an art exhibition at the Karl Alexander Gymnasium. He stares at it.

EXT. STREET TAXI RANK. DAY.

Henry getting into taxi. The Taxi Driver is a man in his sixties.

INT. TAXI. DAY.

> HENRY
>
> Hotel Am Schlossgarten.

The taxi drives off.

Suddenly Henry leans forward, taps the Driver on the shoulder, points to a street.

> Up there.

> TAXI DRIVER
>
> Hotel Schlossgarten?

> HENRY
>
> No, no. Up there!

The Driver shrugs and turns left.

EXT. STREET. DAY.

The taxi driving uphill towards the Strauss house.

INT. TAXI. DAY.

> HENRY
>
> Stop.

The taxi stops. Henry sits staring at the house. The Taxi Driver looks at his watch and clicks his teeth.

(*Quietly.*)
That was my house. My parents died there. You understand?

The Taxi Driver turns his head.

TAXI DRIVER
(*in German*)
What?

HENRY
Do you understand?

TAXI DRIVER
Nein.

HENRY
My parents died there. They killed themselves there.

TAXI DRIVER
(*in German*)
I don't understand.

HENRY
My father fought for Germany. But he was a Jew. They died of despair. Do you understand?

TAXI DRIVER
Nein.

HENRY
What do you mean? What do you mean, nein?
(*Savagely, in German.*)
What do you mean, nein? Of course you understand! You understand perfectly well! He was Jewish! You understand that perfectly well! You bastard!

TAXI DRIVER
(*in German*)

You get out.

He opens Henry's door. Henry gets out.

EXT. STREET. DAY.

The taxi drives away. Henry stands still for a moment. He walks away down the hill.

INT. PEOPLE'S COURT, BERLIN. 1944. DAY.

Black and white.

Judge Freisler enters the courtroom. The court rises. Freisler gives the Nazi salute and sits.

INT. CEMETERY: OFFICE. DAY.

Henry walks into the office. A Man looks up from a table.

MAN
(*in German*)

Yes?

HENRY
(*in German*)

I believe there are some Jewish graves in this cemetery.

MAN

Jewish? Some. Yes.

HENRY

I would like to look at them, please.

The Man leads Henry to the door. They go out.

EXT. CEMETERY. DAY.

The Man points to a far corner of the cemetery.

MAN

Some Jews over there. Behind the trees.

HENRY

Thank you.

Henry begins to walk towards the trees.

INT. PEOPLE'S COURT, BERLIN. 1944.

Black and white.

A man stands before Freisler. He is unshaven, wears an open-necked shirt, is holding his trousers up. He is heavily set, in his fifties.

FREISLER
(*in German*)

The German people spit on you. You are standing in the People's Court of Germany and the German people spit on you.

EXT. CEMETERY. DAY.

Henry arrives at the Jewish graves. He examines them. They are overgrown, almost buried.

He bends to one, pulls twigs and leaves away from it. He finally discerns a faint inscription: 'Captain and Frau Strauss May 1934'. He stands upright and remains looking down.

INT. PEOPLE'S COURT, BERLIN. 1944.

Black and white.

Another Man stands in front of Freisler. He is short, in his forties.

FREISLER

Are you *proud* of his act? Do I hear *pride* in your voice?

REUNION

MAN
I don't see –

FREISLER
Answer the question!

MAN
We had good reasons –

FREISLER
Good reasons! You stinking traitor! Your soul burns with pus! You have broken your oath not once but twice! You are a criminal hypocrite and a filthy liar! The Reich knows what to do with vermin like you!

EXT. SCHOOL. DAY.

Milling students. Henry walking towards the school.

INT. SCHOOL. HEADMASTER'S OFFICE. DAY.

Brossner, a man in his forties, casually dressed.

BROSSNER
Herr Strauss. Hello. How are you?

They shake hands.

HENRY
We spoke on the telephone.

BROSSNER
Yes, yes. I know. Sit down.
(*He laughs.*)
It isn't often I meet 'old boys' from so long ago. In fact I'm not sure I ever have.

HENRY
(*looking around*)
But this . . . isn't the same school.

BROSSNER

It was totally destroyed.

HENRY

No, I meant . . . you have girls here now . . . for example.

BROSSNER

Oh, yes. Of course.
                    (*Pause.*)
You haven't been in this country at all . . . since then?

HENRY

No. Not since I was a boy. I've had no contact with
Germany at all, in fact, until now. I haven't read a
German book or a German newspaper. I haven't spoken
a word of the German language . . . in all that time.

Brossner grunts.

BROSSNER

You wanted to know about the class of '32. Many died
in the war. We collected information about them . . .
about all the dead . . . over the years. It's in this book.

He shows Henry a book with a plain soft cover.

But we also have a war memorial. Would you like to see it?

Henry is silent for a moment.

HENRY

Yes.

EXT. SCHOOL TERRACE. DAY.

*A group of tall schoolboys kicking a ball about. Brossner, holding
the book, brings Henry through glass doors on to the terrace and
points to a wall.*

*Attached to the wall a large war memorial, containing over one
hundred names.*

Henry stands, looking at it.

HENRY
How did Bollacher die? Is it known?

Brossner looks in the book.

BROSSNER
Bollacher ... on the Russian front.

HENRY
And Erhardt?

BROSSNER
Erhardt ... shot down – over London.

Henry looks at the list of names beginning with L. There he sees 'Konradin von Lohenburg'.

He turns to Brossner.

HENRY
And Lohenburg?

Brossner stares at him.

BROSSNER
Lohenburg?

INT. EMPTY EXECUTION ROOM. DAY.

The room is bare. Two windows at the back. Winter sunshine slanting in. A rafter along the ceiling in front of the window. Butcher's hooks hanging down.

Over this Brossner's voice.

BROSSNER
(*VO*)
You don't know? He was implicated in the plot against Hitler. Executed.

The butcher's hooks glint in the light from the window.